Turning Points
in Analytic Therapy

Turning Points in Analytic Therapy

The Classic Cases

Gerald Schoenewolf, Ph.D.

JASON ARONSON INC.
Northvale, New Jersey
London

The author gratefully acknowledges permission to reprint excerpts from the following:

Fragment of an analysis of a case of hysteria, by S. Freud (1905); Analysis of a phobia in a five-year-old-boy by S. Freud (1909). Both appear in *Collected Papers of Sigmund Freud.* Copyright © 1959 by arrangement with Hogarth Press. Reprinted by permission of Basic Books, Inc., New York.

The Case of Ellen West, by L. Binswanger in *Existence, a New Dimension in Psychiatry and Psychology.* Copyright © 1958 by Basic Books, Inc., New York.

Library of Congress Cataloging-in-Publication Data

Schoenewolf, Gerald.
    Turning points in analytic therapy / Gerald Schoenewolf.
       p.   cm.
    Includes bibliographical references.
    Contents: The classic cases.
    ISBN 0-87668-819-9
    1. Psychoanalysis—Case studies.   2. Psychoanalysis—History.
I. Title.
    [DNLM: 1. Psychoanalysis—history—case studies.
2. Psychoanalytic Therapy—case studies. WM 40 S365t]
RC509.8.S36 1990
616.89'17'09—dc20
DNLM/DLC
for Library of Congress   89-17949
                                             CIP

Manufactured in the United States of America. Jason Aronson Inc. offers books and cassettes. For information and catalog write to Jason Aronson Inc., 230 Livingston Street, Northvale, New Jersey 07647.

To Chinda

CONTENTS

Preface   ix

1   The Discovery of the Cathartic Method   1
Joseph Breuer and Anna O. (1895)

2   Dream Interpretation with Hysterics   21
Sigmund Freud and Dora (1905)

3   The Oedipus Complex   43
Sigmund Freud and Little Hans (1909)

4   Obsessional Neurosis   63
Sigmund Freud and the Rat Man (1909)

5   The Primal Scene   83
Sigmund Freud and the Wolf Man (1918)

6   Jungian Dream Analysis   105
     Carl G. Jung and the Philosophy
     Student (1928)

7   The Inferiority Complex   123
     Alfred Adler and the Dominating Woman,
     the Suicidal Medical Student, and the
     Pampered Physician (1929)

8   Active Therapy   141
     Sandor Ferenczi and the Hysteric (1919),
     the Music Student (1920), the Fantasizer
     (1924), and the Regressed Patient (1931)

9   The Development of Child Analysis   161
     Melanie Klein and Erna (1932)

10   The Masochistic Character   179
     Wilhelm Reich and the Masochist (1933)

11   Existential Analysis   197
     Ludwig Binswanger and Ellen West
     (1944–1945)

Afterword   219
References   223
Index   233

PREFACE

The turning points in psychoanalytic theory and psychotherapeutic technique have come out of the treatment of individuals. For example: Joseph Breuer discovered the cathartic method while treating Anna O. Sigmund Freud understood the roots of obsessional neurosis when he studied the Rat Man. Melanie Klein broke new ground in child therapy through her analysis of 6-year-old Erna. Ludwig Binswanger opened the doors to existential analysis while working with Ellen West.

A review of the classic case histories of psychoanalysis and psychotherapy, this book looks beyond theory to the people who helped shape a new science. The participants—therapists and patients alike—were the pilgrims of psychoanalysis. Their cases provided the advances that made psychoanalytic therapy what it is today.

Chapters are divided into two sections. In the case summaries I show how new advances in theory and technique were discovered while emphasizing the psychodynamics of the relationships between therapists and patients. In the interpretation sections I summarize reviewers' interpretations and assess the importance of each case in the light of current understanding. Each chapter is designed to illustrate a particular advance in our understanding and treatment of individuals with mental and emotional problems.

Acknowledgments

I would like to thank Jason Aronson, M.D., for his invaluable support and assistance in shaping this work, as well as Mary E. Remito, M.S.W., for her ongoing encouragement; David Glassman, Ph.D., Gerd Fenchel, Ph.D., David Belgray, Ph.D., and Jacob Kirman, Ph.D., for their support and feedback on this project; and to Tess Elliot for helping with the preparation of the manuscript.

Turning Points
in Analytic Therapy

1

THE DISCOVERY OF THE CATHARTIC METHOD

Joseph Breuer and Anna O. (1895)

A few days before Christmas in 1880, the Viennese physician Joseph Breuer was summoned to the home of a wealthy Orthodox Jewish family. There he found a beautiful pale young woman of 21 stretched out on her bed, her eyes closed, her arms and legs paralyzed. Every now and then she would open her eyes and squint, unable to recognize the people around her. She had a deep cough.

"I'm afraid she has tuberculosis," her mother told Breuer. Her fears were not unfounded, for there was an epidemic of tuberculosis in Vienna at the time. She looked anxiously at Breuer, explaining that her daughter also complained of migraine headaches and spoke of seeing things such as snakes and skeletons. She also told him of the other calamities that had beset her family: her husband had fallen ill some six months earlier and was now near death in another part of the house, and her two daughters had passed away some years earlier. She asked him if he thought it was

1

tuberculosis, as both looked at the hapless figure of her youngest and only remaining daughter.

Breuer examined her and shook his head. He was a soft-spoken man of 40 with a slightly balding head and a long dark beard. His sensitive brown eyes had a sad glint in them. It was not tuberculosis, he told her, but hysteria. Among his colleagues he was known as "the doctor with the golden touch" (Freeman and Strean 1981, p. 134) because of his success with difficult patients and his skill at diagnosing illnesses. Studying the girl a bit longer, he decided to hypnotize her.

He talked her into a trance and then suggested that when she awoke she would feel better. Suddenly, with her eyes shut tight, she began to mumble. "Tormenting . . . tormenting . . . torment-ing . . . " she said. Breuer leaned closer. She mumbled on in seemingly disconnected phrases about a girl who was tormented, sitting by a bed, fetching water, taking care of somebody who was very sick. Breuer turned to the mother and asked what the girl was talking about.

She was talking about her father, the mother explained. Until recently she had been in charge of taking care of him. Now she had fallen ill herself, and she continually mumbled in the third person, telling the story of a girl taking care of her father, as though she were reading a story from a children's book.

At last Breuer succeeded in awakening her from the trance. She looked up at him with her dark, intelligent eyes, and Breuer spoke to her a bit shyly because of her beauty. He said he would be back to check on her the following day.

From that moment on Breuer could not stop thinking about her. He was of course smitten by what Freud would later call "countertransference." The girl had aroused a strong erotic counter-transference, and Breuer had gotten swept up in these erotic feelings (though unconscious of them) and also perhaps by a narcissistic need to rescue a damsel in distress. She had, in effect, entranced him, and for the next eighteen months she would become his obsession.

Her name was Bertha Pappenheim (Breuer would later name her Anna O. in his case history, to preserve her anonymity), and she was born in Vienna in 1859. Her father was a wealthy businessman. In addition to the two older sisters who had died, she had a younger brother, Wilhelm. Like most upper-class women of that time, she had been educated in the arts and languages; when Breuer met her she was already fluent in French, Italian, and English. The first page of his case history (Breuer and Freud 1895) is filled with superlatives about her:

> She was markedly intelligent, with an astonishingly quick grasp of things and penetrating intuition. She possessed a powerful intellect which would have been capable of digesting solid mental pabulum and which stood in need of it—though without receiving it after she left school. She had great poetic and imaginative gifts, which were under the control of a sharp and critical common sense. [p. 21]

One can glean his adoration of Bertha, particularly of her mind, in this description, as well as his empathy for her intellectual frustration. This frustration was tied to the fact that her younger brother had been allowed to go to college, while she was denied that opportunity. This was the custom in those days, as men were expected to be providers and women mothers and homemakers. With respect to her sexuality he says only that she was able at times to forget her own illness by looking after "a number of poor, sick people, for she was thus able to satisfy a powerful instinct." He does not say what instinct he is referring to, but a few sentences later he adds, "The element of sexuality was astonishingly undeveloped in her" (p. 21). This he attributed to an "extremely monotonous existence in her puritanically-minded family," which "influenced her decisively in the direction of her illness, by indulging in systematic day-dreaming" (p. 22). Here Breuer is alluding to psychical processes that Freud would later name "repression" and "conversion hysteria." In analyzing Bertha's astonishing lack of sexual development a few years later, Freud (1905a) explained, "The character of hysterics shows a degree of sexual repression in excess of the normal quantity, and intensification of resistance against the sexual instinct (which we have already met with in the form of shame, disgust and morality), and what seems like an instinctive aversion on their part to any intellectual consideration of sexual problems" (p. 164). Due to her puritanical household and to the puritanical values of the society in which she lived, Bertha had repressed her sexuality and converted frustrated libidinal energy into her various symptoms, including the tendency to daydream.

Breuer diagnosed Bertha's illness as a hysterical psychosis. Today she would more likely be diagnosed as a schizophrenic with a split personality. Her gradual breakdown began when her father, of whom Breuer states she was "passionately fond," fell ill of a peripleuritic abscess which failed to heal, and to which he succumbed in April 1881. During the first few months of his illness, which began in July 1880, Bertha devoted herself to nursing her father. She was at his bedside every night and every morning, leaving only to take afternoon naps. Her mother attempted to persuade her to curtail her nursing activities for the sake of her own health, but the young woman would not listen. It was not surprising to anybody when she became sick.

She grew weaker and weaker. She developed a cough and the cough became worse. She became increasingly anemic. Then she acquired a distaste for food. It was at this point that her mother forced her to stop nursing her father. Her afternoon naps became longer, and were followed in the evening by trances in which she would mumble what seemed like nonsense. When she awoke from these trances she would be "highly excited." By December 11 she had taken to her bed, where she would remain for several months, developing one new symptom after another. Breuer wrote of a left-sided occipital headache, convergent squint (diplopia), complaints that the walls of the room were falling over, disturbances of vision, paresis of the muscles of the front of the neck, and contracture and anaethesia of the right upper and the right lower extremity.

It was at this point, in late December, that Breuer took on Bertha's case. He began seeing her twice a day, once in the morning and once in the evening. At first his method of treating her consisted simply of hypnotizing her at each visit and suggesting that she would feel better. Hypnosis was just beginning to be used with hysterics and other patients in those days, and was still frowned upon by the medical establishment. Until then, nobody had understood the psychological causes of mental illness; it had been attributed to genetics, to the devil, to evil spirits within, and it had been treated with electric shock, diet, drugs, and various rites of exorcism performed by Catholic priests. (Unfortunately, today some psychiatrists are returning to the use of electric shock and drugs in treating mental patients, and there is now a trend toward dismissing psychological factors and disdaining long-term psychotherapy.) By using hypnosis, Breuer was already taking a new path. However, this would only be the starting point on the road to a completely new way of understanding and treating mental patients.

He was a good listener. During his twice-a-day visits to Bertha's bedside he listened raptly to everything she said and observed her every movement. Before long he had noted that she presented two very distinct personalities, which he called states of consciousness. The first state, in which she was alert and pleasant, he called her normal state. The secondary state, in which she was "excited" and "nasty," he referred to as an "absence," viewing it as a form of autohypnosis. In describing this secondary personality's effect on the normal personality, he used the term "unconscious" for the first time in psychoanalytic literature, saying that the "products" of the secondary state acted as a stimulus "in the unconscious" (p. 45). (Freud also used this term later in the same book.) The "absences" had begun gradually. She would stop in the middle of a sentence, repeat her last words, pause vacantly, and then go on talking as though nothing had happened. These lapses grew longer, until she developed the secondary state of consciousness.

At one moment she might look at herself in a hand mirror and chirp, "How good of you to visit me so often, Dr. Breuer. But I do hate to inconvenience you in this way. Is it a terrible inconvenience? You can be honest with me, my dear Dr. Breuer, I can see it in your eyes anyway. Your eyes are quite transparent, you know. . . . " Then suddenly she might change, gasping at her image in the mirror, her face turning pale, her eyes dark, and her voice taking on a sinister edge. Now she would again repeat the phrase, "Tormenting . . . tormenting . . . tormenting . . . " and spout out seemingly nonsensical phrases. Sometimes she spoke of snakes being in her hair, of people in the room trying to get at her, of going mad. She would tell him she was evil and laugh and laugh at him as he stared at her, bewildered. Sometimes she would throw a pillow or tear off the buttons of her blouse. Sometimes she would scream.

Breuer would try to get her attention by calling her name or asking her questions.

Then, just as suddenly, she would come back to her normal state. She would ask him what she had said, and tell him that she felt as though she had just lost some time. During the normal times, she could speak quite objectively about her illness. She told him that she thought she had a good and a bad self, and that she could sense a profound darkness somewhere in her head.

Despite his efforts, her condition worsened. Her days fell into a routine. In the mornings when he made his first visit, she would be normal but excited, and he would hypnotize her to calm her down. In the afternoons she would fall asleep, and go into a state of "autosuggestion." In the evenings Breuer would call on her again, and she would awaken in her absent stage, which seemed to be a kind of hysterical mania. Breuer would again put her in a trance and encourage her to "talk herself out." Lying back on the bed, her eyes shut, her face contorting, she would tell more stories about sick girls nursing sick fathers, or repeat certain English fairy tales. After she had drained away her excitement under the trance, she would calm down until morning. However, her paralysis grew worse, and her speech gradually deteriorated. Breuer noticed that she was increasingly at a loss to find words, had trouble with grammar and syntax, no longer conjugated verbs, and eventually used only infinitives, for the most part incorrectly formed from weak past participles. She also omitted both the definite and indefinite article. After a while she put words together out of four or five languages and became almost unintelligible. Breuer's description of her speech not only provides a graphic portrait of her deterioration, but also a moving testimony of Breuer's attention to the minutest details of her behavior.

Soon she stopped speaking altogether. For two weeks she was mute. She made great efforts to speak, but could not. For the first time, Breuer began to understand the "psychical mechanism of the disorder" (p. 25). He realized that she had felt offended over something (something he said, most likely), and she had made up her mind not to speak about it.

"You're offended by what I said, aren't you?" he probably asked her at last. "Would you tell me about it?" She probably shook her head obstinately. "Tell me. You'll feel better if you do."

"There's nothing to tell."

"Isn't there?"

She tormented him with silence a while longer before she verbalized the anger she had been suppressing, describing how he had hurt her two weeks earlier. (Breuer does not say how he hurt her.) From that moment on she was able to talk again, and this change also brought about a return of the power of movement to her left arm and leg; in essence, he had analyzed her resistance. However, a few days later a new form of resistance appeared; she began to speak only in English. "Why are you speaking in English?" Breuer asked.

"I'm not. I'm speaking German, my dear Dr. Breuer," she answered. "Can't you tell?" She thought she was speaking German when she was speaking English.

On April 1 she got up for the first time. On April 5 her father died. This sent her into a profound stupor, lasting several days. Afterwards she was more subdued. She was less anxious, and the remaining contracture of her right arm and leg was diminished. The squint remained, however, and she complained of how difficult it was to recognize people. "I have to do such a laborious amount of recognizing work," she told him. "I have to constantly say to myself, 'this person's nose is such-and-such, and his hair is such-and-such, so he must be So-and So'" (p. 26). Still everybody seemed like a wax figure to her, somehow unconnected to her world, except for Dr. Breuer. She always recognized him the moment he entered her room. However, even with him, she had to feel his hand before she could acknowledge him.

She became more and more attached to him. When at one point she stopped eating completely, the only one who could convince her to eat was Breuer, and then only if he hand-fed her. When a consulting physician was called in, she completely ignored him. Breuer had her demonstrate all her peculiarities, including reading from a French text aloud in English. "This is like an examination," she said cheerfully in English. She laughed as she read, and the consulting physician moved his hand before her eyes but could not get her to look at him.

The consulting physician tried speaking to her. She spoke only to Breuer. Finally the physician blew smoke in her face.

She suddenly saw a stranger before her, rushed to the door to take away the key and fell unconscious to the ground. There followed a short fit of anger and then a severe attack of anxiety which I had great difficulty in calming down. Unluckily I had to leave Vienna that evening, and when I came back several days later I found the patient much worse. She had gone entirely without food the whole time, was full of anxiety and her hallucinatory *absences* were filled with terrifying figures, death's heads and skeletons. [p. 27]

She acted out the hallucinations as though she was experiencing them, and her mother and the servants had become quite alarmed by the time Breuer returned. On occasions such as this, Breuer reported that he would sometimes resort to the drug chloral to calm her down.

It was in July that, quite by chance, he made his two most important discoveries. He found that her current symptoms were connected with memories from the recent past—the period in which she had nursed her father. Then he found, after experimenting with different approaches to her ramblings, that if he got her to talk about these memories from the past and she brought forth the repressed emotions connected with them, the symptoms would disappear. Freud later alluded to this phenomenon with his famous line, "Hysterics suffer from reminiscences" (1910, p. 16).

The discoveries occurred at summer's end, after she had stopped drinking water for a period of many weeks. When Breuer (1895) questioned her about why she could not drink, she could not explain it. She just knew she could not stand the taste of water anymore. Every time the longed-for glass of water touched her lips, she would gasp and push it away with disgust. For six weeks she lived on fruit such as oranges or melons. Then one day, while under hypnosis, she began grumbling about her English lady-companion. She really did not care for this woman at all, she told Breuer. The woman was so disgusting. It really was not polite to say such things, she knew, but the woman really was terribly disgusting.

Breuer asked for an explanation, sensing a connection.

She began to describe "with every sign of disgust, how she had once gone into that lady's room and how her little dog—horrid creature!—had drunk out of a glass there" (p. 34). She had said nothing about it at the time, not wanting to be impolite.

After relating this anecdote, she asked for something to drink, and drank a large quantity of water without any difficulty. The drinking disturbance vanished, never to return.

Patient and therapist together had discovered what Breuer would call "the cathartic method" and the phenomenon of "psychic determinism" (symptoms being linked with past traumas). It had happened very simply, as discoveries usually do. Bertha had talked about the memories and feelings locked inside her, and Breuer had listened, now and then asking a pertinent question. In one sense she seemed to know instinctively what she needed in order to cure herself (although in another sense—in the transferential sense—she did not), and Breuer was willing to go along with her. So she had talked and he had listened, and the symptoms had disappeared. For hundreds of years physicians had been treating such patients in all kinds of ways, some more bizarre than others. Yet the very method that seemed to offer the best hope for a cure was the one that seemed the simplest.

Once they had discovered this method, her symptoms began to disappear in quick succession. For instance, one day he hypnotized her and asked her if she could remember the first time she had had trouble seeing. She remembered a time when she was sitting at her father's bed. She was wondering if he was going to die, and as she did so her eyes filled with tears. At that moment her father awoke, and asked her what time it was. Not wanting him to see her crying (afraid that he would guess she was thinking of his death), she tried to fight back the tears. She picked his watch up from the table, brought it up close to her eyes, and squinted at it. In telling Breuer this memory, tears welled up in her eyes and she began to sob. The next day she no longer squinted, and could see perfectly.

One of the most important memories, and one of the last to be discovered, was related to both her paralysis and her tendency to speak English. She described another evening she had spent sitting by her father's bed. She was exhausted from lack of sleep, but tried to keep awake in case he needed anything. Despite her efforts, she fell asleep for a few minutes. When she awoke she felt guilty. What if he had died while she was asleep? she asked herself. (Psychoanalytic research has since shown that very often an obsessive concern about somebody's death masks an unconscious wish for that death.) Suddenly she thought she saw a large black snake slithering across the wall behind her father's bed, ready to attack him. (There were, indeed, such snakes behind the house.) She tried to keep the snake away, but found that her right arm was paralyzed. It had been hanging over the back of her chair and had gone to sleep. She looked at her rigid arm and hand, and then the fingers turned into little snakes with death's heads. Breuer wrote:

When the snake vanished, in her terror she tried to pray. But language failed her: she could find no tongue in which to speak, till at last she thought of some children's verses in English and then found herself able to think and pray in that language. . . .
    Next day in the course of a game . . . a bent branch revived her hallucination of the snake, and simultaneously her right arm

became rigidly extended. Thenceforward the same thing invariably occurred whenever the hallucination was recalled by some object with a more or less snakelike appearance. [p. 39]

Again, once she had recalled this memory and relived it emotionally, the symptoms vanished. But it had taken a long time and a lot of therapy work to get there. Breuer explained that it was "quite impracticable to shorten the work by trying to elicit in her memory straight away the first provoking cause of her symptoms" (p. 35). She would just grow confused, and things would proceed even more slowly. Generally he asked her to focus on a particular symptom and recall past incidents during which she had experienced the symptom. In each case many incidents came to her mind before she recalled the initial trauma that led to the formation of the symptom. For example, in working on her inability to hear people when they came into her room, she recalled 108 separate detailed instances of this before remembering the first—not hearing her father come in. She had many memories of her cough before she reached the original one, a time when she heard dance music as she was sitting at her father's side and wished she could be at the dance. She was overcome with guilt and began to cough. Thereafter, whenever she heard music she would cough. In addition, during the last six months of the treatment, she developed symptoms that were connected with events that had happened a year earlier. For instance, one day she told Breuer she did not know why, but she was angry at him. It turned out that she had been angry at him on precisely the same day a year before.

As the work proceeded, she became more and more cheerful. It was on one of these cheerful days that she coined the term "the talking cure." While he was working with her, she said something like, "Well, here we go again with the talking cure."

"Talking cure?" He beamed at her. "Yes, that's a good name for it all right."

"It's like chimney sweeping," she said. "You're sweeping my chimney. Sweeping all the blackness out of my head" (p. 30).

The Talking Cure. Chimney Sweeping. These phrases would become famous as characterizations of the "radical" new method of treatment Bertha and Breuer had discovered.

Unfortunately, the case had an abrupt and somewhat unhappy ending. Breuer had become so engrossed in treating Bertha that he not only neglected other cases, but his wife as well. Jones (1957) wrote that Freud later found out from various sources what had actually happened (but was not reported in Breuer's case history). As the case reached its final stages and Bertha's symptoms disappeared, Breuer's wife became morose. Freud speculated that she had grown jealous of Bertha. She had been forced to endure eighteen months listening to her husband go on and on about the intelligence, attractiveness, and insight of his special patient. In those days it was highly unusual for a physician to spend so much time with a single patient. Not only Breuer's wife, but also his colleagues saw this as strange. (Breuer would not tell Freud about the case until five months after it had been terminated, and only then would he find an appreciative listener.) When Breuer finally guessed the meaning of his wife's moroseness, it "provoked a violent reaction in him" (Jones, p. 143), and he decided to bring the treatment to an abrupt end. The following morning he informed Bertha that she was well, and that he would not be seeing her any longer. She seemed to be able to accept this pronouncement. However, he was called back that evening.

In a letter to Stefan Zweig on June 2, 1932, Freud speculated on what happened on that last visit:

> On the evening of the day when all her symptoms had been disposed of, he was summoned to the patient again, found her confused and writhing in abdominal cramps. Asked what was wrong with her, she replied: "Now Dr. B.'s child is coming!"
>
> At this moment he held in his hand the key that would have opened the "doors to the Mothers," but he let it drop. With all his great intellectual gifts there was nothing Faustian in his nature. Seized by conventional horror he took flight and abandoned the patient to a colleague. . . . [E. Freud 1960, p. 413]

Jones wrote that Breuer was shocked at discovering his patient in the throes of an hysterical childbirth (pseudocyesis). He managed to hypnotize her and talk her into a state of calm before fleeing the house "in a cold sweat." The next day he and his wife left for a second honeymoon in Venice, "resulting in the conception of a child" who was to commit suicide sixty years later in New York. Breuer never treated Bertha again, although he continued to take an interest in her case.

She had a few relapses after her treatment with Breuer was terminated. She spent some time in a sanatorium in Gross Enzersdorf, where Jones says "she inflamed the heart of the psychiatrist in charge." Breuer visited her there, and he confided to Freud that "she was quite unhinged and that he wished she would die and so be released from her suffering" (Jones, p. 144). This statement is an indication of how guilty Breuer felt, and how angry he was at her for arousing this guilt in him. Bertha went on to live an illustrious life. At the age of 30 she became the first social worker in Germany, and founded a periodical and several institutes for children. She never married and became devoted to feminism and religion. Noted for her acid sense of humor, she wrote five witty obituaries for various periodicals, foretelling her own death.

She remained bitter toward both men and psychoanalysis throughout her life. "If there will be any justice in the world to come," she once said, "women will be lawgivers and men will have to have babies." And, when asked if a disturbed girl in one of her institutions should be psychoanalyzed, she answered, "Never! Not as long as I am alive" (Freeman and Strean 1980, p. 137).

It took nine years for Freud to convince Breuer to publish his case history about Bertha. This was probably because Breuer had so many unresolved countertransference feelings about her, and also because he was afraid of getting a negative reception from his contemporaries. According to Jones, Freud was able to convince him by confiding that one of his own patients had thrown her arms around him during treatment, and by explaining to Breuer his theory about transference. Breuer then agreed to a joint writing venture with Freud, saying of transference, "I believe that is the most important thing we both have to make known to the world" (p. 160). Breuer was 49, Freud 35 when their first paper on the treatment of hysteria appeared in *Neurologisches Centralblatt*, the principal German neurological journal, and was reprinted in a Viennese medical journal. It set off hostility against them that for the next two decades would be open and intense. Their book, *Studies in Hysteria*, sold only 626 copies in its first thirteen years. Breuer would eventually break with Freud in the face of this hostility to the cathartic method and to Freud's theories about the sexual etiology of hysteria. "I confess," Breuer wrote to the psychiatrist August Forel on November 21, 1907, "that plunging into sexuality in theory and practice is not to my taste" (Freeman and Strean 1981, p. 139). Freud's love and admiration for his former mentor would turn first to resentment, then to bitterness, and he would continue to explore the "forbidden" realms of human behavior on his own.

Interpretation

While Freud was the founder of psychoanalysis, Breuer was the first psychoanalyst. His work with Bertha led to the initial formulation of some of the basic concepts of psychoanalysis: repression, psychic determinism, the unconscious, resistance, the sexual etiology of hysteria, psychic trauma, conversion, and transference. Breuer admitted in *Studies in Hysteria* that he had "suppressed a large number of quite interesting details" (p. 41) about Anna O., but it was nevertheless the first case history of its kind.

Still, one wonders what "quite interesting details" he suppressed and why? It might be that these details had to do with the erotic transference and countertransference which he had denied until the last minute, and about which he felt guilty. Bertha had obviously transferred her repressed infantile feelings for her father onto him, and he had countertransferred feelings onto her. Freud later coined the term "transference" in describing Bertha's behavior toward Breuer, and explained the intense rapport created through the use of the cathartic method as "a complete prototype" of transference (1914a, p. 12). Spotnitz, noting the strong feelings narcissistic patients induce in their therapists, analyzed Breuer's relationship with Bertha and concluded that "Breuer's conduct in the final phase of the relationship could now be identified as the prototype of countertransference" (1985, p. 222). Transference and countertransference were factors in the treatment's success and causes of its failure.

Attempting to understand what went wrong in the "Anna O." case, Balint (1968) denotes two kinds of regression, benign and malignant, and places Bertha in the second category. He sees her as suffering from a severe form of hysteria, contriving to derive a secondary gain from her illness and treatment. He asserts that with this type of patient, "As long as the patient's expectations and demands are met, the therapist is allowed to observe most interesting, revealing events and *pari passu* his patient will feel better, appreciative, and grateful" (p. 140). However, the patient's demands never end. The therapist finds himself always in demand, and "in the case of Miss Anna O., this sort of experience seemed to be interminable. A kind of vicious spiral developed; as soon as some of the patient's 'cravings' had been satisfied, new cravings or 'needs' appeared, demanding to be satisfied, leading eventually to a development of addiction-like states" (p. 141). Balint cannot explain this phenomenon. I would suggest that this type of hysteric, by denying aggressive feelings, can never satisfactorily merge with the transference object, and therefore constantly needs more and more reassurance of the object's loyalty.

Olsen and Koppe (1988) compare Breuer's cathartic method with a Catholic confession, but add that while confessors remember what they have confessed, patients under hypnosis do not. They also call attention to the fact that Bertha had a split personality similar to that portrayed in the novel *Doctor Jekyll and Mr. Hyde*, in which an intellectual scientist by day changes into a bestial murderer at night. Through the defense of splitting, she dissociated her "evil" personality from her "good" personality. Although Breuer was able, through hypnosis, to help Bertha obtain temporary relief through abreaction, he did not succeed in integrating these two personalities. This may provide us with an additional clue as to why her "cravings"—as Balint has aptly put it—could never be satisfied.

Freud's understanding of Bertha's hysterical symptoms centered on her repressed sexual feelings. He wrote that ". . . the fact has emerged that symptoms represent a substitute for impulses the source of whose strength is derived from the sexual instinct" (1905a, p. 164). Elsewhere he used the term "strangulated affects" to explain Bertha's repression of forbidden thoughts and feelings about her father, which "manifested themselves in physical symptoms" and then had to be abreacted in therapy in order "to restore the organism to its normal functioning" (1910, p. 18). Freud did not yet recognize the importance of repressed aggression in the etiology of hysteria. Spotnitz, studying the case material in the light of present understanding about the aggressive instinct, concluded that Bertha "had strong feelings of hatred for her father that she did not want to recognize" (1985, p. 223). It is likely that Freud would have come to the same conclusion had he reinterpreted the case in light of his later theories.

Both sexual and aggressive conflicts are evident in the reminiscences that emerged during the course of her treatment. In the memory in which she was sitting at her father's bed, wondering if he was going to die, she stated that she was afraid that her father would guess she was thinking of his death. She tried to hide her eyes, which were full of tears, by squinting at his watch. Why would she be afraid that her father would guess she was thinking of his death? Perhaps because she unconsciously wished for his death. In another memory, while sitting by her father she heard dance music, and wished that she could be at the dance. She was overcome with guilt, and began to cough. This memory may again contain a death wish (if only he were dead I could dance), and it may also contain a wish to act out (at the dance) her incestuous wishes toward her father (on an infantile, oedipal level she may have wished to take her father away from her mother). In the final memory, in which she fell asleep at her father's side and felt guilty, she again thought about his death, asking herself, "What if he had died while I was asleep?" Then she saw a large black snake slithering across the wall behind his bed (both a phallic and a death symbol, as in the hand of death). When she tried to raise her hand, she found that her fingers had turned into little snakes with death's heads (again both a sexual and a death symbol).

Although we do not know the details of Bertha's early childhood, it seems apparent that she had a strong attachment to her father, and that it was most likely of a reaction-formation type. She had an intense, loving loyalty to him (only she could nurse him), which perhaps compensated for her unconscious aggression toward him. The symbolism of her memories, replete with phalluses and death heads, her obsession with her father, her envy of her younger brother, her lifelong bitterness toward Breuer and toward men, and her crusade for women's liberation, may all be seen as signs of unresolved penis envy. Her father had been the dominant force in the household until his illness, and she had wanted his approval and acceptance. As an infant, she would have wanted him to give her a penis. This wish, of course, was frustrated, and later transformed into the phallic imagery of her hallucinations. She was also frustrated by him oedipally; not only did he refuse her a penis, but he also refused to marry her, and to give her a baby. The wish for a penis (for male acceptance and power) and for a baby (confirmation of her femininity) was transferred to Breuer, who at first seemed to give her what she wanted, but then at the last moment turned out to be another frustrating object like her father. Her father's death represented his final betrayal of her, his ultimate frustration of her infantile wishes. "Then let him die quickly!" she may have thought. Yet her superego with its ego ideal of the loving daughter who must not have any "evil" thoughts of death or sex fought against the admission of such sentiments, leading to the hysterical conversion symptoms. Breuer's "betrayal" served to reinforce her father-fixation.

Neither Breuer nor Freud properly understood the connection between adult psychopathology and infantile sexual traumas, another area in which current advances have thrown a brighter light on the etiology of hysteria. Recent research on split and multiple personalities has shown that in most cases such patients have been sexually abused as infants (O'Regan 1985). The severity of Bertha's case suggests that this may also have been the case with her.

Some have suggested that Bertha's illness was entirely caused by the societal oppression of women. Marion A. Kaplan (see Rosenbaum and Muroff 1984), for example, asserts that "if Bertha Pappenheim lived today she would probably not have become Anna O., the patient," maintaining that her illness was a "cultural construct," the product of the "suffocating lot" of nineteenth-century women (p. 101). Views that attempt to blame female emotional problems on male oppression tend to be extreme. Bertha's hysterical psychosis was probably caused by a combination of factors: an innate disposition towards emotional illness; pathological relationships with her father, mother, and brother; a repressive familial environment; and the repressive environment of nineteenth-century Vienna. Indeed, Bertha might not have become a patient today, but it does not mean she would not have been hysterical. Today's hysteric differs from the hysteric of the past century precisely because of the cultural influence on the kind of symptoms a hysteric develops. Women in those days were socialized to suppress their sexual and aggressive drives, resulting in widespread conversion hysteria. In Western society today women are allowed more freedom of expression than men and, in my opinion, are prone to acting out their hysterical rage through vehicles such as radical lesbianism or feminism.

Today the improvement of Bertha's condition during the therapy might be explained, in part, as a transference cure. This would shed light on her relapses after Breuer referred her to a colleague. However, she was much more than hysterical; indeed, several authors in a recent study of the case have diagnosed her as a schizophrenic, or as someone undergoing a profound pathological mourning (Rosenbaum and Muroff 1984). Breuer helped her to get over the pathological mourning, but he barely scratched the surface in terms of modern psychoanalytic technique, for he left untouched the infantile material that formed the core of her father-complex. Hence, she would remain bitter toward Breuer, psycho-analysis and men for the remainder of her life (a displacement of her bitterness toward her father), and Breuer would experience a proportionate guilt and animosity toward her (a displacement, perhaps, of his own unresolved infantile conflicts). His wish, after he visited her at the sanatorium, that she would die and "be released from her suffering" might have been a countertransference response to her unconscious wish for her father's death.

In her later life Bertha was able to sublimate with some success. Although he had not helped her resolve the infantile roots of her complexes, Breuer had nevertheless assisted her in function-ing competently in the world of work. His pioneering treatment of her was instrumental in providing a framework for later psy-choanalysts to build upon, particularly underscoring the impor-tance of transference and countertransference. In specific, his work with Bertha served as a graphic illustration of the hazards of "the talking cure." He himself did not reap the rewards of his discov-ery; rather, for the rest of his life he had to endure the enmity of his patient, his own guilt, and the hostility of his contemporaries, who saw him as a quack and a pervert.

It is understandable, when the case is seen in this light, why most psychiatrists even today would rather treat mental patients with drugs. Simply relating to a patient is more difficult and riskier. Yet, despite the fact that Breuer's work with Bertha achieved only minimal results, it was a springboard for a new, more humane, and genuinely curative form of treatment. As Freud wrote in the last chapter of *Studies in Hysteria*: ". . . much will be gained if we succeed in transforming . . . hysterical misery into common unhappiness" (p. 305).

2

DREAM
INTERPRETATION
WITH HYSTERICS

Sigmund Freud and Dora (1905)

In 1894, twelve years after Breuer's treatment of "Anna O.," a handsome man in his late thirties came to Dr. Sigmund Freud with complaints of "confusion." Freud linked this symptom with syphilis, which the man said he had contracted before he was married, and prescribed an "energetic" treatment for it. Four years later the man returned to introduce his daughter, who he felt had "meanwhile grown unmistakably neurotic" (Freud 1905b, p. 27).

The man was Philip Bauer, a wealthy manufacturer who owned two textile mills. His daughter was Ida (whom Freud would later give the pseudonym Dora in her case history). She was 16 when Freud first met her, a girl "of intelligent and engaging looks" who may have glanced at him with suspicion when they were introduced. She did not like doctors, nor did she have much respect for men. Freud was 42 and nearing his prime. He was in the process of writing what he would later come to regard as his best work. He had been married for twelve years, and had fathered six children, three boys and three girls. His practice at 19 Berggasse in Vienna was well established. He probably sized up this engaging girl with his brown, penetrating eyes as her father told him about the chronic cough from which she had been suffering. Immediately after he gave her an examination, he suggested that she go into therapy with him, but she refused to do so.

Two years later, after she had turned 18, her father brought Ida back to Freud, explaining that she had left a suicide note and had had fainting spells. He was beside himself. He said that Ida had been making outrageous accusations and demands. She claimed that his best friend, Mr. K., had made advances to her, and she was convinced that he, her father, was having an affair with Mrs. K. He felt she had lost her senses, and he practically pleaded with Freud to take his side:

> "She keeps pressing me to break off relations with Herr K. and more particularly with Frau K., whom she used positively to worship formerly. . . . I myself believe that Dora's tale of the man's immoral suggestions is a phantasy that has forced its way into her mind; and besides, I am bound to Frau K. by ties of honourable friendship and I do not wish to cause her pain. The poor woman is most unhappy with her husband, of whom, by the by, I have no very high opinion. . . . We are just two poor wretches who give one another what comfort we can by an exchange of friendly sympathy. You know already that I get nothing from my own wife. But Dora, who inherits my obstinacy, cannot be moved from her hatred of the K.s. . . . Please . . . bring her to reason." [pp. 34–35]

Freud soon took on the case. By then *The Interpretation of Dreams* had been published. It was either hailed or damned, but not taken lightly. He had tasted fame and was confident of his therapeutic prowess, but he was still in need of patients. Indeed, one of his aims in working with Ida was to practice his newly discovered art of dream interpretation; like all discoverers, he was going through a period of infatuation with his new method. He had already made plans to write a book before the analysis had been completed, a work that would supplement his book on the interpretation of dreams "by showing how an art, which would otherwise be useless, can be turned to account for the discovery of the hidden and repressed parts of mental life" (p. 136).

Interpreting dreams was the newest aspect of the therapy process he now called psychoanalysis. He had gradually developed this way of working since breaking with Breuer, abandoning hypnosis because "even the most brilliant results were liable to be suddenly wiped away if my personal relation with the patient became disturbed," noting, moreover, that "the personal emotional relation between doctor and patient was after all stronger than the whole cathartic process, and it was precisely that factor which escaped every effort at control" (1925, p. 26). These observations were based not only on Breuer's work with "Anna O.," but also on his own subsequent work with hysterics. The final decision to abandon hypnosis had come about when an attractive young woman had thrown her arms around him while she was in a trance and at that moment a servant had walked into the office, causing Freud a great deal of embarrassment. Immediately thereafter he began experimenting with other methods, wanting more control of what he had defined as the "transference relationship." For a time he had his patients close their eyes while he would press his fingers to their foreheads, and ask them to tell him whatever they could about a particular symptom. Later this "concentration method" was dropped, and he simply asked them to free-associate without censoring themselves. Free association, he found, was a method "by whose means alone the pure metal of valuable unconscious thoughts can be extracted from the raw material of the patient's associations" (1905b, p. 134). Dreams were another aspect of free association.

When he started her treatment, Freud described Ida's symptoms as "dysponoea [breathlessness], *tussis nervosa* [nervous cough], aphonia [inability to utter sounds], and possibly migraines, together with depression, hysterical unsociability, and a *taedium vitae* which was probably not entirely genuine" (p. 32). Various methods had been used to treat her up until then, including hydrotherapy and the local application of electricity, but to no avail. "The child had developed into a mature young woman of very independent judgement, who had grown accustomed to laugh at the efforts of doctors, and in the end to renounce their help entirely" (p. 30). Neither hydrotherapy nor electricity were part of Freud's treatment plan. Instead he instructed her to come to his office six days a week from 10:30 until 11:30 A.M. and lie on his couch with her eyes closed, while he sat behind and slightly to her right, puffing on his cigars. From this vantage point he could see her, but she could not see him. His initial instructions to her were to say whatever came to her mind without censoring herself, and to tell him her dreams so that they could interpret them together. Like a dutiful daughter, she complied.

Lying on his couch with that suspicious glint in her eyes, a world-weary pout on her face, and her long Victorian gown wrapped around her shapely legs, she told him a tale the complexity of which might match the plot of any romance novel or soap opera. Her world-weary posture (the *taedium vitae* mentioned by Freud) was no doubt a defense against her infantile feelings, and she was already by then quite entrenched in it. One can imagine her lying back, sighing with resignation, assuming from the outset that Freud was on her father's side, wondering how she could either sway him to hers, or extricate herself from the situation entirely. Nevertheless, while the fumes of Freud's cigars wafted above her, she talked.

Ida's family was Jewish and came from Bohemia. Her father was the dynamic figure in the family, a charming, intelligent, agreeable man of 40 whom she had once adored but now disdained. Her mother, Käthe, an uneducated and unintelligent woman whom she despised, had no interest in her husband or children; her days were spent in "cleaning the house with its furniture and utensils and in keeping them clean—to such an extent as to make it impossible to use or enjoy them" (p. 28). Her brother Otto, whom she had idealized as a child but now resented, was a little over a year older than her. From the age of 6, she remembered her father going through a series of illnesses. At one point, he contracted tuberculosis and they moved south. At another time he suffered from a detached retina. During his illnesses, Ida was the one who nursed him. Her mother would not go near his sickbed. Ida had been tenderly attached to her father, and her brother was devoted to their mother. While living in the south, the Bauers had become friendly with the K.s, a younger couple with two small children. Her father and Mrs. K. seemed taken with each other, and before long Mrs. K. had become her father's devoted nurse and confidante. Ida did not terribly mind being replaced by Mrs. K. for she admired her and enjoyed taking care of her children. Even after she became convinced that her father and Mrs. K. were having an affair, Ida did not mind. In the beginning she approved of this relationship, and perhaps enjoyed it vicariously through her own close and confidential relationship with Mrs. K., who became a surrogate mother to her. She took wonderful care of the K.s' children, and often managed things so that her father and Mrs. K. could be alone—all without ever mentioning to her father or Mrs. K. what she knew. As time went on, Mr. K. began paying attention to Ida. They wrote many letters to each other when he traveled, and he brought her small gifts when he returned. He began to court her and she was flattered, until he started making his "disgusting" advances. "I think my father handed me over to Mr. K. in exchange for Mrs. K.," Ida contended with bitterness as she recalled these incidents. She knew Freud would think she was exaggerating, but she really thought her father and Mr. K. had made some kind of arrangement. Freud did not reply.

When she was 14, Mr. K. made his first advance to her. There was a church festival, and Mr. K. invited her to meet him at his office, which was near the festival. When Ida arrived, she found herself alone with him; he had persuaded his wife to stay home and had dismissed his clerks. As she stood in his office, he suddenly clasped her to him and pressed a kiss upon her lips. This kiss was quite disgusting to her, and she tore herself away from him and rushed out of his office. Neither of them mentioned the scene again, and from that time on whenever she saw couples embracing on the street she would walk in the other direction. However, she continued her friendship with Mr. K. Four years later, while she and her father were staying with the K.s at a lakeside resort, Mr. K. proposed to her. He offered to divorce his wife and marry the 18-year-old Ida, complaining "You know I don't get anything from my wife." Again she was disgusted. She slapped him, and when her father had to leave for business reasons a few days later, she demanded that he take her with him. It was soon after this incident that she leveled her accusations about Mr. K., demanded that her father break off with the K.s, and left the suicide note, saying that she could not go on with life. At first her father had called Mr. K. to account, but he denied the whole thing, suggesting that Ida had been reading romance magazines. Mrs. K. backed Mr. K., naming magazines she knew the young woman had been reading, which she thought had put romantic ideas in her head. In the end her father believed them instead of Ida. That is when he brought her to see Freud.

"Why did that first kiss disgust you so much?" Freud wanted to know.

She had no answer.

He could not help but think that such a response to her first kiss was hysterical. A normal girl of 14, he reasoned, would have been sexually excited by her first kiss from a man who had been courting her (and to whom she had been responding) for some time. In analyzing the situation, he speculated that during the kiss she had felt Herr K.'s erect penis pressing against her, and something about that may have revolted her. His erect penis may have stimulated her clitoris, "and the excitation of this second erotogenic zone was referred by a process of displacement to the simultaneous pressure against the thorax and became fixed there" (p. 39). He further speculated that such feelings of disgust were originally a reaction to the smell and sight of excrement. The genitals acted as a reminder of the excremental functions, "and this applies especially to the male member, for that organ performs the function of micturition as well as the sexual function" (p. 40). (Freud had not yet discovered the castration complex, and how the envy of the penis can turn to disgust toward that organ, and toward sexuality in general.) As to why Ida would displace her feelings from her clitoris to her thorax and develop a chronic cough, Freud reasoned that such a displacement safeguarded her "against any revival of the repressed perception" (p. 39). That is, it kept her safe from the disgusting memory of their sexual arousal. Later, he discovered another clue to the nature of this displacement and the formation of her coughing symptom.

"Mrs. K. only loves my father for his money," Ida continually insisted. "She only loves him because he's *ein vermögender Mann.*" She said this over and over, and Freud noted to himself that the word *vermögender* meant both "rich" and "potent." Because of her choice of words and the way in which she said them, he decided that "behind this phrase its opposite lay concealed, namely that her father was '*ein unvermögender Mann.*' This could only be meant in a sexual sense—that her father, as a man, was without means, was impotent" (pp. 58–59). He presented her with this interpretation and asked her if, to her knowledge, her father was in fact impotent.

She said she believed he was.

He then pointed out the contradiction. "If on the one hand you continue to insist that your father and Frau K. are having a love-affair, and on the other hand you maintain that your father is impotent, or in other words incapable of carrying out such an affair, that would seem to be a contradiction, wouldn't it?" he asked.

She blushed. "I know very well," she told him, "that there's more than one way of obtaining sexual gratification" (p. 59).

He asked her how she had learned such a thing.

She said that she did not remember.

He speculated that her sexual knowledge had been obtained through her relationship with the governess who had once worked for the K.s. Ida had been very intimate with her, sharing sexual secrets, until she found out that the governess had had an affair with Mr. K. After that, she would have nothing more to do with the woman.

Was she referring to organs other than the genitals? he pressed her further.

She said she was.

"In that case she must be thinking of precisely those parts of the body which in her case are in a state of irritation—the throat and the oral cavity" (p. 59).

She must have let out a sound or in some other way shown dismay; according to Freud, she would not hear of going so far as this in recognizing her own thoughts.

> But the conclusion was inevitable that with her spasmodic cough, which, as is usual, was referred for its exciting cause to a tickling in her throat, she pictured to herself a scene of sexual gratification *per os* between the two people whose love-affair occupied her mind so incessantly. A very short time after she had tacitly accepted this explanation her cough vanished. [p. 49]

This interaction provides a concise view of the process of psychoanalysis as Freud had begun to practice it. By analyzing the unconscious thoughts, memories, and associations that lay beneath a symptom (the nervous cough) and by bringing what was unconscious to consciousness, he had helped Ida to understand herself and to get rid of the symptom.

However, he encountered much more resistance when he tried to interpret another of her symptoms, the obsessive habit she had of reproaching others. She would go on and on, session after session, castigating her father, her mother, Mr. and Mrs. K., her brother, the governess, and various other people who had offended her. However, her father was the chief target of her reproaches. "I can think of nothing else," she told him one day. "I know my brother says we children have no right to criticize this behaviour of father's. He declares that we ought not to trouble ourselves about it, and ought even to be glad, perhaps, that he has found a woman he can love, since mother understands him so little. I can quite see that, and I should like to think the same as my brother, but I can't. I can't forgive him for it" (p. 67). Probably she wished to gain Freud's sympathy. Instead, noting this "supervalent train of thought," he saw these reproaches as covers for her self-reproaches.

Her reproach of her father for being in love with Mrs. K. was at the same time a reproach of herself for being in love with her father, and her reproach of her father's using his illness to manipulate was a self-reproach for her own similar inclinations. Likewise, her reproaches of Mr. and Mrs. K. covered self-reproaches for harboring illicit feelings of sexual attraction to both of them, while her reproaches of her mother's denial of reality concealed a reproach of her own denial of reality. Writing of Ida's love for her father, Freud explained that he had "learned to look upon unconscious love relations like this (which may be recognized by their abnormal consequences)—between a father and a daughter, or between a mother and a son—as a revival of germs of feeling from infancy" (p. 69). Here he alludes to the Oedipus complex, which he would propound more fully in later writings. Ida had always been drawn to her father, and Freud believed that his many illnesses were bound to have increased her love for him. "He had been so proud of the early growth of her intelligence that he had made her his confidante while she was still a child" (p. 69). One day he confronted Ida with this interpretation, telling her that he could not avoid supposing that her affection for her father must at a very early age have amounted to her being completely in love with him.

She gave him her usual reply: "I don't remember that." But she went on to tell him something analogous about a 7-year-old cousin with whom she identified. "Recently my little cousin witnessed—not for the first time—a heated dispute between her parents, and when I came to see them shortly afterwards, she whispered in my ear: 'You can't think how much I hate that person!' (pointing to her mother), 'and when she's dead I shall marry papa'" (p. 70). Freud took this as a validation of his interpretation, explaining that he was accustomed to regarding such parallel associations as a confirmation from the unconscious of his interpretation.

Later, when he presented her with the interpretation that she was in love with Mr. K. but had an unconscious conflict about loving him which caused her to deny this love, he was met with an adamant "No!" Again he took this adamant "No!" as a confirmation. "The 'No' uttered by a patient after a repressed thought has been presented to his conscious perception for the first time does no more than register the existence of a repression and its severity; it acts, as it were, as a gauge of the repression's strength" (p. 71).

Another confirmation of her love for Mr. K. came a short time later. After having been consistently cheerful for several days, she arrived at her session in the "worst of tempers." It turned out that it was Mr. K.'s birthday. Freud recalled that a few days before, on her own birthday, none of the handsome presents she had received had given her pleasure. One had been missing: Mr. K.'s. This memory was behind her bad temper on his birthday. Yet she still denied her love for him.

Freud never got around to presenting her with his interpretation about Mrs. K. He had concluded that she was also in love with Mrs. K., but he did not think that she was ready to hear such an interpretation. He noted that Ida had occasionally praised Mrs. K.'s "adorable white body" in accents appropriate to a lover, and that whenever she stayed at the K.s' she had shared a bedroom with Mrs. K. while her husband slept in another room. "When, in a hysterical woman or girl, the sexual libido which is directed towards men has been energetically suppressed, it will regularly be found that the libido which is directed towards women has become vicariously reinforced and even to some extent conscious" (pp. 73–74). Through Mrs. K., Ida had been able to vicariously live out her oedipal fantasies about her father. However, at the last moment Mrs. K., her dearest friend, had also betrayed her. Even Mrs. K. refused to believe her accusations about Mr. K., and even she had turned traitor by revealing some of their most intimate conversations about sex, and the names of the magazines she had read. Ida must have felt as though everyone she loved had betrayed her.

And now, here was Freud, apparently no more sympathetic toward her than the others had been. Here was another older man, similar to her father and Mr. K. Was she also in love with Freud? Would he betray her, too? These were the questions Freud asked himself when she brought in her first dream.

He had been awaiting her first dream, and then it happened quite suddenly during the course of a session. She reported that she had once again had a dream which she had had many times before.

"Tell it to me," he said.

> A house was on fire. My father was standing beside my bed and woke me up. I dressed myself quickly. Mother wanted to stop and save her jewel-case; but Father said, "I refuse to let myself and my two children be burned for the sake of your jewel-case." We hurried downstairs and as soon as I was outside I woke up. [p. 78]

After two months work, Freud must have been silently overjoyed to get this dream. It was a dream whose symbolism was fairly clear, and which offered many new clues to Ida's unconscious motivations. He had determined in *The Interpretation of Dreams* that not only daydreams, but night dreams as well, represented wish-fulfillments. Even nightmares such as this one were expressions of wishes, or, as he would put it many years later, after critics had heaped objections upon him for this theory, "a dream is an *attempt* at the fulfillment of a wish" (1933, p. 30). He had also learned to divide dreams, considering both their manifest content, which linked them to present events, and their latent content, which linked them with the events of early childhood.

He was able to discover the manifest content of Ida's dream fairly quickly. He asked her when she had had the dream, and she said she believed she had first dreamed it while staying with the K.s at the lakeside resort where Mr. K. had proposed to her. In fact, after he had proposed and she had slapped him, she took a nap; she awoke to find Mr. K. standing beside her bed. He said that he had just come into "his own bedroom" to find something. However, she was quite upset by the episode, and asked for a key to the room, only to find that there was none. She had the dream for the next few nights—until she left unexpectedly with her father—and she had it again a few days before telling it to Freud. Thus the manifest content of the dream was a wish to be rescued by her father from Mr. K.'s advances (the fire of his passion, and hers). The jewel-box represented, according to Freud, her virginity. In analyzing why she had had the dream again a few days before, Freud interpreted that Ida must once again have begun to feel sexually threatened, and he believed that the threat was now coming from Freud himself, another older man who was making advances at her, forcing her to reveal to him her innermost sexual secrets. He told her these interpretations, explaining, "The dream confirms once more what I had already told you before you dreamed it—that you are summoning up your old love for your father in order to protect yourself against your love for Herr K." (p. 86). He elaborated on this idea and then added that he saw the recent reappearance of the dream as a sign that the same situation had arisen once again, and that she had decided to give up the treatment (run from another burning house), a treatment to which her father made her come.

She could not accept these interpretations, and he let them drop for the moment. However, his premonition about her stopping therapy turned out to be quite correct, for within a few days she had done just that. Indeed, his failure to handle the transference he had begun to interpret may have been one of the factors that led to her hasty exit. As Glenn (1980a) noted, it was following his explanation of autoerotic activity that "she had the first dream which contained a determination to leave a dangerous house; she must have been terrified that her wishes [about Freud] would come true" (p. 32). However, for the remaining few days, Freud continued unabashedly to work on this and a second dream.

He proceeded to analyze the latent content of the dream. One of the phrases kept going through his mind—*that it might be necessary to leave the room; that an accident might happen in the night.* When he thought about accidents that happen in the night, he thought about bed-wetting. In a paternalistic way, he veered Ida toward this subject by asking her to look at a table and tell him if she saw something new there. She said she did not. He said there was a box of matches on the table, and asked her if she knew why children were told not to play with matches. "Yes," she replied. "On account of the risk of fire" (p. 87). That was not the only reason, he told her. They were warned not to "play with fire" because there were supposed to be certain consequences. Again she did not know what he meant. He explained that children who played with fire were said to wet their beds.

Upon pursuing this theme, he discovered that she had been a bed-wetter, and that her father used to wake her up in the middle of the night in order to "rescue" her from bed-wetting (put out the fire). Freud took it further. He discovered that before she had been a bed-wetter she had been a masturbator, another activity which her father had discouraged (rescued her from). Since water was needed to put out fire, Freud associated her bed-wetting to the fire in the dream, and, at the same time, saw the wetting as a symbol of sexual excitation, as when Ida became excited by Mr. K.'s kiss. Again, when Freud presented her with his interpretation, she could not accept it.

A session or two later he found another way to broach this interpretation. On that day she wore a small reticule at her waist— a fashion ornament that had recently come into style—and as she spoke she kept playing with this reticule—opening it, putting a finger into it, and closing it—without paying attention to what she was doing. Freud looked on this piece of behavior as a "sympto- matic act," an unconscious expression of a desire to masturbate. When he asked her why she was wearing the reticule and what she thought her actions meant, she replied, "Why should I not wear a reticule like this, as it is now the fashion to do?" (p. 93). The more she resisted his interpretations, the more Freud seemed to persist.

Still, she seemed to be cooperating when she brought in a second dream, and Freud quickly analyzed the second dream with the same enthusiasm he had shown for the first.

I was walking about in a town which I did not know. I saw streets and squares which were strange to me. Then I came into a house where I lived, went to my room, and found a letter from Mother lying there. She wrote saying that as I had left home without my parents' knowledge she had not wished to write to me to say that Father was ill. "Now he is dead, and if you like you can come." I then went to the station and asked about a hundred times: "Where is the station?" I always got the answer: "Five minutes." I then saw a thick wood before me which I went into, and there I asked a man whom I met. He said to me: "Two and a half hours more." He offered to accompany me. But I refused and went alone. I saw the station in front of me and could not reach it. At the same time I had the usual feeling of anxiety that one has in dreams when one cannot move forward. Then I was at home. I must have been traveling in the meantime, but I know nothing about that. I walked into the porter's lodge, and inquired for our flat. The maidservant opened the door to me and replied that Mother and the others were already at the cemetery. [pp. 114–115]

They worked on this dream for three days. The prominent wish in this dream, Freud decided, was a fantasy of revenge against her father, which was expressed by her father's illness, death, and burial. Moreover, behind this fantasy lay concealed an unconscious wish for revenge against Mr. K., who had made "obscene" passes at her and then betrayed her. Her refusal to let the man in the dream accompany her was both an act of revenge against Mr. K. and against Freud, as though she were telling them that since they treat her like a child she would go her own way, and not marry.

At the beginning of the third session of work on this dream she announced, "Do you know that I am here for the last time today?"

"How can I know, as you have said nothing to me about it?" Freud replied.

"Yes. I made up my mind to put up with it till the New Year. But I shall wait no longer to be cured" (p. 127).

Freud must have felt annoyed at this pronouncement, but he chose not to take it seriously. He told her that she was free to leave the treatment whenever she liked, but for that day they would proceed in interpreting her dream. Perhaps, from his part, he was thinking that if she was really going to leave, at least he wanted to get as much out of her as he could in order to complete his analyses of her dreams. On a deeper level, he was no doubt effected by his countertransference. However, it was during this session that an important bit of information emerged: Mr. K.'s affair with the governess. He used this new information, plus a piece of information she had given him a few days earlier (she had had an attack of appendicitis exactly nine months after the incident at the lake, which Freud saw as a symbolic pregnancy) to once more interpret that she was in love with Mr. K., that she took his marriage proposal seriously, but that wounded pride (his treating her like a governess) had led her to reject him. He elaborated on this interpretation at length and she listened to this new interpretation "without any of her usual contradictions," knowing it was her last day. True to her word, she did not return. The entire analysis had lasted barely over eleven weeks.

She paid him a visit sixteen months later, on April 1, 1902, after reading in a newspaper that he had been given the title of professor by the University of Vienna. She reported that for about a month after she had stopped seeing him she was "in a muddle," but since then she had become absorbed in her work. In addition, she had during the interim secured a confession from Mrs. K. that she had in fact had an affair with her father, and from Mr. K. that he had in fact tried to seduce her. (One can imagine her smiling triumphantly as she said these things.) She asked about starting treatment with him again, but Freud did not take her request at face value, interpreting that her real motive was simply to let him know that she was right and he was wrong about the K.s.

Like Breuer with "Anna O.," Freud was able to relieve some of "Dora's" symptoms, but her premature termination limited what he could accomplish. It is reported (Olsen and Koppe 1988) that she went on to lead a relatively normal existence. In 1903 she married an employee of her father's mill. He was said to be a quiet type who wanted to become a composer, and on at least one occasion Philip Bauer hired an orchestra to play one of his son-in-law's compositions. Ida had one son, to whom she was reportedly quite devoted, but refused to have any more children, citing the delivery pains as an excuse. Her brother, Otto, became a leading figure in the Austrian Socialist Party and served as minister of foreign affairs from 1918 to 1919.

In 1923 Freud found out that Ida had been ill again, and had been treated by Felix Deutsch, who recognized her from Freud's case history and told him about it. Deutsch claimed that he cured her of her anxiety by identifying it as related to her son's absence. An informant later told Deutsch that her husband had died of being "tormented by her paranoid behavior" and that she had moved to New York in the 1930s, where she had tormented her son with endless demands and reproaches. She died in New York in 1945, and was epitomized by Deutsch's informant as "one of the most repellent hysterics he had ever known" (p. 286).

Interpretation

Freud's case history about "Dora" has probably been analyzed and interpreted as much as any in the history of psychoanalysis. This may be due in part to the mystery which surrounds the case, since many of the riddles Freud himself posed were not solved. Like the enigmatic Mona Lisa, Ida continues to haunt psychoanalysts long after she herself died. In addition, interpreters have been quick and often zealous in pointing out the many mistakes Freud made in his work with her. What greater pleasure can there be than discovering that the "king" has faults?

Feminist writers have usually viewed Ida as a victim of male oppression, pointing not only to "abuse" by her father and Mr. K., but also to Freud's seductive and overbearing analytic style. Janet Malcolm (1981), for example, contends that Freud conducted himself more like a police inspector interrogating a suspect than a doctor helping a patient. "Aha! I know about you. I know your dirty little secrets. Admit that you were secretly attracted to Herr K. Admit that you masturbated when you were five. Look at what you're doing now as you lie there playing with your reticule . . ." (p. 73). In pondering Freud's choice of a pseudonym, she reflects: "Who could Dora be but Pandora? The case rattles with boxes; you practically trip over one wherever you turn. There is the jewelry box in the first dream (which Freud wasted no time in connecting with the female genitals); there are two boxes in the second dream, whose respective disguises (of key and railroad station) Freud quickly penetrates; and there is the above mentioned reticule . . ." (p. 96). She concludes that the case history is in reality a parable of defloration, of good (Prometheus) against evil (Pandora).

Rieff (1959) chastises Freud for concluding that Ida was hysterical because she responded with disgust to Mr. K.'s advances. It seems to him that Freud was saying that all aversions betray their opposite, which he feels is not at all true. To uncover acceptance beneath each rejection, he argues, would be to refuse to accept human goodness. "Dora could have turned down Herr K. for several good reasons," he writes. "Perhaps, at fourteen, she had not yet quite the aplomb to relish an affair with the man who was, after all, the husband of her father's mistress. Possibly she did not find him attractive" (p. 81).

Erikson (1962) sees Ida's plight in terms of a search for the truth, which he thought to be typical of adolescents. He asserts that her view of the truth was different than Freud's—she sought a historical truth, while Freud was concerned with psychic truth, and so the two clashed. He suggests that this clash, along with Freud's failure to appreciate her adolescent idealism, led to the failure of the analysis, as well as to her return a year later.

Glenn (1980a) summarizes five reasons why Dora left therapy:

1. Distrust of Freud because he reminded her of his father
2. Fear of Freud as a seducer who discussed sexual matters prematurely

3. Fear of her sexual wishes toward Freud
4. A need to turn from passive to active out of a fear of desertion or betrayal
5. Revenge against Freud as an acting out of her transference.

Like Erikson, he concludes that Freud did not understand the special needs of an adolescent patient. "I suspect," he writes, "that Freud did not properly evaluate Dora's teenage hostility and that he responded too intensely to it" (p. 34). Her therapeutic alliance, he says, was based in part on the hope of finding a neutral, nonincestuous, noncorrupt object who could serve as a mentor. Not only did Freud refuse to be her mentor, he also refused to be her analyst. Glenn cites, as an example of this, Freud's acceptance as a fait accompli of Ida's announcement that she was leaving therapy. "He did not offer appropriate advice to continue in conjunction with analyzing her resistances and conflicts. He did not attempt, as we would now, to discover the basis for her statement" (p. 34).

Schlesinger (1969) and Langs (1980a) emphasize the pathogenic aspects of Ida's environment. Schlesinger looks at the interactions among members of her family, noting that none of them were communicating with one another honestly. The adult denial of the truth, he argues, was a threat to her "ego-cognitive powers." Langs points out that Ida's psychoanalysis was headed for failure from the beginning because of deviations in analytic technique resulting in "misalliances." Specifically, he cites Freud's relationships with Dora's father, her father's sister and brother, and Mr. K. "In these ways, Freud did not maintain the one-to-one relationship with Ida that many analysts would currently establish" (p. 61).

Commenting on Freud's countertransference, Freeman and Strean (1981) speculate that he may have found Ida's rejection of him difficult to cope with. He may have therefore rationalized his rejection of her by viewing her as untreatable. "He seemed to underestimate her affection and desire for help, while overestimating her desires for revenge. There is the impression he used her hostile feelings as a justification for terminating the treatment" (p. 185). Grinstein (1980) takes it a step further, suggesting that Freud had erotic interests in female patients whom he unconsciously considered as forbidden Oedipal substitutes. In his discussion of Freud's Irma dream, in which Irma, a patient, is given an injection, Grinstein interprets the injection as Freud's unconscious wish to inject Irma sexually. If seen in this light, Freud's rejection of Ida would appear to have been an attempt to deny the erotic feelings the young woman had aroused in him.

Freud himself pondered his failure to reach Ida. In a postscript he lamented the fact that he had not succeeded in mastering the transference in good time. He realized from the beginning that he was replacing her father, and he consciously tried to be straightforward with her, knowing that her father hardly ever was. However, that was not enough, and after the first dream had warned him that she was feeling threatened by the treatment, he regretted that he did not heed the warning and say to her, "Now it is from Herr K. that you have made a transference on to me. Have you noticed anything that leads you to suspect me of evil intentions similar (whether openly or in some sublimated form) to Herr K.'s?" (1905b, p. 142). It was this analysis of the transference that might have saved the relationship, he thought, and prevented her from "acting" her feelings by leaving therapy.

He also regretted that he failed to discover in time and inform the patient that her homosexual "gynaecophilic" love for Mrs. K. was the strongest unconscious current in her mental life. The longer he thought about it, the more he realized that there was something significant about the fact that the very person who had betrayed her the most, her friend and confidante, Mrs. K. (who had revealed to her father their secret conversations about sex), was the one person she hardly ever reproached. The second dream, he said, had given him the final clue. The remorseless craving for revenge in that dream concealed the current that ran contrary to it—"the magnanimity with which she forgave the treachery of the friend she loved" and the manner in which she kept secret "the fact that it was this friend who had herself revealed to her the knowledge which had later been the ground of the accusations against her" (p. 143). Freud added that before he had learned the importance of the homosexual current in neurotics, he was often brought to a standstill in his work with patients.

I think Freud's fascination with dream interpretation may have caused him to lose sight of Ida the person while focusing on Ida the dreamer, who provided him with the wondrous symbols with which he could "strut his stuff." Over half of the book is devoted to analyzing and interpreting two dreams, and at times Freud's pursuit of the farther reaches of symbolic connections seems a form of intellectual abandonment which might have added to Ida's disenchantment. In a letter to Wilhelm Fliess written on June 12, 1900 (a few months before starting treatment with Ida), Freud wrote, "Do you think that one day there will be a marble tablet on this house, saying: 'In this House on July 24, 1895 the Secret of Dreams was revealed to Dr. Sigmund Freud'?" (E. Freud 1960, p. 116). This letter shows how profound was Freud's devotion to dreams, as well as to the achievement of fame.

It may well be that all these criticisms, including Freud's own, are to some degree valid. However, despite its apparent flaws, his "Fragment of an Analysis of a Case of Hysteria" is a milestone in psychoanalytic history. It is the first illustration of the use of dream interpretation in therapy. It also serves to introduce or graphically demonstrate many other important psychoanalytic concepts, all discovered and named by Freud, including transference, the sexual etiology of hysteria, repression, acting out, symtomatic acts, reversal of affect, displacement, switch words, somatic compliance, and reactive thoughts.

It should be remembered that Freud, like Breuer, was a pioneer. He was bound to make mistakes in his development of psychoanalysis, just as an engineer will develop many flawed designs before he comes up with a smoothly working model. Furthermore, the mistakes that Freud made with Ida and other patients are the same mistakes any beginning psychoanalyst will make. Unfortunately, Freud's honesty was both an endearing and a provocative quality. To my knowledge, no other psychoanalyst wrote so openly about himself, revealed so many of his own dreams, presented so many cases in which his work, with all its flaws, was there for all to see, and provided such candid criticisms of his own work. In a sense, he had to have a strong ego to be so open; but in another sense he may have been acting out a masochistic aspect of his personality, one which unconsciously invited sadism (in the form of criticism). An individual who is too open and too self-critical attempts to use this posture as a defense against the threat of being criticized by others. Freud used this posture throughout his writings and in his lectures, but whether it represented a masochistic character trait or a normal defense against the expressions of Victorian oppression his work met is an arguable point. Actually, his self-reproaching trait was the opposite of Ida's habit of reproaching others, and this may have been another reason for their clash.

Finally, it may well be that Freud's contention that she was untreatable was not so far off the mark; when Felix Deutsch treated her in 1925, he reported her to be similarly resistant. The compulsive suspiciousness and reproaches that Freud attempted to analyze may have been, on a deeper level, the beginnings of paranoia. We tend to judge young people differently than older people—and all the more so if they are young and pretty—usually viewing them as underdogs and/or victims, being charitable about such things as judging paranoid trends in their personalities. However such trends, when seen in the perspective of their overall life cycle, take on another meaning. If she was in fact a hysteric with paranoid features, Freud indeed had a difficult patient. Paranoids are one of the most resistant types, because they do not trust enough to form a therapeutic alliance.

Of all Freud's writings, the most fascinating and instructive are his five case histories. These book-length cases are not only poignant accounts of his discoveries, but also great literature. They are rich with clinical material, dynamic formulations, and theoretical constructions, presented in Freud's elegant style.

"Fragment" was the first of these histories, and like his other early writings, it shocked the Victorians who read it; they saw it as a kind of psychoanalytic pornography. Today there is no longer anything shocking about a doctor talking to a teenaged girl about sex, and the fact that this case history has endured after its shock value has diminished is another testimony to its greatness.

3

THE OEDIPUS COMPLEX

Sigmund Freud and Little Hans (1909)

At the time Freud began his psychoanalysis of Little Hans, he was just coming out of professional seclusion. The hostility toward him and his work had continued for about ten years following the publication of his first papers on hysteria in the early 1890s, and during those ten years he was stigmatized and isolated by the medical and psychiatric communities. He would later refer to this period as one of "splendid isolation" (Jones 1957, p. 233). During these years after Breuer had abandoned him there was no other professional in his field with whom he could even talk about his theories. They all thought him mad or perverted or morally despicable. However, soon after *The Interpretation of Dreams* came out, a group of supporters began to gather around him. In 1902 Wilhelm Stekel suggested that Freud start a discussion group, and the "Psychological Wednesday Society" was born. It was later known as the "Vienna Psycho-Analytical Society."

In 1903 Max Graf, a noted music critic, joined this group. He was the father of the boy who would become known as "Little Hans." Freud stated in his preface to *Three Essays on the Theory of*

Sexuality (1905a) that he had drawn his conclusions predominantly from psychoanalytic investigations with adult patients, and hoped that knowledge drawn from studies in other fields would eventually be used to test his theories. One of the first things he did in his new Wednesday night discussion group was to request that members gather direct observational data on the sexual development of children. Accordingly, in 1906, when Little Hans was 3, Max Graf began supplying Freud with written reports of his son's sexual development. Later, at the age of 4 years, 9 months, Little Hans developed a neurosis, the chief symptom of which was a phobia, and Freud diagnosed the boy's condition as "anxiety hysteria." He then began advising the father on how to treat the boy and became, in essence, the father's supervisor. Some years earlier he had psychoanalyzed the boy's mother, and so he had direct knowledge of each member of this family. *Analysis of a Phobia in a Five-Year-Old Boy* appeared early in 1909, with the consent of Little Hans's parents.

The reports of Little Hans began when he was almost 3 years old. He was a "cheerful, good-natured, and lively little boy" (Freud 1909a, p. 154), who had begun to take a special interest in his "weewee-maker." Like all children who are going through this phase of development, he had become quite curious about who had penises and who had not. He asked his mother if she had a weewee-maker (she said yes), he asked his father, and he asked various other people. Once, standing before a lion's cage in the zoo, he shouted out with glee, "I saw the lion's weewee-maker" (p. 152). When he saw a cow being milked, he exclaimed to his father that there was milk coming out of the cow's weewee-maker. When he saw water being let out of a train engine, he thought the engine was weeweeing and wondered where its weewee-maker was. Eventually, he understood that animate objects had weewee-makers and inanimate ones did not. Freud compared these sexual researches of Little Hans to the philosophical inquiries of the philosopher Wundt. "In the view of that school, consciousness is the invariable characteristic of what is mental, just as in the view of little Hans a weewee-maker is the indispensable criterion of what is animate" (p. 155). However, the boy's interest in weewee-makers was not purely scientific. He had also become fascinated with touching his penis. When his mother caught him, at the age of 3 years, 6 months, she threatened him with castration: if he played with himself, she told him, she would ask Dr. A., their pediatrician, to cut off his weewee-maker. What would he weewee with then? she asked. He replied, "With my bottom" (p. 152).

"He had made this reply," Freud noted, "without having any sense of guilt as yet. But this was the occasion of his acquiring the 'castration complex', the presence of which we are so often obliged to infer in analyzing neurotics, though they one and all struggle violently against recognizing it" (p. 152). He had noted in *Three Essays* that there was a tendency on the part of boys to think that both males and females had penises, and to deny all evidence to the contrary. Behind this denial was the assumption that females had been castrated, and that there was thus a danger of losing their own penises (1905a).

It was at around the same age that the great event of Little Hans's childhood occurred: his sister Hanna was born. Now his Oedipus complex—another phenomenon of which Freud had just begun to write—first emerged, and it eventually led to the formation of neurotic symptoms. His sister's arrival banished him from his parents' bedroom, where his crib had been kept until then, and took his mother's attention away from him. A few days after his sister's birth he became sick with a fever, and remarked, "But I don't want a little sister" (1909a, p. 154). He began to take an interest in her weewee-maker. Watching her being given a bath when she was seven days old, struggling with his castration complex, he said, "But her weewee-maker's still quite small. When she grows up it'll get bigger all right" (p. 155). Watching her again several months later he observed, "She has got a tiny little wee-wee-maker" (p. 157). He also showed a marked interest in where his sister had come from. His parents told him that the stork had brought her, but he was not so sure about that. In his fantasies his playmates became his own children, whom he could master and dominate. "My children Berta and Olga were brought by the stork too," he told his father (p. 156). If his mother could reject him for other children, he could do the same to her.

His neurosis developed during the next year, as repression gradually set in. In the meantime, he enjoyed sexual attractions to both girls and boys (confirming Freud's theory of a primary bisexuality). He liked to see his playmates urinate, and for them to see him do it as well. He also liked to see his mother urinate, and to look at her weewee-maker. Sometimes, if he begged her enough, she would take him to the toilet with her. Sometimes, when his father was away, she would let him sleep with her. He liked to sleep with his mother and cuddle with her. He liked the way her breasts felt against him, and the way she smelled. He liked it when she touched him, too, while giving him a bath, and when she put powder on him. He wanted her to touch his weewee-maker:

> As his mother was powdering round his penis and taking care not to touch it, Hans said: "Why don't you put your finger there?"
>   *Mother*: "Because that'd be piggish."
>   *Hans*: "What's that? Piggish? Why?"
>   *Mother*: "Because it's not proper."
>   *Hans*: "But it's great fun." [p. 162]

At the age of 4 years, 9 months he developed a phobia, and his father wrote to Freud appealing for his help. "My dear Professor, I am sending you a little more about Hans—but this time, I am sorry to say, material for a case history." He explained that Hans had developed a nervous disorder that had made him and his wife most uneasy because they had not been able to dissipate it. He told Freud that he would call on him the next day but in the meantime he was enclosing the material at hand. "No doubt the ground was prepared by sexual over-excitation due to his mother's tenderness," he continued. "He is afraid that a horse will bite him in the street" (p. 165).

During their meeting in January, 1908, the father spoke with Freud about Hans's problem. It had begun one morning with an anxiety dream: Hans had awakened in tears, and told his mother that while he was asleep he thought she was gone and he had no Mummy to cuddle with. He had been expressing such fears for a few weeks, Graf reported, and when he got into an "elegiac mood of this kind" his mother would usually take him to bed with her. A few days later, while walking to the park with his nursemaid, he began to cry and asked to be taken home to cuddle with Mummy. The following day his mother went out with him herself. Again he started to cry. He told his mother, "I was afraid a horse would bite me" (p. 167). Later he told her he was afraid the horse was going to come into his room. Thinking this phobia was connected to masturbation, his mother asked him if he put his hand to his weewee-maker. He said he did every morning while still in bed.

Freud listened to the father relate this information and decided that the boy was suffering from a repressed erotic longing for his mother. He explained this to the father, and added that the reason he knew it was repressed rather than normal longing was that the anxiety did not subside when the object of the boy's longing (his mother) gave him what he wanted. It may be (although we do not know for certain) that Graf asked Freud to take on the case. However, at that time Freud believed children could not be psychoanalyzed because they did not have the capacity for introspection. He decided, instead, to act as a consultant, advising Mr. Graf on how to treat his child. Ironically, the interventions he advised were often more behavioral than psychoanalytic.

The two men sat face-to-face in Freud's office. Freud leaned thoughtfully and characteristically back in his chair, while the horses were clammering and carriages jangling on the street below. "Here's what I'd suggest you do," he told Graf. "Tell the boy that all this business about horses is just a piece of nonsense and nothing more. Tell him the truth is that he is very fond of his mother and wants to be taken into her bed" (p. 171). The boy pretends to be upset about horses, Freud explained, so she'll take pity on him. Graf probably nodded approvingly at this advice, for he himself felt that his wife was to blame for the outbreak of the phobia. However, Freud steered clear of placing blame. "I'd also suggest," he went on, "that you tell him the reason he's afraid of horses is that he has taken so much interest in their weewee-makers. Tell him even he knows that it's not right to be so very much interested in weewee-makers, including his own weewee-maker, and he's absolutely correct, it's not right. I'd further suggest that you begin giving Hans some enlightenment about sex" (p. 171). Freud further explained that the boy's behavior justified the assumption that his libido had become attached to a wish to see his mother's sexual organ. He advised Graf that he should take away this goal by informing Hans that his mother and all other females (as he could see from his sister Hanna) had no weewee-makers at all. "However, I wouldn't tell him this last piece of information until a suitable occasion when it has been led up to by some question or chance remark on Hans's part" (p. 171).

In those days, Freud was still trying to discover how masturbation and anxiety were linked. That is why he advised telling Little Hans not to masturbate. In a paper written before his work with Little Hans, he asserted that masturbation provided incomplete discharge, and therefore led to neurosis, while the complete suppression of masturbation led to the transformation of libido into anxiety (Freud 1895). However, in the case history itself, he wrote, "States of anxiety are not produced by masturbation or by getting satisfaction in any shape" (1909a, p. 170).

Almost as soon as he completed his consultation with Freud, Graf went home and began instructing Hans as Freud had advised. He told the boy that the business about horses was nonsense, and that he used it to sleep with his mother. Apparently he also explained about sex, but there is no record of what he said, or how the boy reacted to this information.

For a few days after his enlightenment Hans's phobia seemed to wane. He went merrily out to the park each day, his fear of horses transformed to an obsession with looking at them. Then he caught influenza and was bedridden for two weeks, after which it was decided that he needed to have his tonsils removed. After the tonsilectomy, he was required to stay indoors another week. When he was finally well enough to go outside again, he refused. Now he said that he was afraid of white horses. Asked by his father why he was afraid of white horses, he replied that his friend Lizzi's father had once told her (within earshot of Hans): "Don't put your finger to the white horse or it'll bite you."

"I say," the father countered, "it strikes me that it isn't a horse you mean, but a weewee-maker, that one mustn't put one's hand to."

"But a weewee-maker doesn't bite," Hans replied (pp. 172–173).

His father kept up the pressure about masturbation. One morning after the boy had just gotten out of bed, Mr. Graf reminded him again that if he stopped putting his hand on his weewee-maker his "nonsense" would go away.

"But I don't put my hand to my weewee-maker any more."

"But you still want to."

"Yes I do. But wanting's not doing and doing's not wanting" (p. 174).

The following Sunday, as they were walking down the street, Mr. Graf told Hans that neither Hanna nor his mother nor any female had a weewee-maker. Hans seemed to take it in stride, asking only if his father had a weewee-maker. His father reassured him that he did. He then asked how little girls weewed, if they had no weewee-maker. Mr. Graf explained that their weewee-makers were smaller. Hans nodded.

His moods seemed to change from day to day. The following day his mother took him for a walk and he was very frightened again. The next day he was cheerful. The following night he was restless, and he woke up at six o'clock. His father asked him what was wrong, and he replied that he had put his finger to his weewee-maker "just a little." He said he had dreamed that he had seen Mummy quite naked in her chemise, and she had let him see her weewee-maker. Freud interpreted this dream to mean that Hans had not accepted the information he had been given about the fact that women had no penises. Recalling when his mother had threatened Hans with castration, Freud concluded that the boy's enlightenment had had a shattering effect on his self-confidence and had exacerbated his castration complex, rekindling memories of the threat made by his mother. Hans was struggling with the realization that there were beings who did not possess penises, and that his own could actually be taken away, as his mother had suggested. Presumably he explained this to Mr. Graf.

Soon Hans reported another dream. *A big giraffe was in his room, and a little, crumpled one. The big one called out because he took the crumpled one away from it. Then he sat down on the top of the crumpled one.* His father questioned him about the dream and interpreted that the big giraffe represented himself (Hans's father), and the crumpled giraffe, either his mother or the mother's genital organ. He recalled that during the previous night the boy had been seized with longing for his mother, and had come into his parents' bedroom for that reason. The dream represented the boy's wish to take his mother away from his father. As his father wrote down this interpretation, the boy's blond brows wrinkled.

"Why are you writing that down?" Hans asked.

"Because I shall send it to a Professor, who can take away your 'nonsense' for you."

"Oho! So you've written down as well that Mummy took off her chemise, and you'll give that to the Professor too" (p. 181).

Mr. Graf then asked the boy to tell him quickly what he was thinking. He said, "Raspberry syrup." Then he added, "A gun for shooting people dead" (p. 181). His father recalled that Hans was given raspberry syrup as a reward when he went to the "potty," and that sometimes he confused the words "shooting" and "shitting."

Next Monday, March 30, 1908, father and son visited Freud together. At first the boy did not want to visit the professor, but his father persuaded him by saying that Freud had a pretty little daughter. Upon seeing the boy again, Freud was struck by the self-assurance and irreproachable manners of this "queer little chap." The consultation was a short one, perhaps sandwiched in between his regular sessions. Freud sat in his usual chair, and father and son sat in upright chairs opposite him. A late winter sun beamed down from the high windows along the Berggasse.

When Freud received the report of this development from Hans's father, he concluded that the immediate exciting cause of the phobia was indeed when this horse pulling a bus fell down. He interpreted this to mean that the boy unconsciously wished that his father might fall down in the same way, and be dead. This wish, being forbidden, was immediately repressed, resulting in a fear of being bitten by a horse (his father). However, Freud wondered if there were other, still deeper meanings to this new fear, and he pondered the significance of the horse's making a row with its legs.

On the evening of April 7, Graf once again called on Freud to seek his advice about Hans. He, too, was curious about Hans's new memory. "I wonder what he could have been reminded of by the fallen horse kicking about with its feet?" he asked.

Freud's eyes brightened. "What do children do when they hold on to their urine? They stamp their feet, don't they?"

"That's very true." Graf recalled that in the early days, when Hans had to be put on the potty, he would protest by stamping his feet in a rage, and sometimes throwing himself on the ground (p. 196).

Freud suggested that he find out more about the stamping.

The following morning, Graf told Hans that he had been to see the Professor the night before. He told the boy the Professor wanted to know more about one thing. He reminded the boy that there were occasions when he stamped his feet, and the boy agreed that when he was cross or he had to do "lumf" he would stamp his feet. In the middle of this conversation, the boy suddenly ran away, saying, "Oh, I must weewee" (p. 197). Freud interpreted this abrupt need to urinate as a confirmation of his interpretation linking the stamping of feet with retaining urine. Later that day when father and son went out to the street Hans added one more bit of information, telling his father that he was also afraid of coal-carts.

From this point on, Hans's phobia gradually began to subside as more material came to the surface and was analyzed by his father, with Freud's help. At first his phobia seemed to become transformed into an exaggerated loathing for excrement. Then one day Hans said "ugh," when his mother showed his father a new set of yellow underwear she had just bought. His father wanted to know why he said "ugh," and Hans replied that he was disgusted by his mother's yellow underwear, and also by her black underwear; they reminded him of "lumf." Freud interpreted this disgust as a sign of Hans's repression of his erotic feelings about his mother. A few days later Hans had another dream. "*I was in the bath, and then the plumber came and unscrewed it. Then he took a big borer and stuck it into my stomach*" (p. 208). His father translated the dream as follows: The boy was in bed with his mother. Then his father came and drove the boy away with his big penis.

Hans began to grow increasingly preoccupied with babies. He said again and again that he did not want his mother to have any more babies, and he began to have many more fantasies in which he was the mother and his playmates were his children. Once he told his father to pay the stork not to bring any more babies from "out of the box" where babies come from. The father now made a connection between the furniture vans and buses which the boy had been afraid of and his mother's "baby box." Later Hans expressed a fear of the bathtub, and recalled his mother's giving Hanna a bath. His father asked if he ever wanted his sister dead. Hans replied, "H'm . . . well."

> *Father*: "That was why you thought when Mummy was giving her her bath, if only she'd let go, Hanna would fall into the water. . . ."
> *Hans*: ". . . and die."
> *Father*: "And then you'd be alone with Mummy. A good boy doesn't wish that sort of thing, though."
> *Hans*: "But he may think it."
> *Father*: "But that isn't good."
> *Hans*: "If he thinks it, it is good all the same, because you can write it to the Professor." [p. 215]

For Hans, everything had changed since the birth of his sister, and it became apparent that his fear of vans or wagons tipping over was a fear of the delivery of new babies. He was angry at Hanna for taking his mother's attention away from him, at his mother for abandoning him, and at his father for possessing his mother the way he wanted to possess her. In addition, he was growing more and more angry at his father for badgering him about these matters. Like Freud with Ida, Graff was overzealous in his use of psychoanalysis, something that Freud himself had noted. In an aside, Freud pointed out that the father was asking too many questions, and leading the boy toward presumed answers, rather than letting him say whatever he was thinking. He advises novice analysts not to try to understand everything at once, but to "give a kind of unbiased attention to every point that arises and to await further developments" (p. 207). He had learned a few things since working with Ida.

Despite Graf's clumsy use of psychoanalysis, Little Hans steadily improved. Freud first advised Graf to try to trace Hans's phobia back to the thoughts and wishes occasioned by the birth of his sister. Later (when the boy began having "lumf" fantasies), he advised Graf that according to the theories of children, a baby is a "lumf"—a piece of excrement. This explained Hans's fear of coal-carts, which he saw as carts full of "lumf." On April 24 Graf and his wife sat down with the boy and told him the real facts about birth: that children grow inside their mummies, and are then brought into the world by being pressed out of her like a "lumf."

In the afternoon when they took him out to the street there was visible improvement in his state. He ran after carts and only showed a trace of anxiety—a reluctance to stray from his neighborhood.

On May 2 he had another dream, and ran to his father to tell it to him: *The plumber came; and first he took away my behind with a pair of pincers, and then gave me another, and then the same with my weewee-maker* (p. 240). Hans's father immediately grasped the meaning of this dream, and told the boy that the plumber had given him a bigger behind and a bigger weewee-maker, like Daddy's. The boy nodded, and added that he also wanted to have a moustache and hair on his chest, the way Daddy did.

By the following week Graf was able to report to Freud that the phobia was gone. In less than four months, Freud and Graf had cured Hans. At the same time, his castration and Oedipus complexes had also diminished. He was able to withdraw gradually from the oedipal rivalry for his mother's love, and to relate to his mother, father, and sister with gradually lessening ambivalence.

In a postscript added to the case history in 1922, Freud wrote that he had run into a "strapping youth" of 19 who introduced himself as "Little Hans." Although the publication of this first analysis of a child had, Freud said, caused a great stir and indignation because the poor little boy had been "robbed of his innocence" and made the victim of psychoanalysis, Hans had in fact grown to be a healthy young man. Hans declared that he was perfectly well and suffered from no troubles or inhibitions. His parents had been divorced and each had remarried, but he was on good terms with them and had successfully undergone this ordeal without damage to himself. However, Hans did not remember anything about his psychoanalysis. Freud attributed this to childhood amnesia.

Freud lost contact with Little Hans soon after he published his case history. In the case history, he had been openly critical of Graf's treatment of Little Hans and had refused to side with him against his wife as Graf had seemed to want. Forty years later, Graf reported that Freud had, in the early days, been a good friend who had carried a large rocking horse up four flights of stairs on Hans's third birthday (an omen of things to come?), but that their friendship had eventually ended because of Freud's authoritarianism. "I was unable and unwilling to submit to Freud's 'do' or 'don't'—with which he once confronted me—and nothing was left for me to do but to withdraw from his circle" (1942, p. 475). Graf became a professor of music in 1909, and his break with Freud came soon after; perhaps there was a connection between his professorship and his impatience with Freud's "authoritarianism."

He also may have been jealous of his son's idealization of Freud.

Hans, whose real name was Herbert Graf, went on to become a noted stage director for the Metropolitan Opera in New York. He wrote three books and several articles about opera and lived a productive life.

Interpretation

Although this was the first instance of child psychoanalysis, the case of Little Hans is not known for its therapeutic technique. As Olsen and Koppe (1988) point out, childhood phobias generally disappear by themselves, although they can sometimes develop into compulsion neuroses. They believe that the success of the case was due not to the technique, which was faulty, but to the positive transference that Hans was able to develop toward Freud. While his feelings for his father oscillated between love and hostility, and his trust was shaken by the misinformation given him about sex and babies, his feelings about Freud remained constant: Freud became a parent-ideal. "Freud ('the Professor') as he was called in the letters Hans dictated to him was totally good and omniscient and did not misuse the boy's confidence" (p. 291).

Others echo their sentiments about Freud's (and Graf's) faulty technique. For example, Glenn (1980b), focusing on the advice Freud gave to Graf, sees much of it as misguided. When Freud had Graf tell Hans about his incestuous wishes, for example, he believes it complicated rather than helped the treatment. Glenn argues that children often experience interpretations by their parents as license to express their drives, and, moreover, such interpretations may interfere with their development. "Accurate interpretations create the impression that the omniscient parents can read the child's mind, thus interfering with his sense of privacy, his sense of reality, and eventually, his sense of autonomy. Difficulty in separating self- and object-representations can occur" (p. 123). Freud's second suggestion, Glenn adds, that Hans be told that he was right in thinking he should not be so interested in penises, was not only puzzling in view of Freud's liberal attitude toward masturbation, but also was bound to "increase the child's guilt . . ." (p. 123). The final suggestion, that Graf tell Hans that females lack penises, was "bound to frighten the child as it interfered with his use of denial" (p. 125). In fact, Glenn asserts, the information that Freud offered to Hans was incomplete and distorted; he was told that females have no "weewee-makers," rather than that they have a different kind of "weewee-maker." This misinformation increased his distrust for his father, who had already misled him about childbirth.

Silverman (1980) is critical of Freud's lack of attention to Mrs. Graf's seductive and intrusive behavior, which interfered with Hans's passage through the stages of separation-individuation. Silverman notes that in a discussion of the case during the Wednesday evening meetings, Freud said that Mrs. Graf's only serious error was in taking Hans to the toilet with her. Did Freud's feelings toward Hans's mother, a former patient, prevent him from evaluating her seductiveness properly? Silverman asserts that Mrs. Graf not only took Hans to the toilet with her, but she also bathed, dried, and powdered him daily, taking care not to touch his penis even when he was 5 years old. When her husband was away, she allowed him to sleep with her. "Hans's mother infantilized and seduced him into a dependent and increasingly eroticized attachment to her," Silverman notes, "which must have been very powerful" (p. 102). This, in turn, would have impeded Hans's normal separation from her.

Slap (1961) calls attention to Freud's failure to notice the impact of Hans's tonsillectomy on his neurosis. He points out that after the tonsillectomy Hans began to fear *white* horses—which he links with the white uniforms doctors and nurses wear in hospitals. He also relates the tonsillectomy to Hans's plumber dreams, and to his distress at seeing black leather straps around the mouths and eyes of some horses. At that time, black surgical masks were in vogue in Vienna hospitals. Silverman (1980), agreeing with Slap, adds that Hans's playfully "operating" on a rubber doll is another indication of the impact of the tonsillectomy. "A child analyst today probably would address himself initially to the reality aspect of the tonsillectomy as a recent trauma which has imposed a demand upon the ego for repair and mastery" (p. 107). Silverman expresses surprise that Freud, who usually started at the surface, did not do so with respect to Hans's tonsillectomy.

Rieff (1959) comments on the unempathic manner in which Hans is treated by Freud and Graf. "Freud's great case study of infantile sexuality, 'Little Hans,' seems as much a study of infantile intellectuality. There is clever Hans tracking down the mystery of how babies are born, despite the frustrating lies of his parents and the baffling intrusions of a professor who likes to collect his stories" (p. 92).

Schur (1972) points out that when Freud was working on the Little Hans case, he had not yet accepted the presence of a separate aggressive drive. He did pay considerable attention to Hans's aggression, and its impact on his neurosis, stating, for example, that "The fear which sprang from this death-wish against his father . . . formed the chief obstacle to the analysis until it was removed during the conversation in my consulting room" (1909a, p. 112). Nevertheless, his recognition of the negative Oedipus complex and the negative transference toward the father was limited, since at the time sadism was not seen as a fusion of libidinal and aggressive drives, but as a form of libidinal expression; therefore he paid too much attention to masturbation and not enough to aggression.

Not only did Freud's theories about drives change over the course of the years, but so also did his theories on the structure of the mind. At the time he worked with Hans, he viewed mental processes from the standpoint of the topographical theory, his aim being to bring the unconscious material to consciousness. Later he made aggression an instinct and shifted to the structural theory; his motto then became, "Where there was id, there shall ego be." When he reevaluated Hans's pathology in *Inhibitions, Symptoms, and Anxiety* (1926), he saw his phobia as resulting from ego defenses mobilized to guard against forbidden drives—sexual and aggressive—and the attending anxiety. He identified anxiety as a signal of danger arising in the ego, and relegated repression to one of several defense mechanisms, rather than the umbrella term used for all such mechanisms. However, he still felt that Hans's conflict was centered in the oedipal phase.

Nowadays, psychoanalysts would put more stress on pregenital issues. They would pay attention not only to the oedipal conflicts but also to the preoedipal factors that paved the way and contributed to the formation of the castration and Oedipus complexes. Roiphe and Galenson (1981) and Mahler and colleagues (1975), for example, have conducted research showing the importance of the "anal-rapprochement" phase of development, a stage in which children must master their bowel movements and adjust to the discovery of the differences in sexual anatomy between the two genders. It is not clear from the case history when Hans first discovered the difference in sexual anatomy, as he continued to deny this difference long into the phallic stage; however it is quite clear that this difference was on his mind, and it is also clear that he was much concerned with excretion. There is ample evidence that the anal stage was problematic for him (his father alludes to the fact that he was fed syrup as a laxative, and used to stamp his feet and make a row when he had to stop playing and go to the potty). Today's psychoanalysts would want to know more about this stage and about the earlier oral stage of development.

Finally, today's psychoanalysts might take a closer look at what Silverman refers to as Hans's passive-feminine identification with his mother's child-bearing and nurturing activities. It would have been helpful for him to have been given more guidance and less interrogation by his father, guidance about the male's *active* use of his penis and testicles in the process of procreation. Indeed, as I have emphasized (Schoenewolf 1989), the castration complex in boys is comprised not only of castration fear and denial of the difference in the sexes, but also of womb envy. Hans's passive-feminine identification with his mother was, among other things, an acting out of this womb envy. He envied and resented his mother's capacity to bring more people into the world, to take care of them, and to have control over them. At one point in the case history, he tells his father he wants to have babies, but that his mother should not have any more. Hans's father should have analyzed this womb envy in order to help Hans understand and value his masculinity.

Nevertheless, *Analysis of a Phobia in a Five-Year-Old Boy* remains a classic of psychoanalytic literature because the case provided Freud with a direct confirmation of many of the theories about sexual development and infantile sexuality with which he had been grappling. He had barely touched on the castration and Oedipus complexes up to that point; in this case history he was able to demonstrate and elaborate on them. He was also able to point to the importance of such factors in psychosexual development as "erotogenic zones" (a term he had previously invented) and the bisexual dispositions of children. Commenting on Hans's blissful fantasies of having babies, taking them to the toilet, making them "weewee," and wiping their behinds, Freud noted that during the period when Hans himself had been an infant these performances had given him pleasure. "He had obtained this pleasure from his erotogenic zones with the help of the person who had looked after him—his mother, in fact; and thus the pleasure already pointed the way to object-choice" (p. 250). Observing how Hans showed affection to both boys and girls, he said, "Hans was a homosexual (as all children may very well be), quite consistent with the fact . . . that he was *acquainted with only one kind of genital organ*—a genital organ like his own" (p. 252).

The case also provided an illustration of how repression sets in during the phallic stage and leads to neurotic symptoms. Beginning with his mother's castration threats, Hans's repression grew larger and deeper as more of his impulses and feelings were assaulted by his intrusive parents. These included hostile and jealous feelings against his father, and sadistic impulses (premonitions of copulation) toward his mother. "For Hans horses had always typified pleasure in movement," Freud explained, "but since this pleasure in movement included the impulse to copulate, the neurosis imposed a restriction on it and exalted the horse into an emblem of terror" (p. 280). Hence the instincts repressed in the unconscious (id) became transformed into anxiety in the conscious (ego). Freud would later view phallic repression as crucial to the formation of the superego; he foreshadowed that development in this work by making the observation that "analysis replaces repression by condemnation" (p. 285).

While Ida provided a means for showing the technique of interpreting dreams in an actual case, Little Hans gave Freud a way to illustrate the theme he had explored in his second great work, *Three Essays on the Theory of Sexuality.* Little Hans also paved the way for the development of child psychoanalysis, not only as a legitimate method for treating children, but also as an important new way of gathering psychoanalytic data.

4

OBSESSIONAL NEUROSIS

Sigmund Freud and the Rat Man (1909)

"I've suffered from obsessions ever since my childhood," a young law school graduate told Freud (Freud 1909b, p. 158) at his initial interview on October 1, 1907. "But for the last four years these obsessions have become stronger. Mainly I worry that something might happen to two people who are most dear to me—my father and a lady I very much admire." He went on to say that he was aware of having what he supposed Freud would call compulsive impulses. Sometimes he had an impulse to cut his throat with a razor. At other times he found himself prohibiting himself from doing the most trivial things, in order to prevent certain ideas from occurring in his mind. He had wasted years fighting against these ideas, and had lost much ground in pursuit of his goals. He'd tried various treatments, but none was of any use to him except a hydrotherapy treatment at a sanatorium—and this was probably helpful only because he made an acquaintance there, with whom he had regular sexual intercourse. The young man looked intently at Freud, his face pale and his brow furrowed, as though waiting for a response. Freud said nothing, and he went on speaking quite articulately about himself, almost as if he were speaking about somebody else. "Here in Vienna I've had intercourse only at irregular intervals. I feel disgusted by prostitutes, so that route to satisfaction isn't open to me. Altogether my sexual life has been stunted. I haven't even masturbated that much, except for a period during my sixteenth or seventeenth year, which I understand is normal. I first had sexual intercourse at 26" (p. 258).

"The Rat Man" (whose real name was Ernst) began his treatment with Freud the following day. In fact, Freud began working with him during the same period in which he was indirectly treating Little Hans, and this case became the first ongoing case presentation in the history of psychoanalysis. Freud first discussed Ernst at the Wednesday meetings of the Vienna Psycho-Analytical Society on October 30. During these presentations, he referred to his treatment of Ernst as an example of a "changed technique" in which "the psychoanalyst no longer seeks to elicit material in which he is interested, but permits the patient to follow his natural and spontaneous trains of thought" (Nunberg and Federn 1962, p. 227). Later he presented the case at the first International Psycho-Analytical Congress, held on April 26, 1908, in Salzburg—a meeting which also included presentations by Ernest Jones, Franz Rilkin, Karl Abraham, Isidor Sadger, Wilhelm Stekel, Carl Jung, Alfred Adler, and Sandor Ferenczi. By this time Freud had published six books and many papers, and his fame was spreading throughout the world.

In his early fifties, he had just begun to show signs of grayness. Jones (1957) provides a deft description of him during this period:

He had a strikingly well-shaped head, adorned with a thick moustache, and a full pointed beard. He was about five feet eight inches tall, somewhat rotund—though probably his waist did not exceed his chest measurement—and he bore the marks of a sedentary profession. . . . He had a lively and perhaps somewhat restless or even anxious manner, with quick darting eyes that gave a serious and penetrating effect. I dimly sense some slightly feminine aspect

in his manner and movements, which was perhaps why I developed
something of a helping or even protective attitude toward him
rather than the more characteristic filial one of many analysts.
[p. 251]

Freud described Ernst as a youngish man (although he was
nearly 30 when he entered analysis) who gave the impression of
being clearheaded and shrewd. He was born in 1878, the son of a
mother who came from a wealthy industrial family and a father
who was a low-ranking military officer. He had three older sisters,
a younger brother, and two younger sisters. His father died when
Ernst was 21 years old, and it was then that his neurotic symptoms began to grow. He managed to get a law degree, though not
without some delay, and to become enamored of an older woman
who did not return his affections. Later, during a military exercise
he took part in as a reserve officer, his obsessive neurosis became
full-blown. This led him to Freud.

At the beginning of their first session, Freud made him
"pledge himself to the one and only condition of the treatment—
namely, to say everything that came into his head, even if it was
unpleasant to him, or seemed unimportant or irrelevant or senseless" (p. 159). The Rat Man's very first communication—to
which Freud, agreeing with a point made by Adler, attached
particular significance—was about his relations with men.

"I have a friend of whom I have an extraordinarily high
opinion," the Rat Man began, speaking in his nervous, articulate
manner. "I used always to go to him when I was tormented by
some criminal impulse and ask him whether he despised me as a
criminal. He'd always assure me that I was a man of irreproachable
conduct" (p. 160). He gazed around the room, his eyes furtively
alert, always on guard. He went on to tell Freud that when he was
younger—about 14 or 15—there had been another man who filled
the same role in his life. This man was a 19-year-old student
whom Ernst thought to be a genius, and who seemed to have taken
a liking to the younger boy. He became Ernst's tutor, and raised
his self-esteem to an extraordinary degree; for a time he made

Ernst feel he was a genius. "Then he suddenly changed and began treating me as though I were an idiot. Finally I noticed that he was interested in one of my sisters, and realized he had been using me to gain admission into the house. This was the first great blow of my life" (p. 160).

Freud listened carefully to what he said and how he said it. He no longer had patients close their eyes, nor did he take notes; instead he jotted down his recollections in the evenings after work, and suggested other analysts do likewise to avoid "the consequent withdrawal of the physician's attention" (p. 159). He observed silently that Ernst's opening words "laid stress upon the influence exercised over him by men, that is to say, upon the part played in his life by homosexual object-choice . . ." (p. 160). However, he did not understand the transferential aspect of this communication, as he might have done a few years later. The Rat Man was unconsciously telling Freud that he wanted him to be like the friend he trusted, and not like the man who had disappointed him. In other words, he wanted Freud to be an omniscient, omnipotent, and kindly pre-oedipal father, not a rivalrous oedipal father who might turn on him.

The patient spent the remainder of this first session talking about his "sexual life." When he was 5 years old he persuaded his governess, Fräulein Peter, to let him creep under her skirt and finger her genitals. Afterwards he had a "burning and tormenting curiosity to see the female body" (p. 160). He recalled other instances of peeping at naked women, including another governess, servants, and his sisters, and remembered that by the age of 6 he "suffered from erections, and I know that once I went to my mother to complain about them" (p. 161). At this same age he began to have the feeling that his parents knew his thoughts. He was always thinking about wanting to see girls naked, and at the same time he feared that something bad might happen if he thought such things. He became convinced that he had to do all sorts of things to prevent these thoughts from entering his mind. When Freud asked him what bad thing might happen, he replied, "For instance, that my father might die" (p. 162), and confessed that thoughts of his father's death had preoccupied him from an early age.

In reviewing this first session, Freud speculated that the patient was under the domination of a component of the sexual instinct, the desire to look (scopophilia), that is, to see girls who pleased him naked. This intense wish was linked with the obsessive fear that something dreadful would happen—that his father would die—if he had such thoughts. He observed, "Obsessional neuroses make it much more obvious than hysterias that the factors which go to form a psychoneurosis are to be found in the patient's infantile sexual life and not in his present life" (p. 165).

The following day Ernst recalled the incident about the rats which had brought him to Freud. The previous summer he had been required, as an officer of the reserve, to take part in maneuvers. He wanted very much to prove himself to the regular officers, "to show the regular officers that people like me had not only learned a good deal but could stand a good deal too" (p. 165). He was so eager to prove himself that when he lost his lorgnette during a rest stop he did not even stop to look for it; instead he wired his optician to send another by postal express. During the same halt he sat next to a captain toward whom he felt a dread, and who "was obviously fond of cruelty." As Ernst spoke of this man, his face became paler than usual, and his words came out hesitantly. "I do not say he was a bad man," he continued, "but at the officer's mess he had repeatedly defended the introduction of corporal punishment, so that I had been obliged to disagree with him very sharply" (p. 165). Now, as he sat with this dreaded captain, the latter began telling him about a specially horrible punishment he had read about, used in the East. Suddenly Ernst broke off and got up from the sofa; he began to pace around the office in a state of agitation. "Please, spare me a recital of the details. Please." He looked at Freud imploringly.

Freud sat in his chair observing the patient with somewhat anxious eyes. He assured Ernst that unlike Captain M., he had absolutely no taste for cruelty, and no intention of tormenting him unnecessarily. But, at the same time, he could not grant him something which lay beyond his power. Freud began explaining that the overcoming of resistances was the law of treatment, one that could never be dispensed with. He, in turn, would do all he could to guess the full meaning of any clues he was given.

Ernst lay back down on the couch, hugged himself, and turned away from Freud, clearly in a daze. Freud described his questioning of the patient at this point to learn more about the "horrible punishment":

Was he perhaps thinking of impalement?—"No, not that; . . . the criminal was tied up . . ."—he expressed himself so indistinctly that I could not immediately guess in what position—". . . a pot was turned upside down on his buttocks . . . some rats were put into it . . . and they . . ." —he had again got up, and was showing every sign of horror and resistance—". . . bored their way in . . . "— "into his anus," I helped him out. [p. 166]

As Ernst mumbled his story, his face took on a strange expression, which Freud interpreted as one of horror at pleasure. He proceeded to talk with difficulty, saying that at the moment the captain told him about this punishment, an idea flashed through his mind that it was happening at the same time to a person who was very dear to him. Freud asked if Ernst himself were carrying out this punishment, and Ernst said no, that it was being carried out "as it were impersonally" (p. 166). He then acknowledged that it was being carried out against a certain "lady friend" he admired; upon more questioning he admitted that it was also being carried out against another person—his father, who had died many years before.

Ernst then related that later on during the maneuvers, when his new lorgnette had arrived, the cruel captain informed him, mistakenly, that he owed Lieutenant A. money for the postage. Ernst became obsessed with paying back Lieutenant A., feeling that unless he did so, the rat punishment would actually be carried out on the lady. He made a vow to himself to pay back this lieutenant, even though deep down he knew that he did not actually owe him money. (In fact, he was in the debt of the woman at the post office.) He devised an elaborate scheme for paying back the money, a scheme that involved going first to one train station and then to another, giving the money to one officer who would give it to a clerk who would give it to another officer, and so on and so forth, the entire story being so confusing that Freud had trouble following Ernst's babblings, and had him repeat it three times. Freud attempted to point out the confusion and obscurity of his thinking, but to no avail. At the end of the session Ernst, still in a daze, repeatedly addressed Freud as "Captain."

When Freud first presented this case to the Vienna Psycho-Analytic Society, the members must have shaken their heads and perhaps had a good laugh or two about the rat punishment, for from that time on the patient became known as "the man with the rats," and later simply as the "Rat Man." In making his notes for the second session, Freud recalled that the patient had spoken not only of punishments in this world, but also in the next world, and observed that his religious sentiment provided a certain indeterminateness to his thinking. One of the components of obsessive thinking is its obscurity; the elaborate and confused ponderings of the obsessive-compulsive are aimed at defending against the truth—the truth in this case being that Ernst was in a rage at his lady friend and at his father and wished them to die horribly. The obsessive ritual of paying back the money was an attempt to atone for such wishes.

In the third session Ernst babbled on about his attempt to repay Lieutenant A. He said that he had actually gotten on a train to set his labyrinthine plan in motion. Then he had changed his mind, and, for complicated reasons, got off the train and went to see his friend, confiding the scheme to him. The friend held up his hands. "Can there be any more doubt that you're obsessed?" he asked. His friend managed to calm Ernst down, and even went with him to the post office, to dispatch the 3.80 crowns to the branch where the lorgnette had arrived. However, Ernst could still not give up the obsession. He decided that what he needed was to find a doctor who would give him a certificate stating that, in order to recover his health, it would be necessary for him to reimburse Lieutenant A. in a particular ritualized manner. Though Freud could get him to acknowledge that he did not in fact owe Lieutenant A. anything, and had already sent the money he did owe to the post office, Ernst would give up neither the notion of paying back Lieutenant A., nor the link between this repayment and his own health.

The next day, Ernst spoke about his father's death. When his father had been on his deathbed, Ernst had asked the doctor how much longer he had to live, and the doctor had told him two more days. Ernst napped for an hour, and when he awoke, at 1:00 A.M., his father was dead. (A few months after his father's death, while studying for his law exam, Ernst had developed the ritual of keeping the front door open from midnight until 1:00 A.M. in order to let his father's ghost in. During that hour, he would often stand before a mirror and gaze at his erect penis, as though flaunting himself before his father.) It was after his father's death that he became obsessed with the idea that he was a criminal. He spoke to his friend, who always reassured him he was not a criminal, and that his self-reproaches were exaggerated.

Freud disagreed with Ernst's friend. Perhaps in some way he *was* a criminal. He told Ernst his self-reproaches were not exaggerated:

"No. The affect is justified. The sense of guilt cannot in itself be further criticized. But it belongs to another content, which is unknown (unconscious), and which requires to be looked for. The known ideational content has only got into its actual position owing to a mistaken association. . . . Moreover, this fact of there being a mistaken association is the only way of accounting for the powerlessness of logical processes in combating the tormenting idea." [pp. 174-175]

Ernst did not like what he heard. He had wanted Freud to reassure him, as his friend had. "How," he asked somewhat crossly at the next session, "could the information that my self-reproaches, my sense of guilt, is justified have a therapeutic effect on me?" (p. 176). Freud replied with another brief explanation of the unconscious, and Ernst then remembered having had the thought, at the age of 12, that if his father died the little girl with whom he was in love would take pity on him. Freud interpreted that he had a wish for his father's death, and this wish lay beneath his obsessional neurosis. "How could that be?" Ernst asked, but then he remembered that six months before his father's death he again had had the thought that if his father were dead, he could have the affections of a female—the lady whom he admired and wanted to marry. His father had opposed the marriage on the grounds that the lady was too poor, and Ernst had thought that if his father died, he would inherit his money, and be rich enough to marry her. Again Freud interpreted a wish for his father's death, and Ernst protested, "I merely feared my father's death, I did not wish it."

"According to psychoanalytic theory," Freud continued, "every wish corresponds to a former wish which was now repressed" (p. 180).

Ernst asked incredulously how that could be. He maintained that he had loved his father more than anybody in the world.

It was precisely such intense love, Freud said, that was the condition of the repressed hatred.

But, Ernst replied, he and his father had always been the best of friends, and always agreed on all but a few subjects.

Which subjects did they disagree on?

Only about the lady he wanted to marry, but Ernst never really had the "sensual desires" toward her he had had toward girls when he was a boy.

"You have just produced the answer we were looking for," Freud told him (p. 181). He had just discovered, Freud pointed out, the third great characteristic of the unconscious, the source from which his hostility to his father derived its indestructibility. This source had to do with the sensual desires. Ernst must have felt his father as in some way interfering with his sensual desires, and wanted to get rid of him for that reason.

The Rat Man left shaking his head in disbelief. The next day, his seventh session, he said he still could not believe that he had ever wished his father dead. He then recalled feeling jealous toward his little brother. On one occasion he had loaded his toy gun with a ramrod, and tricked his brother into looking down the barrel. He had pulled the trigger, and the ramrod hit his brother in the forehead, stunning but not injuring him.

"If you can remember something so foreign to you as this," Freud said, "then how can you deny the possibility of something similar, which you've now forgotten entirely, having happened at an earlier age in relation to your father?" (p. 182). The source for his obsession lay in his early childhood, Freud assured him, but Ernst said that he could not believe this. He believed that his illness had become intensified after his father's death. Freud agreed that his sorrow at his father's death contributed to the intensity of his illness, but it was not the source. "A normal period of mourning would last from one to two years," Freud explained, "but a pathological one like yours would last indefinitely" (p. 185).

As the analysis continued, Freud learned more of the details of Ernst's obsession, and presented him with more interpretations. Once, when his lady friend had not been able to see him because her mother was ill, he had gotten the impulse to cut his throat. Freud interpreted that he actually wanted to kill the mother, but because of the guilt this idea induced, he quickly decided that he himself must die. Another time, his lady friend had been paying a lot of attention to a cousin of hers named Dick. Ernst then decided that he was too fat (the German word for fat is *dick*), and went on a weight-loss campaign which required him to jog to the top of a mountain each day. Once, while standing near a cliff, he received a command to jump.

He also had other obsessive-compulsive rituals, some of which took the form of an overprotectiveness toward his lady friend. One day when they were sitting together during a thunderstorm he became obsessed with the need to count to forty or fifty between each flash of lightening—the unconscious wish being that lightening would strike her dead. On another occasion, he knocked his foot on a stone lying in the road, and had been "obliged" to move the stone over to the side of the road, because "the idea struck him that her carriage would be driving along the same road in a few hours' time and might come to grief against this stone" (p. 189). But a few minutes later he felt that this idea was absurd, and he had been "obliged" to move the rock back into the middle of the road. Freud interpreted that a battle between love and hate was going on inside him, and his removing and then replacing the rock was symbolic of this conflict. On yet another occasion he had an obsession to understand things, which was intended to compensate for a fear of misunderstanding. This fear was aroused when his lady friend said something to him which he construed to mean that she was embarrassed by something he did in public. Later, she was able to prove to him that he had misunderstood her, and that she had merely wanted to save him from being laughed at. From then on, he always tried to understand precisely what anybody said to him (as he did when the captain told him that he owed Lieutenant A. money), to the point that he lost sight of the obvious by focusing on the obscure.

Finally, his obsessions also took the form of revenge fantasies. His lady friend had turned down his first marriage proposal ten years before he had come to Freud; since then she had warmed to him, but he had been unwilling to propose again. Each time he came near to doing so, he would become convinced that he did not really care for her after all. Once, when she was lying ill in bed, he had had a fantasy that she would lie like that forever. He also had a recurring fantasy that she had married somebody else, a high-ranking government official (she seemed to want such a match), and that he joined the same branch of government, and rose to a higher rank than her husband, who then became his surbordinate. One day, this man committed an act of dishonesty, and the lady threw herself at Ernst's feet and begged him to save her. He said that he would, but that he had only joined the service because of her, and now that his mission was complete he would resign. He had fantasies of doing good deeds for the lady without her knowing of them, the magnanimity of these services always designed to disguise the underlying hostility toward her.

Eventually, after several months of work with Ernst, Freud was able to discover what he called "the exciting cause" of the illness. It had occurred soon after his father's death. His mother had told him that it was his father's wish that he marry a wealthy woman, and accordingly she had arranged a match with the daughter of a rich cousin, whose father would offer him a very good position in his firm when his education was completed. This forced him to decide between the lady he admired and the one arranged for him by his mother. Freud wrote, "He resolved this conflict, which was in fact one between his love and the persisting influence of his father's wishes, by falling ill; or, to put it more correctly, by falling ill he avoided the task of resolving it in real life" (p. 199). From the exciting cause in his adult years, Freud found a thread leading back to his childhood. Putting together all the clues Ernst had given him, he deduced that before Ernst was 6 years old, he had been guilty of some sexual misdemeanor connected with masturbation, and that his father had soundly castigated him for it. Such an event would have left behind an ineradicable grudge against his father as an interferer with his sexual pleasure. When he told this to Ernst, Ernst recalled that his mother had repeatedly described just such an event to him, although he could not remember it himself. It had happened when he was between 3 and 4 and coincided with the fatal illness of an older sister. He had, according to his mother, bitten someone—perhaps his nurse or his sister—and his father had given him a beating for it.

> The little boy had flown into a terrible rage and had hurled abuse at his father even while he was under his blows. But as he knew no bad language, he had called him all the names of common objects that he could think of, and had screamed: "You lamp! You towel! You plate!" and so on. His father, shaken by such an outburst of elemental fury, had stopped beating him, and had declared: "The child will be either a great man or a great criminal!" [p. 204]

Even when confronted with this memory, Ernst still refused
to admit that he had wished his father dead. Instead, as the treatment continued into its third and fourth month, he developed
what Freud would later call a "transference neurosis." "Things
soon reached a point," Freud wrote, "at which, in his waking
phantasies, and his associations, he began heaping the grossest and
filthiest abuse upon me and my family, though in his deliberate
actions he never treated me with anything but the greatest respect"
(p. 206). He brought in a dream in which Freud's mother had died
and he was anxious to offer Freud his condolences, but he was
afraid that in doing so he might break into an impertinent laugh.
Freud interpreted that the mother in the dream was really Ernst's
mother, and Ernst angrily asked if Freud were taking revenge on
him with such interpretations. On another occasion, he saw a girl
on Freud's stairway and decided she was Freud's daughter; he
imagined Freud wanted to match him up with her—and draw him
away from his lady friend, just as his father had tried to do. "The
only reason you're so kind and patient with me," he said, "is that
you want me for a son-in-law" (p. 198). He dreamed that he saw
Freud's daughter in front of him and she had two patches of dung
for eyes. Freud interpreted that Ernst wished to marry his daughter not for her beautiful eyes, but for her money (excrement = money).

It was true that Freud was being nice to him. In the notes that
were published posthumously (pp. 253–318), he described interventions that went beyond the scope of what is now called classical
psychoanalysis, and which may have exacerbated Ernst's transference neurosis. For example, he asked Ernst to bring in a photograph of his lady friend, and Ernst responded by threatening to
quit the treatment, apparently viewing Freud's request as an attempt to interfere—as his father had done—with his sexual life.
On another occasion Freud fed Ernst some herring, which took up
a good portion of his session. Four sessions later Ernst complained
that Freud had made a profit out of the meal, since Ernst had lost
time because of it. Still later Freud lent Ernst a book, Zola's *Joie de
Vivre*, because the hero's problems resembled Ernst's. Again,

Ernst was suspicious of Freud's motives. It may well be that Freud, due to his countertransference, was attempting to appease the patient, unsure of how to deal with the negativity that was pouring out of him. Even Ernst felt badly about the abuse. "How can a gentleman like you, sir," he asked, "let yourself be abused in this way by a low, good-for-nothing wretch like me? You ought to turn me out: that's all I deserve" (p. 206). Part of him wanted to be kicked out, and thus spared having to face his conflicts.

Ernst's verbal assault grew more intense and Freud valiantly attempted to analyze the transference. Now, following such assaults, Ernst began to bury his head in his hands, or suddenly jump up from the couch and roam about the room. When Freud asked why he did that, he could not answer. After the pattern had been repeated several times, Ernst finally got in touch with his feelings. "I'm afraid you'll give me a beating" (p. 206). His father, he recalled, had had a nasty temper and had not known when to stop. Being able to understand that he was responding to Freud as though Freud were his father was the turning point of the treatment.

As the months wore on, Ernst was relieved of his symptoms as well as the underlying conflicts. This came about not only through the analysis of Ernst's transference neurosis, but through the analysis of the "rat idea." Freud soon unraveled the meanings of Ernst's preoccupation with the captain's rat story and the instructions to repay the money. Rats, it turned out, meant many things to the patient. His father had been an ardent card-player (*spielratte* or play-rat) when he was in the army. Once a friend had lent him money to pay a gambling debt, and the father had never repaid his friend. Owing money to the young postal service woman, and the feeling that he owed money to Lieutenant A. led to Ernst's identifying with his father; he did not want to be like the father for whom he felt so much hatred and shame.

The captain's description of the rat torture activated Ernst's anal-erotism, and aroused memories of the excitement he felt when he was infected with intestinal worms in childhood. Rats (*ratten*) were anal symbols associated with money (installments = *raten*) and to his payments of Freud's fee. When Freud had initially told him his fee, Ernst had commented, sarcastically, "So many florins, so many rats" (p. 211). Rats were also associated with his symbolic payments to his father's wishes, including his wish for Ernst to marry (*hieraten*) the right woman, and they stood for the penis which, like rats, can transmit disease. Finally, rats were equated, in Ernst's mind, with children, including the patient himself, who used to bite like a rat (and had been severely punished for it).

The treatment lasted a little over eleven months. Once the complicated interweaving of the obsession had been solved, the rat delirium disappeared and Ernst began to think and function in a more normal way. Moreover, as his funds had dwindled by that time, he and Freud agreed to termination. In a note added in 1923, Freud stated, "The patient's mental health was restored to him by the analysis which I have reported upon these pages. Like so many other young men of value and promise, he perished in the Great War" (p. 250). He had served in the regular army during World War I, and was killed at the age of about 36.

Interpretation

Following Freud's presentation of this case in April 1908 at the Salzburg Conference, it quickly became the classic study of the obsessive-compulsive personality. Jones reports that during this presentation Freud sat at the end of a long table and spoke for nearly five hours, without a break. He had wanted to stop midway, but the participants "were so absorbed that [they] insisted on his continuing" (1957, p. 250). Jones sees the main idea in the presentation as the alternation of love and hate that underlies obsessive-compulsive thinking. The early separation of the two attitudes (splitting) results in the repression of hate. "When the two attitudes are of equal strength there results a paralysis of thought expressed in the clinical symptom known as *folie de doute*." Through the years, the "Rat Man" has become one of the prime "teaching tales" of psychoanalytic candidates. However, as psychoanalytic technique and theory have progressed, the case has been reviewed and reinterpreted by new generations of analysts.

Some reviewers have noted Freud's intellectualism. Kris (1951), points out that this case represents an early phase of psychoanalytic theory and technique in which the aim was the "conspicuous intellectual indoctrination" of patients, an outgrowth of the formality and intellectualism of the Victorian era. There was, he feels, little emphasis on reliving in the transference, which classical analysis was later to acquire. Indeed, Freud did not actually introduce the concept of "transference neurosis" until 1914, in his paper, "Remembering, Repeating, and Working Through" (Freud 1914b). Nor had he yet developed the concept of neutrality. The result was that Ernst seemed to do much reliving in the transference, while Freud concentrated on intellectually indoctrinating him.

Rieff (1959) echoes Kris's sentiments, asserting that Freud's own intellectual virtuosity often pervades his interpretations of dreams and other symptoms. In the case of the Rat Man, Rieff notes that Freud concentrated primarily on solving the rat idea, amplifying it through a number of words allied in sound to "rat" which the patient produced. In the end, one cannot be sure if Freud's interpretations reflect his patient's or his own unconscious. "An entire neurosis can take the form of an elaborate pun" (p. 79).

Kanzer (1980a) contends that Freud was not only too intellectual, but too helpful as well. In his zeal to assist the patient in finishing his thoughts and associations, he lost sight of neutrality, and played into Ernst's neuroses. For example, when Ernst haltingly told the story of the rat torture, he was able to draw Freud into a dialogue that was actually a reproduction of the proceedings he was describing. When he got up from the couch and pleaded with Freud to release him from the "pledge" to follow the rule of free association, Freud linked himself with the sadistic captain by saying that he himself had no taste for cruelty, and then finished the phrase "into the anus" for the patient. In doing so "the analyst was being seduced into the role not only of the cruel officer, who told the story, but also of the rats which invaded the victim's body" (p. 139). In addition, the patient now had good reason to feel about Freud as he had felt about his parents: that Freud could read his mind. These factors represented contaminations of the transference that would make Freud's task more difficult. He concludes, however, that despite the fact that Freud had not yet fully developed his stance of neutrality or the skill for directly analyzing transference and resistance, "in retrospect, it may be seen with what skill and intuition Freud's theoretical explanations took cognizance of and dealt with the transference" (p. 143).

Looking at Freud's influence on Ernst, Kanzer, in another paper (1980b), observes a similarity between Ernst's traumatic experience as a child and Freud's. When Ernst was beaten by his father, and he responded by heaping verbal abuse on him, the father had said, "The child will either be a great man or a great criminal." When Freud was 8 he urinated on his parents' bedroom floor, and his father exclaimed, "This boy will come to nothing." Freud later said that this incident haunted him for the rest of his life, and lay behind his accomplishments, as though he were saying to his father, "You see, I have amounted to something after all." In both instances, self-assertion to the father at the height of the oedipal period was "the occasion for substitutive castration and change in personality" (p. 238). This similarity, Kanzer contends, led to Freud's ability to be empathic with Ernst in a way he could not have been with Dora, for example.

Kestenberg (1980), studying Freud's descriptions of Ernst's behavior and drawing on many years of her own research on infant motor development, postulates that Ernst was fixated in the oral-sadistic phase of development. She notes that he did not have good control over the "middle range" of affectivity, veering from agitation to indifference or daze, and from fantasies of achieving high ambitions to feelings of humiliation and abandonment. She calls attention to the fragmentation of Ernst's personality, which was suggestive of the processes of isolation and ego-splitting. Ernst also had a need, she suggests, to control the goings in and comings out of the body, and the rat gnawing its way in might be interpreted as a wish to bear a baby. (Due to the removal of her ovaries, Ernst's lady friend could not give birth.)

Reviewing Freud's technique in terms of its replication of the parent–child dyad, Kestenberg observes that his patience, understanding, and compassion were like that of a good parent, and served to foster the rematuration of Ernst after his fixation points had been loosened. Freud countered Ernst's confused thinking with precise formulations, provided him with new object- and self-images, and served as a dependable model, correcting the undependability of the models he had had in his early childhood.

Shengold (1980) also views Ernst as fixated in the oral-sadistic phase, but emphasizes that he was a seduced and traumatized child who developed cannibalistic fantasies as an adult and found in the rat a symbol of his own ferocious orality. He speculates about the significance of teething, and describes a character type that he calls "rat people," who extensively use alterations of consciousness that produce vertical ego splits consisting of powerful personalities that appear and disappear. "These people operate under the sway of the compulsion to repeat past traumata whose central content appears to be overstimulation" (p. 201).

Olsen and Koppe (1988) contend that Ernst's neurosis could be traced back to an imperfect accomplishment of the active Oedipus complex. "The Rat Man had very few memories from this period in his life," they write, "but his subsequent development was unmistakably evident, in particular, in his anal interests" (p. 294). They point out that he had once seen his oldest sister sitting on the potty, and this had made him aware of the sexual anatomical differences. And the incident in which his father gave him a beating happened right after this sister had died, near the end of the anal and the beginning of the phallic stage. This punishment resulted in Ernst's developing a reaction formation toward his father, manifesting itself in an overconcern for his father's safety. They also see the rat idea as being traceable to the anal stage. Rats are like excrement that is passed from the intestines, they point out, and Ernst's stinginess was an anal trait.

Both Weiss (1980) and Langs (1980b) in separate papers comment on Freud's countertransference. Weiss alludes to the dream Ernst brought in about Freud's mother being dead and his being afraid to offer his condolences because he might laugh impertinently. Freud interpreted this bit of negative transference about his mother by immediately turning it around to the patient's mother, asking Ernst if it had never occurred to him that if *his* mother died he would be freed from all conflicts and could marry whomever he wished. Ernst responded angrily and fearfully, accusing Freud of taking revenge on him with this interpretation. "Is it fair to surmise," Weiss asks, "that the Rat Man by verbalizing a death wish against Freud's mother inflicted pain on Freud and that unconscious anger and hurt were warded off by an interpretation which contained a death wish against the patient's mother?" (p. 207). Weiss sees similar instances of countertransference when Freud asked for a photograph of Ernst's lady friend, and when he offered his patient herring. Langs notes that Ernst revealed at the outset that an unconscious motive for treatment was his wish to receive the same reassurance from Freud as he got from his friend. As a result, he induced Freud into what Langs calls a "sector of misalliance—unconscious shared efforts to achieve symptom relief through means other than insight" (p. 216).

All of these reviewers have made significant contributions to understanding this case. However, I would add one additional observation about the traumatic episode which precipitated Ernst's infantile neurosis and led to his obsessive-compulsive syndrome. Freud and others have stressed the father's beating as the primary cause of Ernst's trauma; I would speculate that his older sister's death was an equally important factor. His need to protect both his lady friend and his father from harm may derive from guilt feelings about somehow causing his older sister's death by having forbidden thoughts or behaving in a forbidden way toward her. He recalled seeing her on the potty and discovering the differences in sexual anatomy; such a scene usually arouses strong feelings of denial, fear, and contempt. She may also have been the person he had bitten before his father beat him. Soon after that she died. As an adult, Ernst had a charming niece who he liked very much, and one day he thought that if he indulged in coitus, something would happen to Ella. Was this a repetition of thoughts he had had at the time his sister died? He also had similar thoughts about his lady friend, and about his father. Research by Bowly (1979) has shown how deep an impact such a death can make on a child.

In his introduction, Freud modestly stated, "The crumbs of knowledge offered in these pages, though they have been laboriously enough collected, may not in themselves prove very satisfying; but they may serve as a starting-point for the work of other investigators, and common endeavor may bring the success which is perhaps beyond the reach of individual effort" (p. 157). However, our understanding of obsessive-compulsive personalities has not changed very much since Freud's landmark case history of the Rat Man. Only the techniques we use for treating them are different, as has been noted by many reviewers of the case. Freud also noted that people with obsessional neurosis do not come in for treatment as often as do hysterics, and this remains true today.

The case is a signpost for a certain phase in the development of psychoanalytic technique—the "intellectual indoctrination" phase. It is also the first case in which a transference neurosis was depicted—although this phenomenon would not be given a name until a few years later. It contains a plethora of material for students who wish to study the remarkable intuitive processes by which Freud explored the psyches of his patients, as well as the clinical experiences that determined the direction analytic theory would take.

5

THE PRIMAL SCENE

Sigmund Freud and the Wolf Man (1918)

Sergesius Pankejeff—whom Freud would nickname "The Wolf Man"—began his first session with Freud by proposing that he defecate on Freud's head and sodomize him (Blum 1980a, p. 343). Freud politely declined. The analysis lasted four years, from February 1910 until the summer of 1914, and was by far the longest analysis undergone until then.

It was a period of Freud's life during which he was increasingly embattled both inside and outside analytic circles. Three of his leading followers, Jung, Adler, and Stekel, were pulling away from him, and the psychiatric establishment had, at the same time, continued its attack on his theories. Not only were his theories under attack, but those of his followers as well. He and his followers were repeatedly denounced at scientific conferences as practitioners of pornography, filth, housewives' psychiatry, and witchcraft, among other things. For example, at the Congress of German neurologists and psychiatrists in Hamburg in 1910, Professor Wilhelm Weygandt banged on the table when Freud's theories were mentioned, shouting, "This is not a topic for discussion at a scientific meeting; it is a matter for the police" (Jones 1957, p. 291).

When Adler and Jung, perhaps reacting to the public outcry, began to challenge his theory of infantile sexuality, Freud decided once again to demonstrate the importance of infantile neurotic factors in a case history. Sergesius—or Sergej—provided him with an array of infantile traumata to analyze; indeed, he would turn out to be the most famous patient in the history of psychoanalysis, treated and written about by several other psychoanalysts and many laypeople after Freud. Freud's case history was written in 1914, but it was not published until four years later, under the title "From the History of an Infantile Neurosis" (Freud 1918). As the title indicates, almost the entire case history is devoted to reconstructing Sergej's childhood, and there is virtually nothing about Freud's therapeutic relationship with Sergej. What we know of that relationship comes from other sources.

Sergej was a Russian, whose family was among the wealthiest landowners in that country. His father was active in liberal politics and suffered occasional bouts of depression. His hypochondriacal mother was kept busy with her various illnesses. Sergej was born on Christmas Day, 1886, a fact which would become significant to his development. His only sibling was a sister, Anna, two-and-one-half-years older than he was. During his childhood the family divided its time between an estate in Odessa and a castle-like manor house in the country. Sergej and his sister were brought up by nannies, governesses, and tutors. A grandmother is believed to have committed suicide; his grandfather vied with his father for his mother's hand in marriage; an uncle who suffered from paranoia died in total isolation on a remote estate; and his sister committed suicide at the age of 21. Such was his family background.

Sergej's psychic problems began in early childhood. At one point he became angry and unmanageable, and showed sadistic tendencies. Then he developed a phobic anxiety of different animals, particularly wolves. Then, after the age of 4, the phobia was replaced by an obsession with religion. At the age of 17 he contracted gonorrhea and had a nervous breakdown. He underwent various psychiatric treatments in the following years, at one point consulting the famous psychiatrist Kraepelin, who diagnosed him as a manic-depressive. While staying in a sanatorium in Munich he met a nurse named Therese, a divorced woman a few years older than he, who had a child. She was such a dominating and moody woman that the doctors, his family, and all his acquaintances opposed his relationship with her. His Russian physician, Dr. Drosnes, who had read about psychoanalysis, recommended that he travel to Vienna and have a consultation with Freud. Sergej set out immediately, accompanied by Dr. Drosnes and a medical student. The student's task was to give Sergej enemas for his digestive difficulties, and to be the third in their card games. Both were supported financially by Sergej.

He was 23 when he met Freud. One of the first things he asked Freud during his initial consultation was whether he should marry Therese. He explained that everybody else was against her. Freud ordered him not to see Therese anymore, and told him flatly that marrying her was out of the question. (At that time, psychoanalysts regularly instructed their patients not to make any big decisions until after they had completed their analysis.) A year later Freud relented and allowed Sergej to visit Therese, but remained steadfast on the question of his marrying her. In an interview with Sergej sixty years after his analysis with Freud, he said that initially he worshiped Freud. "Freud was a genius even though not everything he said was true," Sergej told Karin Obholzer (1982, p. 30). "If you had seen him—he was a fascinating personality. . . . He had very serious eyes that looked down to the very bottom of the soul. . . . When I told him about my various states [of mania and depression] he said: 'We have the means to cure what you are suffering from. Up to now, you have been looking for the causes of your illness in the chamber pot.'" In the beginning, Sergej said, everything about psychoanalysis was exciting and new. Yet he was skeptical. Whenever Freud explained psychoanalytic concepts to him or gave him an interpretation, he would reply, "All right. I agree, but I am going to check whether it is correct."

To which Freud replied, "Don't start that. Because the moment you try to view things critically, your treatment will get nowhere. I will help you, whether you believe it or not" (p. 31).

In the case history, Freud described Sergej as remaining for a long time "unassailably intrenched behind an attitude of obliging apathy":

> He listened, understood, and remained unapproachable. His unimpeachable intelligence was, as it were, cut off from the instinctual forces which governed his behavior in the few relations of life that remained to him. It required a long education to induce him to take an independent share of the work; and when as a result of this exertion he began for the first time to feel relief, he immediately knocked off the work in order to avoid any further changes, and in order to remain comfortably in the situation which had been thus established. [p. 477]

Freud added that it was only after the patient had formed a strong enough attachment with him to counterbalance his "shrinking" from the task that he was able to make any progress. Today's psychotherapists have become familiar with this problem in working with borderline and narcissistic patients (into which category, according to Harold Blum [1980a] Sergej would have fallen). However, despite this attachment, Sergej's resistance was so great that Freud, who diagnosed Sergej as an obsessional neurotic, eventually lost patience with him and resorted to a "parameter"—a deviation in standard psychoanalytic technique: he told the patient that he would end his therapy in six months, no matter what. At first the always suspicious Sergej did not believe him, but when he became convinced that Freud meant it, much new material rose to the surface.

While the therapy moved along slowly and painfully, Sergej lived the life of a wealthy Russian in Vienna; he gambled, took fencing lessons, frequented nightclubs and the theater, had flings with women of lower status, and hired an occasional prostitute for his sexual gratification, preferring anal intercourse. For a time Dr. Drosnes and the medical student stayed with him. Occasionally he would visit Therese in Munich, or she would visit him in Vienna. Yet, despite his self-indulgent existence, his depression remained. He went through the actions of his life, but his attitude was apathetic. Indeed, his first session with Freud seemed a microcosm of his life at the time: his offer to defecate on Freud's head and take him anally was one of his apathetic actions, most likely aimed at shocking or provoking Freud. Freud, as was indicated earlier, did not analyze the Wolf Man's transference toward him in the case history, although this initial interaction could clearly be seen as an enactment of Sergej's father complex.

It would appear, based not only on Freud's statements but also on Sergej's later interview, that Sergej continued to be somewhat seductive and provocative throughout the treatment. He had a habit of turning from the couch to gaze at Freud. On one of those occasions Freud said, "You turn around because you want to show that you have beautiful eyes" (Obholzer 1982, p. 169). From then on Sergej kept his eyes to the fore, not wanting Freud to think him vain. Once he asked Freud why he sat at the back of the couch instead of at the front, and Freud replied that he had once had a female patient who wanted to seduce him, and kept raising her skirt and sitting up to embrace him (p. 169).

At the core of Freud's analysis of Sergej was a dream, from which the patient got his nickname "The Wolf Man." He probably related this dream somewhere near the beginning of the treatment, and eventually Freud (1918) used it to shed light on all aspects of his infantile neurosis. He had the dream on the night before his fourth birthday (Christmas):

> I dreamed that it was night and that I was lying in my bed. (My bed stood with its foot toward the window; in front of the window there was a row of old walnut trees. I know it was winter when I had the dream, and night-time.) Suddenly the window opened of its own accord, and I was terrified to see that some white wolves were sitting on the big walnut tree in front of the window. There were six or seven of them. The wolves were quite white, and looked more like foxes or sheep-dogs, for they had big tails like

foxes and they had their ears pricked like dogs when they are attending to something. In great terror, evidently of being eaten up by the wolves, I screamed and woke up. [p. 107]

The patient said that after he awoke, his nurse came to him, and it took her a long time to convince him that it had been only a dream. The only action in the dream was the opening of the window, he said, for the wolves sat quite still and without any movement on the branches of the tree, looking at him. "It seemed as though they had riveted their whole attention upon me.—I think this was my first anxiety dream. . . . From then until my eleventh or twelfth year I was always afraid of seeing something terrible in my dreams" (p. 499). He added a drawing of the tree with the wolves.

His first association to the dream was a memory of being afraid of a picture of a wolf in a book of fairy tales. His sister used to tease him by holding this particular picture up in front of him, and he would become terrified and begin to scream. In this picture the wolf was standing upright, its claws stretched out, its ears pricked. Freud asked him why the wolves were white, and he thought of the sheep in neighboring estates. Asked how the wolves came to be on the tree, he was reminded of a story that he had heard his grandfather tell about a tailor who was sitting in his room when the window opened and a wolf leaped in. The tailor pulled off the wolf's tail and it fled. Later the tailor was walking in the woods when a pack of wolves came toward him. He climbed a tree, and the wolves tried to reach him by standing one on top of another, with the maimed wolf on the bottom of the pile. Just then the tailor shouted, "Catch the grey one by the tail!" and the tailless wolf ran off, toppling the others.

"Why were there six or seven wolves?" Freud asked. The patient thought of another fairy tale, "The Wolf and the Seven Little Goats." The wolf in the story had a white paw, and at one point he snored under a tree. Sergej remembered his father playing wolf with him, threatening to "gobble him up." He also remembered going out to the pasture with his father when an ovine epidemic was raging and watching the sheep die.

Freud was able to date the dream when he understood, through Sergej's associations, that the tree was a distorted Christmas tree and the wolves were ornaments or gifts in the tree. He had dreamed it the night before Christmas, having gone to bed fantasizing about what kind of gifts he would receive from his father.

Freud and Sergej spent several years interpreting this dream. Eventually, through its interpretation and through other memories, Freud was able to reconstruct a primal scene, which he believed had occurred when the patient was about one and a half. The patient had no memory of this scene, but Freud became convinced that it had happened. Freud speculated that the boy had witnessed the scene while suffering from malaria, when his crib had been moved into his parents' bedroom. In the primal scene his father was copulating with his mother from the rear as dogs do, Freud deduced, allowing for the possibility that the patient had seen dogs or sheep copulating. The scene aroused his castration fear. Identifying with his mother, he had the thought that if he were to take his mother's place he would have to lose his penis and have an open "sore." Castration was depicted in the fairy tale about the wolf who lost his tail. The tailless wolf upon which the other wolves climbed represented the mother, while the wolf in the other story who stood on his hind legs represented the father. Being eaten by the wolf represented copulation, the act having been displaced from the phallic to the oral zone. The window opened by itself in the same way Sergej's eyes did when he gawked at the primal scene, and the wolves stared at him just as he had stared at the primal scene. The wolves were white like sheep and like the wolf's paw in the story, and perhaps like his naked parents in the primal scene. They were motionless, in contrast to the passionate movement of the parents in the primal scene, and had large foxtails, representing the denial of castration.

In his analysis of Sergej's infantile neurosis, Freud divided his childhood into four phases, each of which was precipitated by a particular traumatic event. The first phase began when Sergej was two and a half, when he remembered seeing his nurse, Gruscha, on all fours scrubbing the floor. Apparently the sight of her behind aroused him sexually, and he reacted by urinating on the floor. She jokingly told him that little boys who urinated on floors should have their penises cut off. Freud speculated that Sergej's preference in adulthood for servant girls of lower status and intelligence than he, as well as his preference for anal intercourse, could be traced to a fixation at this point. It was as though he needed to conquer such girls in this way to affirm his manhood.

The second phase, the phallic phase, began when Sergej was seduced by his sister at the age of 3 years and 3 months. They were playing on the floor when his sister grabbed his penis and started fondling it. She explained her behavior by saying that Nanja (their nanny) did the same with everybody, even the gardener. The sister then had him stand on his head and tried to grab his genitals again, but he ran away. Later he tried to seduce Nanja by playing with himself in front of her, and she told him that if he did that he would get a "sore" there—which he took as a castration threat. Then, during a summer vacation while his parents were away on a trip, he underwent a character change; he became aggressive and sadistic where previously he had been passive and masochistic. He was cruel toward both animals and people, and tormented his once dear Nanja to distraction. During this vacation he had been surrounded by women, and he was the smallest child there. This and his seduction by his sister made him feel powerless, and the incestuous play with his sister also aroused guilt feelings. Freud speculated that his aggression was a reaction to the castration threat, and that it was in reality not a form of sadism but of masochism, serving to provoke punishment and pave the way for him to be spanked on his bottom. Freud later alluded to this memory in his paper, "A Child is Being Beaten" (1919). It also represented a transformation of his identification from father to mother and of the active heterosexual object choice of Gruscha to the passive homosexual object choice of the father.

At the age of 4 the third phase began with the wolf dream the night before Christmas. During this phase the patient had an animal phobia. He was not only afraid of wolves but also of the smaller animals he generally mistreated. He recalled once chasing a large butterfly, but just as he was about to catch it he was filled with anxiety and ran off crying. Freud interpreted that each such instance of anxiety represented displaced castration anxiety. During this phase Sergej dealt with the castration threat from his father by further developing a passive phallic, homosexual disposition. His intestinal troubles during adulthood (constipation, diarrhea, pain) were hysterical symptoms related to his conflicted wish to be taken anally.

Phase four began when, Sergej was 4½ and his mother and Nanja began his religious training. Now his sadomasochism and animal phobia were replaced by an obsessive-compulsive religious piety. He said the Lord's Prayer over and over, crossed himself constantly, and kissed all the images of the saints in his room before going to bed at night. Religion assuaged his guilt, appeased the castration threat, and speeded the formation of the superego. In Freud's view, the religious instruction was so effective because the patient identified with Jesus. He and Jesus had the same birthday, and the story of Jesus appealed to his masochism. He wondered if Jesus had a bottom; if he had bowel movements like everybody else; who his father was—Joseph or God. "The boy had some kind of inkling of the ambivalent feelings toward the father which are an underlying factor in all religions," Freud stated, "and attacked religion on account of the slackening which it implied in the relation between son and father" (p. 540). The struggle between his heterosexual and homosexual feelings now manifested itself in this confusion about God:

> His old love for his father, which had been manifest in his earliest period, was therefore the source of his energy in struggling against God and of his acuteness in criticizing religion. But on the other hand this hostility to the new God was not an original reaction either; it had its prototype in a hostile impulse against his father which had come into existence under the influence of the anxiety dream, and it was at bottom only a revival of that impulse. The two opposing currents of feeling, which were to rule the whole of his later life, met here in the ambivalent struggle over the question of religion. [p. 541]

This ambivalence could be detected not only in his confusion over his relationship with God, but also in certain obsessive thoughts that kept occurring to him, such as "God—shit," and "God—swine," which also pertained to his anal eroticism. He also developed obsessive rituals by means of which he atoned for his "blasphemies." Each time he made the sign of the cross he was obliged to breathe in deeply or to exhale forcibly. Since "breath" in Russian was the same word as "spirit," each inhalation meant he was breathing in the Holy Spirit and a strong exhalation represented the expulsion of evil spirits. The intense breathing also reminded him of his parents' intercourse in the primal scene.

After three and a half years, Freud decided to set a termination date for the analysis. He did so because the analysis had been bogged down for a year or so, and he hoped that the threat of termination would force Sergej out of his resistance. The intervention worked; during the next six months much new material emerged. Sergej recalled chasing the butterfly called a "Gruscha," which reminded him of his first nursemaid, "Gruscha," and the memory of urinating on the floor. Another recollection cleared up another one of his symptoms. He had a feeling that he was always seeing the world through a veil, which was broken only when he defecated after an enema. Then he recalled that he had been born in a caul, and had the superstitious conviction of invincibility which broke down when he acquired gonorrhea. Freud interpreted that Sergej's desire to break the veil and see more clearly was a wish to be reborn as a woman, replacing his mother and offering himself anally to his father. He also interpreted the connection between money and excrement and its relation to his intestinal troubles, and in the course of the work, Freud observed, "his bowel began, like a hysterically affected organ, to 'join in the conversation,' and in a few weeks time recovered its normal functions after its long impairment" (p. 552).

Sergej's period of religious obsession ended at about the age of 10, when he succeeded, through a new tutor, in finding another sphere of interest in which his active and phallic attitude could find expression—the military. He then took an interest in broad-bottomed servant girls, and became somewhat promiscuous. It was at this time that he made a sexual advance toward his sister, and she rejected him. When he contracted gonorrhea at 17, his repressed homosexuality returned, manifesting itself in the intestinal troubles. At the same time, he became so obsessed with money that when his sister committed suicide and his father died, he thought only of his inheritance.

Freud's analysis of Sergej seemed to help him to some extent. It freed him from much of the ambivalence toward Therese, so that after a while Freud decided marriage would be acceptable, and it also resolved the homosexual impulses that had been sublimated and bound to aesthetic interests. The patient reported, when asked sixty years later if Freud had helped him, "Well, he enabled me to marry Therese. That was a decision that wasn't easily made, but I did manage. I finished my studies. . . . I conducted myself more or less normally. My depressions had got better" (Obholzer 1982, p. 44).

However, Sergej lost his entire fortune following World War I and the Russian Revolution, and returned to Vienna broken and despondent. Freud treated him for another six months without fee, and took up a collection for him among his friends and colleagues. Sergej got a job as a clerk in an insurance company, where he remained until he retired in 1950. In 1926 he suffered from a relapse and wanted to see Freud again, but Freud had become too ill at the time to take him on and referred him to a trainee, Ruth Mack Brunswick. According to Brunswick (1928), Freud's forced termination of Sergej's case left the patient with unanalyzed and pathogenic feelings and fantasies toward Freud. He developed a full-blown hypochondria, which Brunswick attributed to his identification with his hypochrondriacal mother; a mild case of paranoia, including megalomaniacal thoughts of himself as Freud's closest associate; and a persecution complex focused on a Professor X. who had operated on his nose. After Brunswick had systematically refuted his belief in his favored position with Freud, Sergej became enraged at both Freud and Brunswick, believing them to be conspiring against him, and he threatened to kill them both. Then, after she had analyzed his fantasy of being Christ, positive dreams emerged about Freud and Brunswick, and his delusions were resolved.

Sergej remained closely tied to psychoanalysis for the rest of his life. In 1938, when Therese committed suicide, he sank into another depression and returned to Brunswick for additional treatment. In 1950 he wrote an autobiography, which was eventually included in a book about him by Muriel Gardiner (1971), who maintained continuous contact with him throughout his life. In the 1970s Sergej was interviewed by the journalist Karin Obholzer; at his request her interview was not published until a year after his death in 1979. Another interview by psychoanalyst Kurt Eissler, who also had much contact with Sergej in his later years, has not as yet been made public.

Gardiner, in the final chapter of her book about him, describes Sergej as someone who had generally been prone to "obsessional doubting, brooding, questioning . . . completely engrossed in his own problems and unable to relate to others" (p. 361). She asserts that the defects that remained with the patient from his obsessional neurosis could not be removed completely by either Freud or Brunswick. "However, the positive results of the Wolf Man's analysis are impressive indeed" (p. 365).

He continued to draw people to him even as he neared the end. On his deathbed, he was visited frequently by Obholzer, Gardiner, Albin Unterweger (a friend of Gardiner's), Eissler, who had intermittently analyzed him, Dr. S., the director of the Vienna Psychiatric Hospital and his current analyst, as well as others involved with psychoanalysis. His death seemed to symbolize something to all of them—perhaps the death of an era or of the dimming of a psychoanalytic beacon.

Obholzer recounts that during his last two years he developed a strong need for affection, something she had not noticed in their earlier relationship. Before, she says, "He expressed his feelings toward me by formally kissing my hand when he arrived and when he left. Now, when I sit by his bed, he wants to hold my hand for hours, embraces me when I arrive and leave, and sometimes even kisses me" (p. 247). As he understood that he was dying, he reached out to her, pleading with her to help him. Near the end he complained, "Life was in vain, everything was pointless, we must build something, something new, begin at the beginning once more. . . . Give me some advice!" (p. 247).

On May 6, 1979, at the Vienna Psychiatric Hospital, the Wolf Man took his last breath.

Interpretation

Did psychoanalysis help Sergej? This is the question psychoanalysts and laypeople alike have debated since Freud's case history first appeared. The Wolf Man is the most famous patient in psychiatric history, and more follow-up research is available about him than about any other of the subjects of early psychoanalysis; hence, debates about the efficacy of psychoanalysis often center, perhaps unfairly, on the Wolf Man.

Freud (1916–1917) himself was dissatisfied with the results of the case. He felt uneasy about his emphasis on the infantile material, on reconstruction, and especially on the primal scene. Indeed, he was so worried about the fact that he had attached such importance to a primal scene he had assumed (but which the patient had never actually recollected) that he held back from publishing the case for four years. "I admit," he wrote in a footnote, "that this is the most ticklish question in the whole domain of psychoanalysis. . . . No other uncertainty has been more decisive in holding me back from publishing my conclusions" (p. 584). During the interval between finishing and publishing the case, he thought of still another possibility for explaining the primal scene. The primal scene and other such memories "were once real occurrences in the primaeval time of the human family, and . . . children in their fantasies are simply filling in gaps in individual truth with historical truth" (p. 371).

In addition, since his primary aim had been to refute Adler and Jung, he had neglected the contemporary features of the patient's adjustment and relationship to himself, and he knew it. Immediately afterward, as he explained in "On the History of the Psychoanalytic Movement," he revised his therapeutic approach radically, so as to give the analysis of transference and resistance more emphasis (Freud 1914a). Two decades later, in "Analysis Terminable and Interminable" (1937), he asserted that it was unlikely that an analysis could ever be completely terminated, and it was the case of the Wolf Man that came to his mind. Indeed, according to Strachey (see Freud 1918, p. 5), he referred to the Wolf Man directly in six articles between 1913 and 1937 and indirectly in several others; he remained preoccupied with this case for the rest of his life.

Such detractors of psychoanalysis as Obholzer have pounced on the case in order to prove psychoanalysis to be a sham. Obholzer writes how psychoanalysts surrounding Sergej pressured him not to allow her to interview him in an attempt to protect their investment, and how both Eissler and Gardiner tried to block the signing of the contract for the book. As for the case itself, Obholzer feels that psychoanalysts have distorted the facts in order to demonstrate a cure when in fact there was no cure. Commenting on Brunswick's statement that Freud's time limit had "resulted in the patient's bringing sufficient material to provide a cure, but it had also enabled him to keep just that nucleus which later resulted in his psychosis" (see Gardiner 1971, p. 304), she asks, "Is there such a thing as being cured on the one hand, yet retaining the nucleus of a psychosis which is, after all, something rather substantial?" (Obholzer 1982, p. 20). Obholzer refers to Sergej as a "ward of psychoanalysis," since he was passed on from one psychoanalyst to another during his lifetime. However, it is fair to say that he also had a host of other types of physicians around him, due to his hypochondria. And psychoanalysts have had some justification for being protective about psychoanalysis since, beginning with Freud's first papers, it has continually been under attack. They knew that Obholzer's aim was to debunk psychoanalysis, and naturally wanted to stop her. If psychoanalysts were using Sergej, then so was she.

Many psychoanalysts have wondered along with Freud about the importance of the primal scene. In the years since the publication of this case, it has become a basic concept of psychoanalysis, the significance of which has been taken for granted. Blum (1980b) observes that the concept is seen as a crystallization of the oedipal drama, and the fantasy of the primal scene figures prominantly in movies, plays, novels, ballet, and art. It represents a condensation of the active and passive drives, masculinity and femininity, eros and thanatos. It symbolizes curiosity about pregnancy and birth. And it represents, via displacement and condensation, the conflicts of the oedipal child.

Yet the debate about its relevance in Sergej's case and in general continues. Rosenfeld (1956) asks if Freud may have been troubled by counteridentifications, mixing reactions to his own primal scene with that of Sergej's, and hoping to to recover his own primal scene in that way. Schur (1972), supporting Rosenfeld's contention, points out that Freud's parents lived in a one-room apartment when he was an infant, and Freud would most likely have witnessed his parents' intercourse. Anna Freud (1951) looks at the telescoping effect of memory and the genetically determined coital play of children reared in war nurseries (akin to Freud's phylogenetic memories) and casts doubt about the reconstruction of a single infantile primal scene shock such as that described in Sergej's case. Esman (1973) proposes that the primal scene need not be traumatic at all, and wonders if it explains everything and nothing. Blum (1980a) doubts the accuracy of the reconstruction of the primal scene in the Wolf Man's case, while affirming its central importance in psychoanalysis. A child of one year, six months, he argues, could not have perceived the details of the primal scene, particularly if he were suffering from malaria; and at any rate such a scene would have been only one of many traumatic events such as seductions, illnesses (the malaria itself), castration threats, and perhaps a constitutional vulnerability to overstimulation.

With regard to Sergej's actual analyses by Freud and Brunswick, two analysts, Blum (1980a) and Halpert (1980), assert that Freud misdiagnosed the patient. Utilizing today's advances in diagnostic technique, Blum demonstrates that Sergej's infantile neurosis was "a severe borderline disturbance which provided the foundation for a borderline adolescence and . . . adult borderline personality" (p. 343). He explains that Sergej's development of a transference psychosis with Brunswick fourteen years after his treatment with Freud had ended reflected a typical borderline lack of true ego integration and the consequent vulnerability to regression under stress. Blum also points to other symptoms of borderline personality—Sergej's bizarre offer to defecate on Freud's head and sodomize him during their initial consultation; his chronic hypochondria; his "obliging apathy"; his long-standing depression; his tendencies to act out; and his failures in ego synthesis. Further, he asserts that his infantile neurotic symptoms were similar to those of children who later became borderline or schizophrenic. Many obsessive children, he notes, later develop schizophrenia, and sexually traumatized children often become borderline. The primal scene allegedly took place, he notes, during the rapproachement subphase of separation-individuation, when basic moods, trust, and distrust develop. Finally, he points to the significance of preoedipal pathogenic factors, such as Sergej's having had several "mothers," his real mother's hypochondria, his separations from his father, his seduction by his sister, castration threats by servants, and other preoedipal determinants of passivity, masochism, and compliance. The Wolf Man's fear of helplessness and passivity, according to Blum, are also indications of a wish to be devoured in sleep, to enter a state of symbiotic union.

Halpert notes that Freud himself became unsure of his diagnosis of Sergej when, after the news of his sister's suicide, the Wolf Man displayed hardly a trace of grief, instead rejoicing that he would now be sole heir to the family property. Not only was Freud suddenly confused about Sergej's diagnosis, but he also became alarmed about his patient's analyzability, particularly his ability to form an object cathexis. (Halpert underscores the importance of this capacity in forming an effective transference and working alliance, and observes that such a capacity is generally lacking in borderline personalities.)

Langs (1980c) suggests that there were problems in Freud's therapeutic alliance with Sergej because of Freud's deviations from standard technique. Sergej knew that Freud had a dual interest in him, as both a patient and a research subject. Sergej's knowledge of Freud's double interest in him created a narcissistic misalliance, according to Langs, and was replaced later by a similar misalliance with Brunswick. Freud's setting a fixed termination date, moreover, prompted a sector of misalliance in which "Freud became the God (father), who promised a cure and who brought matters to an end (death), and in which the Wolf Man became the victim, Christ" (p. 375). This resulted in a transference cure rather than a real cure, one which gratified his narcissistic needs. Other deviations, including giving direct advice, confiding personal information to Sergej, meeting Sergej's fiancée, accepting an expensive termination gift (an Egyptian antiquity), providing free analytic sessions, and giving him money, further reinforced Sergej's narcissistic needs and impeded his cure. Brunswick was another gift—Sergej was sent to her by Freud and she also saw him without fee. Therefore, her work with Sergej represented a continuation of the misalliance.

Both Blum (1980b) and Kanzer (1980c) attribute Sergej's development of paranoia fourteen years after his termination with Freud to his losing him as an idealized self-object. Blum feels that Sergej, whose ego stability was threatened by Freud's illness, turned to Brunswick to reestablish his narcissistic equilibrium and reenter a symbiotic relationship. Kanzer observes that Brunswick no doubt disturbed this narcissistic equilibrium when she insisted on refuting Sergej's contention that he was Freud's favorite patient. In fact, there was much evidence that he *was* Freud's favorite patient. Brunswick, who was in treatment with Freud at the time she was analyzing Sergej, could not understand his disturbed behavior or control it.

Kanzer also asserts that Brunswick did not properly utilize a new rendition of the wolf dream that occurred during her analysis of Sergej. In this new dream, the wolves were ranging fiercely up and down behind a wall, and a woman (a partial representation of Brunswick) was apparently planning to open the door to let them in. Brunswick interpreted this dream in terms of the first dream, speculating that the wolves in the first dream represented his father, who is threatening to devour Sergej if he spies on his parents during coitus or tries to take his father's place with his mother. "But is it only the father's rage that is being warded off?" Kanzer asks. "The patient was now visibly raging like a wolf and threatening to shoot Freud and Brunswick. . . . The primal scene rage reaction of the little Wolf Man was finding an outlet at last, the rage that came to be represented in passive staring instead of devouring them, and then in projection of the dangerous oral aggression into the passive staring wolves" (p. 360). Kanzer believes that the second dream warns that the analyst is opening the door and lifting defenses that have long kept the wolves (the Wolf Man's narcissistic aggression) in check. She will be destroyed if this occurs. Brunswick was unable to analyze this negative transference and hence unable to resolve the transference situation.

In a sense Gardiner is right, however, when she asserts that the results of Sergej's analyses were impressive. Before seeing Freud, he had spent time in several sanatoriums, and had it not been for his analytic treatments he would most likely have spent more time in such places, perhaps even been permanently institutionalized. We know now that the treatment of borderline and psychotic patients often requires many more than the four years Freud spent with him—sometimes more than ten years, at times more than twenty. Psychoanalysis kept Sergej functioning in a relatively normal manner for his entire life and alleviated much of his depression. For these reasons the case must still be seen as having a successful outcome.

Freud's Wolf Man remains a favorite teaching case in psychoanalytic institutes, although most psychoanalysts now regard it as somewhat outdated. Kanzer calls it "a path through the wilderness in comparison with a modern highway" (1980c, p. 359), but claims it is still a fascinating introduction to the world of psychoanalysis. This longest of Freud's case histories provides clinical material that touches on a host of issues that have remained a central focus in all forms of psychotherapy: the importance of the primal scene and infantile neurosis, ways of terminating treatment, the limits of analyzability, dream interpretation, the nature of narcissism, and acting out in the transference. Like his other case histories, it is a portrait of the mind of one of humanity's greatest geniuses, one which shows him at work with perhaps his most difficult patient.

The primal scene, while once an important concept, has become less so as psychoanalytic research has shown that many factors contribute to psychopathology. Instead of focusing on isolated traumatic events, today's analysts are more likely to look at an ongoing pattern of pathogenic environmental occurrences, and instead of studying an individual's drive conflicts, they will study the multitude of internal and external stress factors. They are also more aware of the interplay of constitutional and environmental influences. Freud was well aware of this interplay himself, although his definition of constitution was a bit Darwinian. In a letter to Else Voigtländer he wrote, "The question as to which is of greater significance, constitution or experience . . . can in my opinion only be answered by saying that fate and chance and not one or the other are decisive. Why should there be an antithesis, since constitution after all is nothing but the sediment of experiences from a long line of ancestors" (see E. Freud 1960, p. 284).

Moreover, the culture in which one lives also has an impact on one's character. The symptoms of today's hysteric are different from the symptoms of the hysteric of Freud's day. So, too, are the symptoms of male psychopathology. Today homosexuality is more accepted by society, so that there is a rise in homosexuality and a decline in obsessional neurosis, which is often a defense used to ward off ego-dystonic homosexuality. (If Sergej had lived today, he most likely would have been more able to accept his homosexuality.) Another important change in the cultural environment centers around family values. In Freud's day the father was generally dominant in the family, and hence in his case histories the father figures prominently in the etiology of his children's psychopathology. In today's society the mother is more likely to be dominant, and she has correspondingly taken a more important role in child-rearing and has a greater impact on personality development. Finally, in Freud's day corporal punishment of children was the rule, while in Western society today corporal punishment is out of fashion, and permissiveness is in vogue. This has led to a decline in such ailments as conversion hysteria and obsessional neurosis (which stem from oppressive environment) and to a rise of narcissism (which often results from the overstimulation or deprivation of permissive parenting).

However, even though Freud and subsequent analysts have relegated the concept of the primal scene to a less important place in the scheme of things, his Wolf Man case was a turning point insofar as it was the most elaborate study of the link between infantile experience and adult neurosis published at that time. This is important because throughout the history of humankind, and even today, there is a tendency to want to attribute all of our ailments, both physical and mental, to the genes, to the stars, to our diet, and to everything other than our behavior to one another. By doing so, of course, we can avoid taking responsibility for the way we raise our children, the way we express our feelings, how our attitudes affect others, and how they affect ourselves. Freud left behind a legacy for succeeding psychoanalysts and psychotherapists to follow. He provided them with road maps on which many of the roads had been charted, but many more were still to be discovered. Those who followed him could never entirely forget their debt to him.

On September 21, 1939, dying of cancer of the mouth and throat, Freud said to his personal physician, "My dear Schur, you remember our first talk. You promised me then you would help me when I could no longer carry on" (Jones 1957, p. 518). He was given a lethal dose of morphine and died peacefully two days later. Jones notes that Freud died as he had lived—a realist.

6

JUNGIAN DREAM ANALYSIS

Carl G. Jung and the Philosophy Student (1928)

Unlike Freud, who wrote five book-length case histories and several of shorter length, Jung wrote no lengthy case histories. Indeed, within the 17-volume edition of his collected works, one can scarcely find a vignette. Perhaps this is because the case history was too concrete a form for him; he preferred to explore human behavior on a more philosophical and mythological level. "In describing the living processes of the psyche," he writes, "I deliberately and consciously give preference to a dramatic, mythological way of thinking and speaking, because this is not only more expressive but also more exact than an abstract scientific terminology, which is wont to toy with the notion that its theoretic formulations may one fine day be resolved into algebraic equations" (Jung 1951, p. 151). This comment is both a defense of his language and a dig at Freud, who wanted to make psychoanalysis more scientific.

Carl Gustav Jung was born on July 26, 1875, in Kesswil, Switzerland, on Lake Constance. His paternal grandfather was a surgeon and his father, Johann, was a clergyman. His mother came from a long-established Basel family. When he was 4, Jung's parents moved to a suburb of Basel, where his father began educating him in Latin and his mother read to him from an illustrated children's book of exotic religions, containing pictures of Hindu gods. Jung at first considered careers in archeology and theology before entering medical school. His final thesis in medical school was a study of occult phenomenon, a subject that would continue to fascinate him all his life. Indeed, some have attributed his interest in parapsychology to psychotic episodes he had during his youth, including a time when he manifested dual personalities, one of which lived in a past century (Stern 1976).

In 1900, at the age of 25, he was appointed as a staff physician at Burghölzi Mental Clinic, where he worked under Eugen Bleuler. When Freud's *Interpretation of Dreams* came out, Bleuler recommended it to Jung. Jung soon began a correspondence with Freud, and in 1907 he went to visit Freud in Vienna. They met at 1:00 P.M. and talked for thirteen hours. At the time of their meeting Jung was 32 and Freud 51. Jung reports that when Freud came to greet him at the hotel where he was staying with his attractive new wife, he told Jung, "I am sorry that I can give you no real hospitality. I have nothing at home but an elderly wife" (Campbell 1971, p. xvi). Jung says he soon discovered that Freud was "in love" with his wife's younger sister, who lived in the same house. "It was a shocking discovery to me, and even now I recall the agony I felt at the time" (p. xvi).

Freud quickly accepted Jung into the inner circles of psychoanalysis, and confided to him that he was adopting him as "an eldest son, anointing him as successor and crown prince" (p. xvii). However, their association was to be short-lived, for it soon became apparent that they had basic differences. One concerned the sexual etiology of the neuroses—Jung felt that mental illnesses spring from many sources, not just from sexual conflicts—and the other concerned the disparity between Freud's empiricism and Jung's occultism.

Jung relates that when he once asked Freud what he thought about precognition and parapsychology, Freud abruptly replied, "Sheer nonsense!" Freud's statement so angered Jung that he said he had to check "the sharp retort on the tip of my tongue." In describing this incident to Billinsky years afterward, Jung said he had a physical reaction to Freud's words:

> It was as if my diaphragm were made of iron and were becoming red-hot—a glowing vault. And at that moment there was such a loud report in the bookcase, which stood right next to us, that we started up in alarm, fearing the thing was going to topple over on us. I said to Freud: "There, that is an example of a so-called catalytic exteriorization phenomenon."
> "Oh come!" he exclaimed. "That is sheer bosh."
> "It is not," I replied. "You are mistaken, Herr Professor. And to prove my point I now predict that in a moment there will be another such loud report." [p. xvii]

Jung claims there was another "report" from the bookcase, but Freud continued to maintain his skepticism. This incident was to be the first of a series of conflicts between them that would eventually lead to their estrangement in 1913.

An additional factor in the break, along with their theoretical and philosophical differences, was Freud's disillusionment with Jung's character: he was not the successor that Freud had hoped for. As Jones later put it, Jung's personality was more that of "rebel" and "heretic" than leader. "His mentality had the serious flaw of lacking lucidity. I remember once meeting someone who had been in school with him and being struck by the answer he gave to my question of what Jung had been like as a boy: 'He had a confused mind.' I was not the only person to make the same observation" (Jones 1957, p. 247). It also came to Freud's attention that Jung, who had married Emma Rauschenback in 1903, sometimes had affairs with his patients. One of them, Sabrina Speilrein, wrote a letter to Freud, bringing her confused relationship with Jung to Freud's attention, pleading for his assistance. She was a pretty 18-year-old who wore her hair in one long braid down her back when she was first admitted to the mental clinic suffering from a psychosis. Jung treated her without a fee, cured her, and then had an affair with her. He also became her mentor and encouraged her to become a therapist herself. Later he confessed to Freud in writing, "I . . . deplore the sins I have committed . . . In view of the fact that the patient had shortly before been my friend and enjoyed my full confidence, my action was a piece of knavery which I very reluctantly confess to you as my father" (see Donn 1988, p. 93).

After his break from Freud, Jung went through his own self-analysis, from 1913 to 1917, and began to develop his own school of therapy, which he called Analytical Psychology. The aim of Analytical Psychology was not to make conscious that which was unconscious, but to bring about "individuation"—that is, helping individuals integrate all aspects of their selves. Most people, Jung felt, went about life playing a rigid role—they presented a "persona" to the world which represented only a small part of who they were. In order to become completely integrated they had to get in touch with their "shadows" (that part of themselves that they disowned), and, if they were female with their animus (male side), or if they were male with their anima (female side). Jung also stressed the importance of complexes but saw them differently than did Freud. They were not necessarily of sexual etiology, but were like mine fields, which the conscious mind had constantly to look out for, and which drained energy. Finally, and perhaps most importantly, Jung spoke of both the "personal unconscious," which was roughly equivalent to Freud's unconscious, and the "collective unconscious," an underlying structure that he thought was common to all people, comprised of "archetypes" such as God, the Wise Old Man, and the Hero. Such archetypes and the myths attached to them were, Jung felt, embedded in each individual's psyche, and had to be dealt with in therapy.

His analysis of the patient he called the Philosophy Student (Jung 1928) demonstrates his method of treatment and his use of these concepts, particularly the uncovering and interpretation of archetypal themes in a patient's dreams. Jung also uses the case of the Philosophy Student, who came to him in about 1910, to illustrate such concepts as the persona, the authentic self, and the personal and collective unconscious. At the time he wrote about her, some years after the case, he said he had a "particularly vivid memory" of her, probably because of her superior intellectual qualities. She suffered from "a mild hysterical neurosis," the principle cause of which he diagnosed as a "father-complex," by which he meant that her relationship to her father "stood in her way."

In those days Jung, following Freud's example, had his patients lie on the couch. (Later he saw them face-to-face.) Lying in Jung's office which, like Freud's, was replete with antiquities, the Philosophy Student spoke mainly about her problems with her current boyfriend. At the beginning of her treatment she was unaware of the fact that she was fixated to her relationship with her father, and that she was seeking a man like her father, "whom she could then meet with her intellect" (p. 107). With her father, Jung says, she had a "feeling" relationship, not an intellectual one—the implication being that her father was not on her intellectual level. She was searching for a father-figure who could be her intellectual equal, but unfortunately her intellect had "that peculiarly protesting character" that is often encountered in intellectual women. "Such an intellect," Jung explains, "is always trying to point out mistakes in others; it is pre-eminently critical, with a disagreeably personal undertone, yet it always wants to be considered objective" (p. 107). This kind of woman, furthermore, invariably criticizes a man's weak spots, and keeps at it until she exasperates him, with the unconscious aim of forcing the man into a superior position and thus making him an object of admiration. "The man does not as a rule notice that he is having the role of the hero thrust upon him," Jung wryly observes; "he merely finds her taunts so odious that in future he will go a long way to avoid meeting the lady" (p. 107). The only man who can stand such a woman, he observes, is the one who gives in to her from the beginning, and thereby becomes devalued by her.

The Philosophy Student had met such a man, and was involved in a relationship that was ungratifying to her. Despite her
unhappiness, she could not break away from him. It was a comfortable relationship in some respects since she had, from the
outset, brought him to submission. Yet the relationship ran contrary to her unconscious aim of finding a man on her intellectual
level, and she needed Jung to help her end it.

Gradually Jung pointed out to her "the game she was playing," and the "regular romance" that had been going on between
her and her father since childhood. From her earliest years, with
unconscious sympathy, she had played up to "the shadow-side" of
her father—that is, fulfilled his unconscious wishes in a way that
her mother could or would not—and thus became her mother's
rival. All of this came to light during the initial analysis of her
personal unconscious.

During this initial phase of treatment, she began to find
Jung's weak spots, and she heaped criticism upon him just as she
had upon her boyfriend, and upon all men. Since "for professional
reasons" he could not allow himself to become irritated by the
patient's criticism of him, Jung inevitably was cast into the role of
the hero she sought, and the "father-lover":

> My role as a hero was just a sham, and so, as it turned me into the
> merest phantom, she was able to play her traditional role of the
> supremely wise, very grown-up, all-understanding mother-daugh-
> ter-beloved—an empty role, a persona behind which her real and
> authentic being, her individual self, lay hidden. Indeed, to the
> extent that she at first completely identified herself with her role,
> she was altogether unconscious of her real self. She was still in her
> nebulous infantile world and had not yet discovered the real world
> at all. [p. 108]

In the course of the treatment, Jung explains, the patient
transferred her "father-imago" onto him, making him both a
father and a substitute for the man she could not reach—a kind of
lover. Hence he became an object of conflict. In him the opposites

were united, and for this reason he stood for a quasi-ideal solution of the conflict. The patient began to view him as a "savior or a god," and at first this state of transference seemed ideal to the patient. Then, after a time, things came to a standstill. "For although it [the transference] holds out the possibility of a cure, it is far from being the cure itself" (p. 74).

Jung attempted to analyze the transference, explaining to her that she had a father complex and that she was transferring her father onto him. He told her that she had made him into the father–lover, and that he represented an ideal solution of her inner conflict between the part of her that wanted a father, and the part of her that wanted a lover, as well as the conflict between her persona and her real self. She seemed to accept this interpretation.

After a time the patient had "reached the upper limit" and was stuck in the positive transference; the standstill had become disagreeable. "What next?" Jung asked himself. Since interpretations seemed to have had no effect on the transference, and since she seemed in relatively good spirits, he discussed with her the possibility of termination, but as he had become her complete savior, she let him know that it would not only be distasteful but positively terrifying to leave therapy at that point.

"But you simply must," he insisted in so many words. "You really ought to let go of me. You just cannot remain dependent on me forever" (p. 74).

In some cases, Jung claims, such a commonsensical approach works. The patient will be able to make the sacrifice leaving therapy entails because of the "exuberant feeling of buoyancy" she gets from the transference. "If successful—and these things sometimes are—the sacrifice bears blessed fruit, and the erstwhile patient leaps at one bound into the state of being practically cured" (p. 74).

However, this leap did not happen with the Philosophy Student, and Jung was then faced with the problem of resolving the transference. "Here," Jung notes, "psychoanalytic theory shrouds itself in darkness. Apparently we are to fall back on some nebulous trust in fate: Somehow or the other the matter will settle itself" (p. 75). Jung protests that one may look in vain for guidance on resolving the transference in books that "sing the praises" of psychoanalysis.

He told himself that there must be a clear and respectable way out of the impasse. So, even though his patient had long before run out of money—"if indeed she ever possessed any"—he continued to treat her, curious to know by what means nature would find a way out of the transference deadlock. Unable to think of anything commonsensical to say, he suggested to her that they should keep an eye open for signs from that part of the psyche "uncontaminated by our superior wisdom"—that is, from her dreams.

She soon gushed forth a stream of dreams, bringing them like golden gifts to her revered savior. Together they carefully examined them—the daughter wise and wonderful beyond her years and the father-lover for whom she had searched all her life—probing the depths of her psyche for new clues. The majority of the dreams referred to the therapist. However, he seldom appeared in his natural shape, but was generally distorted in some way; at times he was of supernatural size, at other times he was extremely aged, and at still other times he resembled her father while being at the same time "curiously woven into nature." One day the Philosophy Student told him a dream which typified and crystallized the themes that ran through all the dreams:

> Her father (who in reality was of small stature) was standing with her on a hill that was covered with wheat-fields. She was quite tiny beside him, and he seemed to her like a giant. He lifted her up from the ground and held her in his arms like a little child. The wind swept over the wheat-fields, and as the wheat swayed in the wind, he rocked her in his arms. [p. 76]

From this and the other dreams Jung concluded that the patient was holding "unshakably" to the idea of his being the father-lover, so that the "fatal tie" they were trying to break appeared to be doubly strengthened. At the same time, he could not help but notice that her unconscious placed a special emphasis on "the supernatural, almost 'divine'" nature of the father–lover, thus further strengthening the overvaluation caused by the transference. And although the patient was able to distinguish intellectually between the "semi-divine father–lover" and Jung's factual reality, she could not understand it in a deeper way, no matter how Jung tried to explain it. The impasse remained.

He asked himself what the source and the purpose of this "obstinacy" could be. What was the real meaning of her need to endow him with superhuman attributes? If he had to be "gigantic, primordial, huger than the father, like the wind that sweeps over the earth" (p. 77), was he then to be made into a god? Was the patient's unconscious trying to create a god out of the doctor in order to "free a vision of God from the veils of the personal," so that the transference to the doctor might be no more than a misunderstanding by the conscious mind? Did the unconscious longing for a god represent a "passion welling up from our darkest, instinctual nature"—one unswayed by outside influences, stronger than the love for a human being? Was it, in fact, the highest and truest representation of transference love—"a little bit of real *Gottesminne*, that has been lost to consciousness ever since the fifteenth century?" (p. 78).

Jung wondered whether the notion that a fragment of religious psychology should emerge as an "immediate living reality" in the middle of the consulting-room, and be expressed in the "prosaic figure" of the doctor, seemed almost too fantastic to be taken seriously. Yet, he asserts, a genuinely scientific attitude must be unprejudiced. Quoting Freud as having stated that the unconscious can "do nothing but wish," he presents this as an example of a prejudiced and unscientific attitude. "There is no a priori reason why it should not be just as possible that the unconscious tendencies have a goal beyond the human person, as that the unconscious can 'do nothing but wish'" (p. 78).

Somewhat excited by his discovery, Jung presented the Philosophy Student with his new interpretation of the transference and of her dreams. "You see, your dreams are giving us a message from your collective unconscious," he told her. "Your dreams are making me into a doctor of superhuman proportions, a gigantic primordial father, a god who is at the same time the wind, and in whose protecting arms you are resting like an infant" (p. 79). Jung reminded her that she had a critical, agnostic attitude toward religion, and that her conscious conception of God was abstract. In contrast, her dreams described an archetypal god, a nature-demon such as Wotan. In mythology, he explained, God was represented as wind, stronger than any man, an invisible breath-spirit. In her dream she had developed a god-image that was "infinitely far" from her conscious idea of God. It could only have come from a collective unconscious. It was her way of resolving something from her past, so that she could love an ordinary man.

The patient was skeptical of this new interpretation. "I find the earlier view—that you represent my father–lover and as such present an ideal solution to my conflicts—more appealing," she let him know (p. 79). Nevertheless, her intellect "was sufficiently keen" to appreciate his interpretation in theory, and a gradual change began to take place. Now, as if in opposition to his inter-pretations, she started bringing in dreams in which she swelled him "to ever vaster proportions," while at the same time—as Jung perceived with astonishment—there was a kind of "subterranean undermining" of the transference. She had started a new relation-ship with a man, and that relationship began to deepen. Slowly, imperceptibly, she began to pull away from Jung.

Jung observed how, during the termination phase of therapy, the patient's "transpersonal control-point" developed—a guiding function that now invested in her self all the overvaluations that had been aimed at Jung. Gradually it gained influence over the resisting part of the unconscious. The dream, as a self-representa-tion of unconscious developments, allowed the psyche of the pa-tient to grow out of her "pointless" personal tie.

Jung maintains that the patient had seen a vision of God in her dreams, and this vision had, in a sense, told her what to do. Hence, she was cured by the emergence of her collective uncon-scious. He does not provide information as to how long this analysis lasted or how frequently he saw the patient. However, since this was in 1910, it might be safely assumed that he saw her for less than one year, as was the custom then. By the time the termination day arrived, he writes, "It was no catastrophe, but a perfectly reasonable parting" (p. 79).

Reviewing the case, Jung argues that the unconscious contains "other things besides personal acquisitions and belongings." The Philosophy Student, he asserts, had been quite unconscious of the derivation of "god" from "wind" or of the parallelism between the two. This content did not come from her thinking, he reasons, nor had she ever been taught it. The critical passage in the New Testament from which it came was inaccessible to her, written in Greek, which she could not read. Some might contend that this was a case of cryptomnesia (the unconscious recollection of a thought the dreamer had once read). Jung counters that he has seen a "sufficient number" of other cases from which cryptomnesia can be "excluded with certainty." In any case, he asserts that in this case he was dealing with a genuinely and thoroughly primitive god-image that arose in a civilized person's unconscious and produced an effect that might give the psychologist of religion food for reflection. There was nothing about the dreamer's image of god that could be called personal, Jung explains; rather, it was a collective image, the ethnic origin of which is well known, that came into existence again through a natural psychic function—a dream. "We are dealing with a reactivated *archetype*, as I have elsewhere called these primordial images" (p. 79). These ancient images are reanimated by the "primitive, analogical mode" of thinking found in dreams. He is referring not to inherited ideas, but to inherited thought-patterns.

Jung further explains that an "infallible sign" of collective images in dreams is that of the "cosmic element"—such as when dreams or fantasies are connected with temporal and spatial infinity; enormous speed and extension of movement; astrological associations; telluric, lunar, or solar analogies; and changes in the proportions of the body. The collective element is also evidenced by certain images in dreams in which the dreamer is flying through space like a comet; feels he is the earth, the sun, or a star;

feels he is immensely large or dwarfishly small; feels he is dead; is in a strange place; is a stranger to himself; is confused, mad, disoriented, dizzy, and the like.

The forces spring from the collective psyche, Jung adds, have a confusing and blinding effect, dissolving the persona while at the same time releasing involuntary fantasies. As the influence of the collective unconscious increases, the conscious mind loses its power of leadership. "Thus, without noticing it, the conscious personality is pushed about like a figure on a chessboard by an invisible player" (p. 109). This, he notes, is how the resolution of the transference was brought about in his analysis of the Philosophy Student.

His goal, in working with this patient and others, was to help them to achieve individuation. Individuation meant becoming an "in-dividual" and, insofar as individuality embraces our innermost, last, and incomparable uniqueness "we could therefore translate individuation as . . . 'self-realization'" (pp. 121–122). He speaks of the "alienation of the self" that afflicts most neurotics, resulting from the false role they must play in society (their persona), and from the power of the primordial archetypes from the collective unconscious. "The aim of individuation is nothing less than to divest the self of the false wrappings of the persona on the one hand, and of the suggestive power of primordial images on the other" (p. 123).

Toward the end of his life, Jung withdrew more and more from professional life. In 1922 he began building what was known as The Tower, a castle-like structure on Lake Zurich. He worked on this castle for the rest of his life, and in 1946, when he resigned from his last teaching post, he went to live there. His wife's death "smote him hard" (Campbell 1971, p. xxxii), and he responded by commissioning more work on The Tower. In the same year as his wife's death, he wrote a long work about alchemy. In his declining years he also wrote about flying saucers as a modern myth, on the biblical book of Job, and on good and evil in analytical psychology. He died after a brief illness in Zurich in 1961. He was 86 years old.

Interpretation

As is apparent throughout this case, Jung was quite critical of Freud. He cast aspersions on Freud's limited understanding of the unconscious—specifically on his contention that the unconscious can "do nothing but wish,"—on the sexual etiology of neurosis, and on the inability of psychoanalysis to resolve the transference. After their break, Freud also became increasingly critical of Jung.

In *A History of the Psychoanalytic Movement* (1914b), Freud argues that all the revisions Jung made to psychoanalytic theory flowed from his ambition to "eliminate all that is disagreeable in the family complexes" so that it can then likewise be eliminated from ethics and religion. By "all that is disagreeable," Freud meant the libido theory. Freud maintains that for this theory Jung substituted an abstract term which was incomprehensible "to fools and wise alike." According to Freud, Jung makes the Oedipus complex into something symbolic; the mother in the Oedipus complex means "the unattainable" and stands for something that must be renounced in the interests of civilization; and the father is "the inner father," from whom one must become free in order to be independent. Freud also criticizes Jung for replacing the conflict between the id and the ego with a conflict between "psychic inertia" and the "life-task" and for attributing the neurotic's sense of guilt to his not properly fulfilling the life-task. "Thus a new religious–ethical system was created, which . . . must necessarily lead to new interpretations of the actual results of analysis, or else distort or ignore them" (p. 63). In order to preserve this system, Freud claims, Jung had to turn entirely away from empirical observation, and therefore had to avoid confronting the patient's repression. He scoffs at Jung's "disregard for scientific logic," charging that while Jung finds the Oedipus complex not specific enough for the causation of neurosis, he at the same time attributes a specific causal quality to "inertia"—the most nonspecific characteristic of all matter, animate or inanimate!

With regard to Jung's method of interpreting dreams, Freud again takes Jung to task, accusing Jung of focusing his interpretation solely on the latent dream-thoughts. "When one remembers that the dream itself is something different from the latent dream-thoughts which it elaborates, something more, there is nothing surprising in patients dreaming of things with which their minds have been filled during the treatment, whether it be the 'life-task,' or 'being above or below'" (p. 98). He says that Jung turns his back on the sexual symbolism of dreams, preferring to give such symbols a religious or philosophical meaning, urging his patients to detach themselves from the complexes that stem from their libido-cathexis. "This can never be achieved, however," Freud notes, "by turning one's back upon them and urging the patient to sublimate, but only by exhaustive examination of them, so that they may be made fully and completely conscious" (p. 66).

Many have echoed Freud's criticism of Jung. Typical of such views was the study by Stern (1976), which called Jung a "haunted prophet," whose psychotic episodes during his youth led to his later formulating theoretical ideas that were grounded in the mysticism of magical thinking. Stern notes that during his youth, Jung became convinced he was two people—the lonely, only child who was tyrannized by his mother and unsure of himself, and a powerful and wise old man who lived in the previous century, wore buckled shoes and a white wig, and knew things others did not know. According to Stern, Jung was haunted by oedipal anger and guilt toward his father, which got transferred onto Freud and influenced his rebellious attitude toward men. His dismissal of the Oedipus complex was an avoidance of oedipal feelings, and his obsession with religion and philosophy was a way of clinging to his mother, who had encouraged his interest in them.

Blum (1953) points out that Jung did not in fact invent the concept of the collective unconscious, but only the term. Nor was he the first to notice archetypes. In fact, Blum says, Freud spoke of "primal fantasies" that were found so frequently during analysis that they assumed a typical form. At first he felt they could be traced back to real experiences, but later he switched to a phylogenetic view, maintaining that such fantasies might be related to the primeval existence of mankind. Blum adds that "The transmission of 'primal fantasies' via racial inheritance can only be considered of historical interest, in terms of our present-day thinking. Explanations of this kind are sufficiently implausible and untestable to warrant their deletion" (pp. 31–32).

Thompson (1950) cautions that Jung's method takes the patient away from reality toward a mystical, semi-religious fantasy life that can be especially dangerous to psychotics, as it encourages and strengthens their tendency to confuse reality with "autistic thinking." As for his method of dream analysis—in which, through a contemplation of the race, patients find solutions to their present difficulties—Thompson is equally skeptical. "One cannot help thinking that in spite of the interpretations the patient's problem still remains but thinking about something else has been substituted for it. This is the classical mechanism of the obsessional neurosis" (p. 169).

Jung's analysis of the Philosophy Student would be considered naive today, even by most Jungians. When he alludes to the books on psychoanalysis which praise the method without offering concrete techniques for dealing with transference, he shows an ignorance of the growing number of papers that had already been written by 1928, when his *Two Essays on Analytical Psychology* was published. Although he understood that the patient had cast him in the role of father-lover, he apparently did not attempt to interpret this to her, ignoring the erotic transference in favor of the narcissistic—her overvaluation of him. Nor did he properly understand the narcissistic transference. While he eventually linked her overvaluation of him to a search by her collective unconscious for a god-figure, today's therapist, aware of the enormous amount of research on narcissism, would more likely look at her need to devalue or overvalue her therapist in terms of inadequate mirroring in her early childhood. Kohut (1971), in particular, has shed light on this phenomenon.

Moreover, Jung's initial attempt to terminate the patient when she was locked in an erotic–narcissistic transference was ill-advised and may well have been due to countertransference. During the initial phase of treatment he noted that he did not allow her criticism to irritate him "due to professional considerations." The implication here is that she actually *was* irritating him but, due to professional considerations, he could not allow himself to show that he was irritated. If this was so, then perhaps these feelings became acted out through an attempt to get rid of her prematurely. He first tried to convince her to leave him, while she was locked into the erotic–narcissistic transference, suggesting that because she was feeling good she was more or less cured and could do without him. This did not work. Then he tried to get rid of her by interpreting her dreams as attempts to make him into a god. When she began undermining the transference and getting involved with a boyfriend, Jung saw this as the work of the collective unconscious and as some kind of divine intervention. More likely the patient felt rejected by Jung's unwillingness to deal with her on a personal level. He noted that she favored his analytical interpretation about her father-complex over his later interpretation about archetypes and wind and god, yet he did not properly understand this fact. Today's analyst would have analyzed her erotic transference while allowing her to idealize him, without interpreting her need to idealize him until she was ready to hear it. It may well be that Jung also in some way discouraged the patient's expression of aggression, which might have also been a factor in her impasse. Had he encouraged the negative transference, her rage might have come to the surface and offered itself to analysis and interpretation. Because of his countertransference, Jung could not tolerate her idealization of him and was probably afraid of the rage against which this idealization was defending.

Jung's interpretation of the Philosophy Student's dream in terms of the wind-god archetype must also be questioned not only because the patient did not accept this interpretation, but because wind might also be interpreted in many other ways. The correct way to interpret such a symbol is to ask the patient for associations to wind and to then link the interpretation to her associations. For example, she might have associated wind with her mother's "big mouth," in which case the dream could have been interpreted as her wish for a father who could rescue her from her mother's domineering influence, a father who would hold her like an infant while protecting her from her mother's ravages. Similarly, Jung's lists of dream and fantasy symbols that might suggest a "cosmic element" could just as easily suggest other things. For example, if one dreams he is immensely large or dwarfishly small, these could be signs of depersonalization or narcissistic tendencies; if one feels he is dead or in a strange place, or is a stranger to himself, these could be signs of emotional detachment, dissociation, or depression. If one feels confused, mad, or disoriented, these might be evidences of hysteria or psychosis.

To his credit, however, Jung *did* understand that this patient's tendency always to point out mistakes in others, always to go for a man's weak spots, was an attempt to force a man into a superior position. Unconsciously she wanted to find a man who would not put up with her "nonsense" (as her father had), but would stand up to her; she wanted a man on whom she could lean (as she could not do with her father, since she had to let him lean on her). In this sense, Jung was able to see things in a positive light, whereas Freud might have seen them more in a negative way. Jung focused on the little girl who needed a hero, rather than on the little girl who was full of rage against her father and envy toward men. It may well be this positive approach, combined with his disavowal of Freud's libido theory and the castration complex, that has endeared Jung to feminists, despite the well-documented fact that in his professional life Jung tended to sexually exploit his female patients whereas Freud did not.

Indeed, Jung's approach has been quite influential. He was one of the first analysts to use the term "self," and to write about the "false self," the "real self," and "self-realization"—terms that were later developed by Winnicott (1953), Fairbairn (1954), Kohut (1971), Jacobson (1971), Mahler and colleagues (1975), and others, and that eventually became part of the vocabulary of popular culture. Jung's emphasis on the integration of the personality and his use of concepts from Eastern philosophy also had a great influence on a wide range of modern schools of psychotherapy, from existential analysis to psychosynthesis to the "human potential movement" of the 1960s and 1970s.

Campbell (1971), in his Introduction to *The Portable Jung*, labels Jung's work a "treasury of learning" and calls Jung "not only a medical man but a scholar in the grand style, whose researches, particularly of comparative mythology, alchemy, and the psychology of religion, have inspired and augmented the findings of an astonishing number of the leading creative scholars of our time" (p. vii). Jung's writings, according to Campbell, enable readers to gain a new realization of the relevance of the mythic lore of all people to their own "psychological *opus magnum* of individuation."

Despite Jung's flaws as a clinician and as a human being, he managed a prolific output of writing (second in size only to Freud's among psychoanalysts), and his theory of personality, as applied to a wide range of human phenomena, stands as a remarkable achievement. "Everyone makes for himself his own segment of the world," Jung once said, "and constructs his own private system, often with air-tight compartments, so that after a time it seems to him that he has grasped the meaning and structure of the whole. But the finite will never be able to grasp the infinite" (Jung 1927, pp. 23–24). To grasp the infinite—that seemed to be Jung's ultimate goal.

7

THE INFERIORITY COMPLEX

Alfred Adler and the Dominating Woman, the Suicidal Medical Student, and the Pampered Physician (1929)

Alfred Adler's many contributions to psychoanalytic theory are well known. It was Adler who first conceptualized the notion of an aggressive drive in man (1908), and it was he who first spoke of the modification of aggression in the service of social interests—a concept which Hartmann (1958) later called "neutralization of aggression." He was one of the first to look at behavior from an object relations standpoint (although he did not call it that) and to understand the importance of the inferiority complex (which analysts today recognize as being a central element of narcissism). He also was one of the first to delineate the importance of birth order and its relation to character formation, to lay stress on the ego and its defensive functions, and to take a holistic view of the human personality (1931).

Adler's therapeutic technique is less well known. Fortunately, he left behind a book of short case histories, which has become a classic among Adlerians. In this work he demonstrates his radical departure from the standard technique that had been developed by Freud. In contradistinction to Freud's method, Adler's technique emphasized a short-term approach and featured what today would be called behavioral, supportive, and paradoxical interventions.

Adler was born on February 7, 1870, in Vienna, the second of six children. His father was a successful merchant. Adler was a small and delicate child who suffered from rickets, which made him clumsier than other children, and his childhood was beset by death and illness. When he was 3, his younger brother died in the crib next to his. He was twice run over by carriages in the streets, and he almost died of pneumonia at the age of 4—an event that caused him to later think "If this question of life is so doubtful, then I should like to become a doctor myself and see what it is all about" (Orgler, 1963). Because of his fragile condition, he was pampered by his parents, and it was difficult for him to adjust to school.

He passed his medical examination in 1895 and became an eye specialist. His first written work was about organ inferiority—the theory that the body's weakest organs tend to break down first, since those organs are the most susceptible to stress. Later he would develop a psychological theory of organ inferiority: an individual develops inferiority feelings with respect to his physiological deficiencies and compensates by striving for superiority in another area, as when a man with paralyzed legs builds up the muscles in his arms.

Adler was an original member of Freud's Vienna circle. When he first read *The Interpretation of Dreams*, he defended it in a local newspaper, and Freud mistakenly thought they were in agreement. However, from the beginning Adler stood apart from the rest of Freud's followers. Jones writes, "My first impression of Adler was that of a morose and cantankerous person, whose behavior oscillated between contentiousness and sulkiness" (1957, p. 305). By 1911, the differences between Adler's and Freud's views had become apparent, and Adler resigned from the Vienna

Psychoanalytic Society, along with eleven other members. The main source of contention, according to Adler, was Freud's demand that all members of the society accept unconditionally his libido theory. This demand supposedly was made after Adler was invited to express his views to the society in four lectures under the title, "Critique of Freud's Sexual Theory of Psychic Life" (Orgler 1963). These lectures were later incorporated into the seminal paper, "The Differences Between Individual Psychology and Psychoanalysis" (1931).

Adler's main contribution to therapeutic technique was to perfect a pragmatic, short-term approach that laid stress on the uniqueness of each human being's problems and solutions. He saw patients face-to-face, and only once or twice a week. He viewed every person as a participant in an individual drama, striving to develop a successful strategy of interaction with his environment in order to realize his own special goals. In his book of short case histories, *Problems of Neurosis* (1929) he compares the therapist's technique with that of a mother. He instructs therapists to appeal to their patients in a friendly way, coaxing them into a receptive frame of mind. The therapist's task is to give patients the experience of contact with "a fellow-man," and then to help them transfer this awakened social feeling to others. He saw this process as analogous to the maternal function.

Adler does not believe in transference or resistance. "What the Freudians call transference . . . is merely social feeling. The patient's social feeling, which is always present in some degree, finds its best possible expression in the relation with the psychologist" (p. 73). As regards resistance, it is "only lack of courage to return to the useful side of life" (p. 73). Adler asserts that neurosis is caused in one of three ways—through organ inferiority, pampering, or neglect. All three bring about feelings of inferiority, weaken the "social contact," and tend to isolate individuals from other people and interests.

The case of the Dominating Woman demonstrates Adler's analysis and treatment of a 46-year-old depressed patient. He describes her as a "very intelligent woman" who, when she came to him, had suffered from melancholia for three years. She told him that she had been married at the age of 16, tried for ten years to have a child, then adopted one before giving birth to two daughters. She had worked in her husband's office for many years, but after her husband had taken a partner she felt herself to be of "diminished importance," and quarrelled continually with the partner. Then her father fell ill and she withdrew from the business to nurse him. It was when her father's health improved that she developed melancholia.

She became suspicious about her husband's business dealings, and demanded that he tell her everything. Every night she went through the same ritual, demanding that he tell her what was going on, accusing him of keeping things from her, assailing him with crying fits. "She wanted to dominate her husband, and crying was a means by which she sought to subdue him. Crying is usually an accusation against another person" (p. 23). The woman felt excluded and inferior if she did not know all about her husband's business. She was a strong woman, Adler contends, who had married a weak man ostensibly in order to save him but, in reality, to rule him. Instead he had gotten stronger and she could no longer rule him. "The choice of an equal mate generally indicates a higher degree of courage," Adler observes (p. 23). The neurotic, however, chooses either to dominate or be dominated by a mate.

The Dominating Woman showed the "principal signs of a true melancholia": her weight steadily decreased, she could not sleep, and she was always depressed in the morning. She feared that the whole family would someday become impoverished. She constantly obsessed about the possibility that they might all starve.

Adler's first objective in treating her was to try to reconcile her with her husband. He told her that her husband was getting older, and he attempted to persuade her not to be so angry at him. He suggested that she be more diplomatic, explaining that there were better methods than crying to get what she wanted from him. The weaker always puts up some kind of resistance, he told her, as no one can endure constant domination. She was just causing her husband to resist more adamantly. "People must treat each other as equals if they are to live harmoniously together" (p. 23).

Adler notes that he always uses the "simplest and most direct" method possible, but acknowledges that the most direct approach with this woman—that of telling her, "You are a dominating woman, and you are now trying to rule by means of illness"—would offend her. First he had to take her side as much as possible, win her over, and then gradually bring her to face the truth.

During the course of the treatment the Dominating Woman developed a guilt complex. She remembered deceiving her husband with another man twenty-five years earlier, and suddenly felt bad about it. She immediately confessed it to her husband and rebuked herself for it. "This so-called guilt-complex," Adler writes, "which we should wholly misunderstand by the Freudian interpretation, was quite clearly an attack upon the husband who was no longer obedient. She could hurt him by confession and self-accusation" (p. 24). The truth, Adler adds, is often "a terrible weapon" of hostility.

Adler used the same indirect method with this woman as he used with most melancholics. After establishing a "sympathetic relation" he began trying to change her behavior.

"Only do what is agreeable to you," he suggested.

"Nothing is agreeable."

"Then at least do not exert yourself to do what is disagreeable" (p. 25).

Such patients, Adler claims, have usually been told to do various uncongenial things to remedy their condition; surprised and flattered to be asked to do something "agreeable," they sometimes immediately begin to improve. Later, he offered the Dominating Woman a second suggestion, but prefaced it with his standard warning that "it is much more difficult, and I don't know if you can follow it" (p. 25). Whenever he used this intervention he was silent for a moment, and looked at his patient "doubtfully," in order to excite curiosity and get attention. He would then say, "If you could follow this second rule you would be cured in fourteen days. It is—to consider from time to time how you can give [your husband] pleasure" (p. 25). He explained to the Dominating Woman that by doing this she would soon be able to sleep and would have no further sad thoughts. He also assured her that she would begin to feel more useful and worthwhile.

The patient said that it was too difficult a rule to follow, and asked how she could give pleasure to another person when she felt none herself? Adler replied that in that case, she would need "four weeks." The patient complained that nobody was giving her pleasure. Adler then made "the strongest move in the game," telling her, "Perhaps you had better train yourself a little thus: do not actually *do* anything to please anyone else, but just think out how you *could* do it" (p. 26).

Adler notes that often when he suggests to melancholics that they consider how they can give another person pleasure, they inform him that they have been doing that all along. These individuals, he says, are to be suspected of "dispensing favors in order to get the upper hand," and with such people he invariably asks whether they think the people they are favoring are really pleased by it.

Sometimes, if the patient cannot follow these suggestions at all, Adler gives in and offers an easier suggestion, asking her to remember all the ideas she has in the night, and give *him* pleasure by telling them to him the next day. The next day the patient will usually report sleeping soundly and remember nothing, even though she has not previously slept for many nights. He concludes that "Melancholia is an illness in which the people in the environment suffer more than the patient" (p. 26). However, he tries to make the patient's family and friends understand that they cannot scold, force, or criticize, but must assist the patient into a better mood.

Adler does not say what happened to the Dominating Woman, but implies that she overcame her depression and learned to deal with her husband in a more effective way.

In the case of the Suicidal Medical Student, Adler was much more direct, setting out to immediately head off his suicidal impulses. The Suicidal Medical Student was a short young man with an inferiority complex about his height, whose mother had pampered him and thus nurtured his complex. Her marriage to a tyrannical physician had been an unhappy one, and she had turned to her son for comfort. For most of his life, mother, son, and father existed in this "miserable fashion."

One day the cook ran into the living room screaming and crying that the father had made a sexual advance. The mother was shocked. She went into a depression and cried constantly about her sad plight.

The Medical Student came to Adler wanting an explanation. He had become distracted from his medical studies and, in despair, had threatened suicide. He said he had asked his mother, again and again, how she could be so depressed by his father's unfaithfulness when for years she had claimed not to have any affection for him. But each time he had asked her such a question, she interrupted him, screaming, "You cannot possibly understand this" (p. 81).

Adler asked the young man if the father's behavior was still as tyrannical as it had been. The young man, casting a surprised glance at Adler, said that actually his father had become calmer. Adler then asked him if he thought his mother would give up her only means of taming this tyrant, calling his attention to the fact that although she "paid the price" with her depression, she nevertheless felt that she was the conquerer. Then he gave the young man an interpretation:

"You are doing something very similar. . . . You are failing in your work at the university, and are not prepared to be independent, so you wish to impress your mother with your suicidal impulses just

as your mother impresses your father with her depression. You
have been trained, as pampered children often are, to succeed by a
display of weakness." [p. 81]

By confronting him with such interpretations, Adler helped
the student understand and adapt to the situation.

The student's inferiority complex and his need to see himself
as superior in his mother's eyes was central to his problem. "It is,
or used to be, the almost invariable conclusion of Freudian psychologists, that the person who excludes love is repressing his
libido," Adler observes, "but it is a vast improvement both in
diagnosis and treatment when we relate this exclusion to the
individual's goal of superiority" (p. 61). The goal of superiority,
he contends, is the determining factor in every neurosis, and is
itself conditioned by experiences of inferiority. The therapist's
first task is therefore to determine the real causes of the feelings of
inferiority. However, this is not always so easy to do, since inferiority is regarded as a weakness and there is a strong tendency to
conceal it. "Indeed, the effort of concealment may be so great that
the person himself ceases to be aware of his inferiority as such,
being wholly preoccupied with the consequences of the feeling
and with all the objective details that subserve its concealment"
(p. 2). Generally the individual hides feelings of inferiority behind
feelings of superiority.

Often, the most immediate need in the treatment of a neurotic, Adler suggests, is to find out if he is confronted with a
problem that cannot be solved. Invariably, such a patient's struggle
for superiority is blocked in some way, for he has been side-
tracked at some point in his past, usually in early childhood. To
get at his insolvable problem, Adler usually begins by discussing
the course of the patient's life from earliest childhood, "noting
especially the incidents or phases which reveal or conceal the most
painful sense of weakness and impotence: and at the same time I
keep myself alert to signs of organic inferiority" (p. 71). Next he
tries to understand the problem by noticing what activities "of a
kind normally to be expected" are left out of the patient's life.

Once he has grasped the problem, he will often ask the patient, ironically, if all his thoughts, feelings, actions, and characteristics are working toward the exclusion or postponement of the problem. "The accumulated experiences of Individual Psychologists justify us in looking for this unity in the life-plan," Adler says, explaining that a wide knowledge of the literature and working tradition of individual psychology helps to identify typical neurotic factors such as "the lack of social interest, failure in courage and self-confidence, and rejection of common sense" (p. 72). The neurotic tends to blame others in order to maintain his feeling of superiority and "escape from the challenge of life" but does not realize it. The therapist must carefully and sympathetically lead the patient toward meaningful work, a meaningful love relationship, and a broader social interest.

In the case of the Pampered Physician, Adler took note, as he often did, of the patient's birth order. The physician had been the youngest, and, like most youngest children, he had been pampered—in this case by two older sisters. When the physician first came to Adler at the age of 60, he complained that he had not been able to swallow normally for twenty years, and during that time he had been able to eat only liquid food. Recently he had had a dental plate made for him. He constantly pushed the plate up and down with his tongue, a habit that caused chronic soreness. "I'm very much afraid I'm getting cancer," the man told Adler (p. 108).

He had been indulged by his two older sisters from birth, and had never married. He could only eat in the presence of his sisters, and was shy about going out with others. "Every approach to society had been difficult, and he had no friends, only a few associates whom he met weekly in a restaurant" (p. 108). The tension that arose when he was with people other than his sisters, Adler believed, caused him to be unable to swallow food. He lived in a kind of "stage fright," always afraid of making a bad impression.

With regard to the second life-question—establishing a meaningful occupation—his goal was to obtain security. He did

not really like being a physician and sometimes fainted when he
had to take examinations. He had become a physician in order to
obtain a position with a fixed income and a pension. "This attraction to an official position is a sign of insecurity," Adler notes,
"and people with a deep sense of inadequacy commonly aspire to
the 'safe job'" (p. 109).

When he came to Adler, afraid of getting cancer, the patient
spoke often of his now aging sisters. "I don't know what to do
about them," he would say. Adler immediately understood the
problem: "It was clear to me that this man, aging, and spoiled by
two unmarried and much older women, was facing a new situation. He was very much afraid his sisters would die" (p. 109). He
had never been in love, for he could never find a woman who
would spoil him as his sisters had done. His only sex had been
masturbation and a few rare "petting affairs" with girls. However,
recently an older woman had appeared on the scene who wanted
very much to marry him. What should he do? The beginning of a
struggle seemed imminent, but his new dental plate came to the
rescue. And though he himself, as a physician, was very much in
doubt about the cancer, he allowed himself to become preoccupied
with this problem just when the new woman had taken an interest
in him. Adler explains that such preoccupations are carefully
cherished by the neurotic, in order to avoid a direction indicated
by logical necessity. "The logical solution of his problem would
be antagonistic to his style of life, and as the style of life must rule
he has to establish emotions and feelings which will ensure his
escape" (p. 110).

The only logical solution to the patient's problem, of course,
was to find a "trustworthy substitute" for his spoiling sisters
before they passed away. But the patient's "distrustful mind"
could not perceive of this possibility, having spent his whole life
convincing himself that he was not suitable for marriage. The new
dental plate, which should have made his self-esteem rise, had
instead become another impediment to marriage.

Adler tried attacking the physician's belief in the cancer, but
that was useless. So he concentrated his efforts on interpreting his

behavior to him. "You're very afraid your sisters will die and leave you all alone," he told him. "Then what will you do? Who will indulge you like your sisters? Will this new woman indulge you in this way? Deep down you don't feel you really deserve it." Finally the day came when Adler got through to him. The next day the physician rushed in with a dream: "I was sitting in the house of a third sister at a birthday celebration of her 13-year-old son. I was entirely healthy, felt no pain and could swallow anything" (pp. 110–111). Adler interpreted that the man had now understood his predicament, but that the dream was related to an episode in his life that had taken place fifteen years before. Its meaning was, "If only I were fifteen years younger." Thus, the physician was still attempting, despite his new understanding of the situation, to maintain his life-style. It would take a while longer to cure him.

According to Adler, the youngest child, such as the physician, exhibits certain characteristics of style which "we never fail to find." The youngest has always been the baby of the family, and has never "known the tragedy" of being dispossessed by a younger rival. His education is often better, for the family's economic situation often improves in later years. And he is generally the most pampered, for the older children join with the parents in spoiling him. This spoiling may have either of two results: the child may become too indulged or too stimulated. "In the former case (of overindulgence) the child will strive throughout life to be supported by others. In the latter case the child will rather resemble a second child, proceeding competitively, striving to overtake all those who set the pace for him, and in most cases failing to do so" (p. 107). Often the youngest pursues a career that is different from the careers of other members of the family—a sign of "hidden cowardice." If everybody else in the family is in business, the youngest becomes an artist; if they are all scientists, he becomes a salesman. Usually, because of the spoiling, the youngest expects to be taken care of by others, as was the case with the physician.

To the best of my knowledge there were no follow-ups on any of Adler's cases. As for Adler, he went on to have an illustrious career. He married Raissa Epstein soon after he had begun to practice medicine, and they raised four children, three daughters and a son. Soon after his marriage he converted from Judaism to Protestantism, proclaiming that Protestantism was more universal, and his children were raised in the Protestant faith. Like Freud, he was known as a family man.

From the beginning of his life he fought against feelings of inferiority and the prospect of death. As a child he had been afraid to walk near a cemetery because it aroused fears of death, but he forced himself to walk through it ten times to overcome this fear (Orgler 1963). As an adult he compensated for the feelings of inferiority and the fear of death by working from dawn to dusk, writing many books and papers, traveling constantly, and giving lectures all over the world.

Adler remained estranged from Freud for the rest of his life. However, despite being fourteen years older, Freud managed to outlive Adler by two years. During the last month of his life, at the age of 67, Adler gave 56 lectures in four European countries. It may be that due to overcompensation, he drove himself too hard. He collapsed from a heart attack in Aberdeen, Scotland, en route to yet another lecture.

Interpretation

Adler's defection from the psychoanalytic movement, like Jung's, was a bitter blow to Freud. Freud is often blamed for not having been more accommodating toward the disagreements of Adler and Jung, and some have suggested that both may have remained in the movement but for Freud's intellectual tyranny. However, their own personalities may have been such that neither could have tolerated being in anybody's shadow for long. Like Jung, Adler continued to make critical references to Freud for the remainder of his life, and Freud heartily reciprocated.

"Adler's 'Individual Psychology' is now one of the many psychological movements adverse to psychoanalysis," Freud comments in *The History of the Psychoanalytic Movement*, "and its further development is no concern of ours" (1914b, p. 54). He then goes on to present a seven-page attack on Adler's theories. He accuses Adler of formulating a "system," something he had avoided doing, and points out that Adler's system is an example of "secondary elaboration," comparable to the process in which dream-material is censored and transformed by waking thought. Adler looks at behavior exclusively from the standpoint of the ego, Freud contends, but reduces it to terms with which the ego is familiar, then translates, twists, and misunderstands it. "Adlerian theory is characterized less by what it asserts than by what it denies, so that it consists of three elements of quite dissimilar value: the useful contributions to the psychology of the ego, the superfluous but admissible introduction of a new jargon to describe analytical facts, and the distortions and perversions of these facts . . ." (p. 54).

Freud also criticizes Adler's notion that the governing motive of human beings is the "will to power," which he contends Adler has expressed preeminently in the form of a "masculine protest" in character-formation and in neurosis. He is referring to Adler's dictum that both men and women in Western culture view the male role as the superior one, and so both strive to be masculine (superior) as a protest against feelings of inferiority. "This 'masculine protest,' the motive-force at work . . . is however nothing else but repression detached from its psychological mechanism and, moreover, sexualized in addition—which accords very badly with his vaunted ejection of sexuality from its place in mental life" (p. 56). In Adler's system, Freud asserts, the biological, social, and psychological meanings of "masculine" and "feminine" are confused. In Freud's opinion, if the masculine protest does exist, it is traceable to a "disturbance in the primary narcissism" due to threats of castration or early interference with a child's sexual activities. Indeed, Adler carries his theory to such lengths, Freud bitterly adds, that he actually believes that the strongest motive for the sexual act is conquest. "I do not know if he has given vent to these monstrous ideas in his writings" (p. 55). Freud also charges Adler with plagiarism, maintaining that some of Adler's views—

such as the psychological advantages of being ill—were really Freud's earlier insights.

Adler's theory, he concludes, is built exclusively on the aggressive impulse, with no room for love. "It might surprise one that such a cheerless view of life should meet with any attention at all; but we must not forget that, weighed down by the burden of its sexual desires, humanity is ready to accept anything when tempted with 'ascendancy over sexuality' as bait" (p. 57).

More recently Chessick (1989) has expressed similar, though less bitter, sentiments about Adler. He points out that Adler's "will to power" was profoundly influenced by the work of the philosopher Nietzsche, and that Adler's attempt to evaluate psychoanalytic data on the basis of a misunderstanding of Nietzsche's interactive principle resulted in an "intrinsic oversimplification" of all explanations. "I do not employ the concepts of Adler or Sullivan, or of the mystical Jung, in my work, since they represent the direct reading of manifest content, using clinically unverifiable or a priori generalizations" (p. 39).

Thompson (1950) agrees with Freud up to a point. She also feels Adler oversimplified the problem of neurosis, and did not properly consider the latent, or unconscious, aspects of dreams, behavior, or the vicissitudes of childhood. At the same time, she asserts, "Adler's positive contributions to psychoanalysis are significant . . ." (p. 160). She believes he was a "pioneer in applying psychoanalysis to the total personality," and was the first person to describe the role the ego plays in producing neurosis, thus anticipating "ego psychology." He was also the first to understand that a person's goals contribute significantly to his neurotic difficulties, and made important contributions to the understanding of cultural factors and the parent–child relationship. Noting that many analysts no longer use the libido theory, she concludes, "He was the first person to discard the sexual theory of neurosis" (p. 161).

Roazen (1984) points out that "Few within psychoanalysis today would feel entirely comfortable to be identified with Adler's tradition" (p. 21). However, many ego psychologists privately acknowledge their debt to him. His "will to power" has now been accepted, Roazen notes, although it has been converted into a different term—"instinct to master." Roazen credits him with being especially compassionate toward victims of social injustice, asserting that he understood quite well how people with low self-esteem and pent-up aggression can bolster themselves by degrading others. "Adler was ahead of his time in understanding some of the social bases for destructiveness" (p. 21).

Wolman (1960, p. 298) echoes Roazen's praise of Adler's understanding of social problems. "It has to be said that Adler's influence is much greater than is usually admitted. The entire neo-psychoanalytic school, including Horney, Fromm, and Sullivan, is no less neo-Adlerian than it is neo-Freudian. Adler's concepts of sociability, self-assertion, security, self, and creativeness permeated the theories of the neo-analysts."

White (1957) also notes that Adler was a pioneer in the development of ego psychology, and points out that in certain respects, "It is indeed legitimate to say that Freudian psychology is in the process of catching up with Adler."

Reactions to Adler's theories seem to have gone through a cycle over the years, as happens with most controversial writers. At first, spurred by Freud's antagonism toward him, most analysts viewed Adler's work in an extremely negative light. Later there was a reaction of the opposite extreme, in which he was seen as a pioneer. However, the final appraisal of his work will probably land somewhere in the middle. He did take certain steps toward the understanding of ego psychology, aggression, narcissism (the inferiority/superiority complex), and parent–child interactions, but at the same time he also tended to overgeneralize and oversimplify complicated phenomena. For example, to call transference a "social feeling" and resistance "lack of courage to return to the useful side of life" is to ignore the complicated unconscious processes associated with them.

Adler's therapeutic technique, as exemplified by the cases summarized, can be criticized on the same basis as are his theories. In some cases his interventions appear too simple, and do not

recognize the strength of the unconscious. His dismissal of transference and resistance as forces to reckon with, moreover, further
impeded his technique. His approach, similar to today's behavioral
psychologists, is for the most part aimed at alleviating symptoms
rather than affecting characterological changes. In the case of the
Dominating Woman, he utilizes suggestion and paradox in order
to rouse her from her depression. With the Suicidal Student he uses
an interpretative technique that, perhaps anticipating Kernberg
(1989), attacks the patient's ego-syntonic defense, but his goal is
different than Kernberg's. Kernberg's goal in using such techniques with borderline personalities is to establish a therapeutic
alliance so that he can get on with analysis proper. Adler's aim is
to effect an immediate change of view and lifestyle in the patient
through "shocking him to his senses," the underlying notion
being that all individuals have an innate common sense and the
therapist merely needs to give them a shove toward it. The case of
the Pampered Physician is another example of the therapeutic aim
of hammering the patient with a confrontational interpretation and
trying to bring him to his senses.

We have no way of knowing how well Adler's technique
worked, as there were no long-term studies of his patients after
they left him. However, laying that question aside, his approach
brings up certain questions that have been debated by therapists
since Freud: (1) Is it necessary for the patient to have insight into
his problem, and therefore to undergo an in-depth analysis? (2) Is
it necessary to analyze transference and resistance in order to
change an individual's character and bring about permanent cure?
Most psychoanalysts would answer both questions "yes." They
would say that unless the patient has insight and has worked
through his resistance, he has not truly been cured. From this
perspective, Adler's "cures" would be seen as transference cures.
Adler gave his patients some supportive suggestions or a little
psychological "kick in the pants" and sent them on their way;
through the strength of his authority, they became convinced they
could do it. But, once the transference had worn off, would they
develop similar symptoms? However, from Adler's perspective, it

must be noted that he worked with a different kind of patient than most analysts; rather than the rich who frequented Freud's office, his clients tended to be poor working-class men and women. They could not afford long-term therapy, and were of an educational level and social situation that led them to appreciate action rather than words. Also, Adler preferred not to "bury" a patient beneath a lot of psychoanalytic constructions, and thus lose sight of the patient's humanity. He deliberately strived for direct simplicity in interpreting an individual's circumstances—his was a phenomenological, natural-history approach—an approach he felt was most likely to be effective with his type of patient.

The question of which form of therapy is more effective has never been definitively answered. Indeed, Eysenck (1952) conducted a large-scale study of therapeutic outcomes. He included the reports of 24 therapists on more than 8,000 cases, and compared them with the results shown by a control group of housewives untrained in performing psychotherapy. Patient follow-up assessments showed that the housewives' results were as good as those of the therapists, and that in many cases no therapy—"spontaneous remission"—provided even better rates of cure. Of course, studies based on follow-up assessments by patients cannot be taken as ultimate validations, since patient assessments are subjective. The Wolf Man initially believed himself to be cured by Freud, and would undoubtedly have given a glowing assessment of Freud's treatment, until, a few years later, he had his famous breakdown and was referred to Brunswick.

The debate about Adler's contributions to analytic therapy will no doubt continue as long as there is a debate about the effectiveness of various modes of therapy. However, there is no denying Adler's influence on theory and therapy, or that he, along with Freud and Jung, was one of the three founders of analytic therapy. He has had an impact not only on various schools of analytic therapy, but also on the so-called third force in psychotherapy—including such schools as transactional analysis, the person-centered approach, reality therapy, existential therapy, and cognitive therapy.

8

ACTIVE THERAPY

Sandor Ferenczi and the Hysteric (1919),
the Music Student (1920), the Fantasizer
(1924), and the Regressed Patient (1931)

Although Sandor Ferenczi did not write a detailed case history, his papers on "active therapy," which span the period from 1919 until his death in 1933, have become classics. Written in a clear, straightforward, and often entertaining style (as opposed to Freud's somewhat circumlocutory Victorian mode), these papers demonstrate his deviations from standard psychoanalytic technique through a series of brief but illuminating vignettes. He worked with the more severe cases of hysteria and obsessional neurosis as well as with borderline personalities, including split and multiple personalities, in contrast to most other analysts of that era. He felt that standard psychoanalytic technique had become too intellectual and rigid, and eventually came to question Freud's abandonment of active interventions, catharsis, and the seduction theory. His experiments were the forerunners of the vast range of active therapy techniques that exist today, but they did not please Freud and the psychoanalytic establishment.

Ferenczi had originally been a general practitioner of medicine in Budapest, Hungary, where he had experimented with hypnotism. When he read Freud's *The Interpretation of Dreams*, he was immediately seized with the desire to meet its author. According to Jones (1957), Ferenczi wrote to Freud, and was invited to meet him in February 1908. He made such a good impression that he was invited to join Freud and his family during their August vacation in Berchtesgaden. From that time on he became Freud's closest associate, the two exchanging more than a thousand letters from 1908 to 1933.

During his analysis with Freud, Ferenczi complained of having been a middle child, lost among about a dozen brothers and sisters, whose mother had rarely expressed any affection for him and had been severe in her punishment. He also complained of a deep need for love from his father (Masson 1984). (Freud would later interpret that Ferenczi's unresolved need for parental love was responsible for his deviations from standard analytic technique.) After the training analysis, which lasted several months, Ferenczi returned to Budapest to set up a psychoanalytic practice.

At Freud's behest, in 1910 he founded the International Psychoanalytic Association and suggested that it be centered in Zurich, with Jung as its first president. On his own accord, Ferenczi also recommended that the president have the right to approve of all future papers presented at IPA congresses. These recommendations met with a storm of protests from Adler, Stekel, and other Viennese analysts, who had been around longer than Jung, and who felt the center should be in Vienna. However, Freud wanted Jung because he was not Jewish (critics had been charging that psychoanalysis was an extension of Judaism), and he wanted to establish a broader basis for this growing field. As for Ferenczi's attempt to give the president censorship powers, this recommendation was angrily rejected. Afterwards, Freud sent Ferenczi an "epilogue," as he called it, about the Congress, in which he stated:

> Your spirited plea had the misfortune to evoke so much contradiction that they forgot to thank you for the important suggestions

you had laid before them. . . . It would have been easy for you to have entirely omitted the critical remarks and to have assured them of their scientific freedom; then we should have deprived their protest of much of its strength. I believe that my long pent up aversion for the Viennese combined with your brother complex to make us shortsighted. [Jones 1957, p. 267]

Soon after this Congress Freud began laying down, in a series of papers written between 1912 and 1915, what would become known as standard psychoanalytic technique. Ferenczi, his unofficial "second in command," went along with Freud's dicta for a while. These rules limited analysts to making interpretations of patients' dreams and free associations, cautioned them to abstain from any gratification of their own or their patients' needs, and required them to remain neutral and reveal as little of themselves as possible, so that they could function as a blank screen on which patients could transfer and project infantile imagos and feelings. However, Ferenczi's experimental nature could not be held in check, and before long he published his first case history illustrating a deviation in technique.

He writes, in "Technical Difficulties in the Analysis of a Case of Hysteria" (1919), of a young woman, whom he does not name or describe, who tried with "great intelligence and much zeal" to carry out the directions for psychoanalytic treatment. She was an insightful person who seemed, at first, to improve somewhat, which Ferenczi attributed to the transference; then for a long time she made no further progress. Instead, her transference became erotic, and she began spending hour after hour declaring her love for him, describing her sensual fantasies about him, and pleading with him to return her love. His attempts to analyze her transference got nowhere. Finally, following Freud's procedure with the Wolf Man, he set a fixed termination date, hoping that this would force her out of her defensive posture. Again she seemed to make some progress, then lapsed back into the erotic transference. "The hours went by in passionate declarations of love and entreaties on her side, and in fruitless endeavors on mine to get her to understand the transference nature of her feelings, and to trace her affects to their real but unconscious object" (p. 190). When the termination date arrived, he discharged her "uncured," though she herself professed to be content with her improvements.

Many months later she came back, desolately complaining that her earlier problems had returned with "all the old violence." Ferenczi does not say what these problems were. He "yielded to her request" and took her on. After a short time she began "the old game again" and he could make no progress with her. This time "extraneous circumstances" interrupted the treatment, and she was again discharged uncured.

The third time she came to him he decided on a different approach. He noticed something about her manner on the couch:

> In the course of her inexhaustibly repeated love fantasies, which were always concerned with the doctor, she often made the remark, as though by the way, that this gave her feelings "down there." That is, she had erotic genital sensations. But only after all this time did an accidental glance at the manner in which she lay on the sofa convince me that she kept her legs crossed during the whole hour. This led us—not for the first time—to the subject of onanism, an act performed by girls and women for preference by pressing the thighs together. [p. 190]

It was not until some time had passed that Ferenczi first had the idea of forbidding her to lie with her legs crossed. He explained to her that when she lay like that she was "carrying out a larval form of onanism" and that, in effect, she was acting out her impulses rather than verbalizing them. The patient reluctantly ceased pressing her legs together, and the results, according to Ferenczi, were staggering. She was "tormented" during the following sessions by an almost unbearable "bodily and psychic restlessness." She thrashed around on the sofa, spewing out fantasies in a delirious manner, and recalled important events of her childhood; these provided him with clues to the traumatic roots of her illness.

However, after a time the patient seemed to resign herself to the new rule about her posture, and once again "took refuge in the sanctuary of the transference love." Once again progress halted.

Eventually Ferenczi figured out that although she had ceased masturbating during her sessions, she was constantly playing with herself during the rest of each day. Upon questioning her, he learned that she had found ways to "eroticize" most of her house-wifely and maternal activities by unconsciously pressing her legs together, while at the same time having erotic fantasies which she kept unconscious. When Ferenczi instructed her to give up all masturbatory activity in and out of her sessions, she again came forth with more material, and made progress. The progress was, however, not yet "definitive."

"*Naturam expellas furca, tamen ista recurrat,*" he dryly noted.

Soon he discovered that she had found yet another way to masturbate. She had begun to playfully squeeze and handle various parts of her body. Indeed, after a while she succeeded, through these "symptomatic acts," in the complete "shutting off of the libido from any other path of discharge" so that "from time to time it was increased to an actual orgasm at other indifferent parts of the body that are not by nature prominent erotogenic zones" (p. 192).

"You are wasting your whole sexuality in these little naughtinesses," Ferenczi told her, and he asked her to agree for the sake of the treatment to give up these gratifications, which she had practiced since childhood. She agreed, and was immediately smitten by the return of an obsessional neurosis which she had first experienced in childhood. Ferenczi was able to analyze it without difficulty.

The last stage in the analysis was the appearance, during the sessions, of a sudden need to urinate. Once more Ferenczi instructed her to desist. Finally, there came a day when she told him, agitatedly, that she had experienced such a violent itch in her genitals that she could not stand it anymore—she was going to have to rub her vagina, and that was that. He explained that this confirmed his assertion that she had passed through an infantile period of active masturbation. She did not believe him, but later she brought in dreams and thoughts that convinced her that he was right. Gradually she began to enjoy her sex life with her husband, and one by one her hysterical symptoms were analyzed and resolved in the light of this new material. At last, Ferenczi pronounced the patient cured. Unfortunately, there was no follow-up on this woman, so we have no way of knowing whether the results were permanent.

In explaining his new technique, Ferenczi credits Freud. "We owe the prototype of this 'active technique' to Freud himself" (p. 196). In the analysis of anxiety hysterias, Freud had found a similar stagnation and directed patients to confront just those critical situations which usually caused anxiety attacks. By this method Freud had been able to free the "wrongly anchored affects" from their connections, Ferenczi observes, and compares this method to experiments on animals in which the blood pressure in distant parts can be raised by applying a ligature on the large vessels. "So in suitable cases we can and must shut off psychic excitement from unconscious paths of discharge, in order by this 'rise of pressure' of energy to overcome the resistance of the censorship and of the 'resting excitation' by higher psychic systems" (p. 197).

Ferenczi elaborates on his new method in "The Further Development of an Active Therapy in Psycho-Analysis" (1921), asserting that he is not attempting to alter Freud's fundamental rule of free association, but merely trying to help the patient, by means of "certain artifices," to comply more easily with this rule. In other words, he was using active interventions in order to break impasses. He contends not only that Freud used active interventions himself, but that interpretation itself is an active intervention. He alludes to the cathartic method of Breuer, but does not actually embrace it; that will come later. He warns that active therapy is not to be confused with suggestion as used by such nonanalytic therapists as hypnotherapists.

He then presents "excerpts" from another case to "substantiate" his theory. This case involved a beautiful young woman, a musician, who suffered from a host of phobias and obsessional symptoms: when she played the piano, she had the obsessive notion that she must disgrace herself, and often did; when she walked on the street she imagined that her "voluminous breasts" were deformed, and would cross her arms over them (and then imagine that this made people look at her all the more); if men paid no attention to her beauty she was unhappy, but she was "no less disconcerted if they did"; when she exhaled she feared she had bad breath and went constantly to the dentist and laryngologist, who could discover nothing wrong. She came to Ferenczi after having already undergone a previous analysis that went nowhere. She seemed to have a great deal of theoretical insight, but nevertheless made no progress. Things remained on an intellectual level.

One day, after she had seen him for several weeks, she recalled a street song that her older sister (who had tyrannized her) was in the habit of singing. Ferenczi asked her to sing the song. For two sessions she struggled with the tune, singing in a low, uncertain voice and breaking off with embarrassment in the middle of a verse. Ferenczi kept encouraging her and she began to sing in a lovely soprano voice. Still, the resistance to singing continued. She recalled that her sister had usually accompanied the song with "unambiguous gestures," and she made clumsy arm movements to illustrate her sister's behavior. Ferenczi then asked her to get up from the couch and sing the song exactly as she had seen her sister do it. "After endless spiritless partial attempts she showed herself to be a perfect chanteuse, with all the coquetry of facial play and movement that she had seen in her sister" (p. 203). Now she began to enjoy such productions and to fritter away the sessions with them.

When he became aware of this, Ferenczi told her, "We know now that you enjoy displaying your various talents and that behind your modesty lies hidden a considerable desire to please; it is no longer a matter of dancing but of getting on with the work" (p. 204). He was astonished to discover that this intervention brought out new memories of her early childhood. She remembered how she had once been "a little devil," the darling of all her family and friends, displaying her talents before all and taking an uninhibited, sensual enjoyment in "muscular movement." Then her little brother had been born and this had turned her into a shy, anxious, and abnormally good child.

Ferenczi next asked the patient to perform other activities that frightened her. He asked her to conduct in front of him (while imitating the sounds of an orchestra), and subsequent analysis revealed the penis envy by which she had been tormented since the birth of her brother; he asked her to play the difficult piano piece she was to perform for a school examination, and it soon became evident that her fear of disgracing herself was related to masturbation and humiliation during childhood ("forbidden finger exercises"); he asked her to go to a public swimming pool to overcome her phobia about having large breasts, and after doing so she got in touch with her unconscious desire to exhibit herself sexually. After her most hidden tendencies had been exposed, she made another confession. "She acknowledged that during the analytic hour she occupied herself a great deal with her sphincter *ani*; sometimes she would play with the idea of passing flatus, sometimes contract the sphincter rhythmically, and so on" (p. 204). For a time Ferenczi encouraged her to continue and even exaggerate these activities; then he reversed himself and asked her to "give up these games" for the good of the treatment. They then came upon the "anal-erotic explanation" of her anxiety about having bad breath, which aroused another series of memories about being told not to play with her feces. It was not long before the patient had begun to improve in all areas.

Ferenczi describes his technique as having two phases. First the patient was asked to perform activities around which she had a phobia; then, after she had begun to enjoy these activities, she was asked, during the second phase, to stop doing them. The command of the first phase served to bring formerly repressed inclinations to the surface; then when this command was reversed, the patient was put in touch with long repressed material which "had to be interpreted as repetitions of something infantile, and the peculiarities and conditions of the childish procedures had to be reconstructed by the analyst with the help of the other analytic material (dreams, fancies, etc.)" (p. 206).

In "On Forced Fantasies: Activity in the Association-Technique" (1924), he introduces another active technique—that of asking a patient to have fantasies. In one such case, he was working with a young man who was strongly inhibited in his expression of feelings, particularly aggressive feelings toward the analyst. Because of his "ideals," he could only relate to the analyst in a friendly and tender way, and as a result the analysis became "aimless." Ferenczi, at first, attempted to get at these feelings by interpreting "somewhat harshly" the patient's aimlessness and his inhibition of feelings while, at the same time, setting a fixed termination date. But this intervention did not work with "The Fantasizer"; instead of placing the patient in touch with his aggressive feelings, it provoked "several hours that were tedious and without tone or activity" (p. 72). When Ferenczi suggested that the young man must hate him for the harsh way he had been treated, he replied that he felt only friendliness and gratitude.

Finally, Ferenczi suggested that he have an aggressive fantasy about him. At first the patient proceeded timidly. But as more and more fantasies emerged, he became more and more hostile, and as he verbalized them he broke out into a cold sweat. Suddenly he began yelling at Ferenczi about being beaten by, and then about beating the analyst. Then he shouted that he wanted to gouge out Ferenczi's eyes. Then he screamed that he wanted to turn Ferenczi into a woman and rape him.

These fantasies, according to Ferenczi, enabled the patient to reexperience practically all the situations of the Oedipus complex and allowed Ferenczi to reconstruct the patient's early infantile history, which, in turn, brought the case to a satisfactory conclusion.

Ferenczi still maintained in this paper that he was staying within the framework of standard technique. However, to everyone else it was obvious he was deviating markedly. Younger analysts found his work interesting, while his contemporaries were dubious. When, in 1926, his papers on analytic technique were collected into a book, Glover wrote a review (1927) in which he noted that Freud had observed that "The best way to shorten treatment is to carry it out correctly" (p. 417).

In "The Elasticity of Psycho-Analytic Technique" (1928), Ferenczi adds new wrinkles to his active therapy methodology by proposing that analysts actively encourage patients to express their aggressive feelings toward them. He notes that until a patient verbalizes these feelings, he will not truly form a positive transference. "If we do not protect ourselves from this [aggression], but, on the contrary, encourage the only-too-hesitant patient at every opportunity that presents itself, sooner or later we shall reap the well-deserved reward of our patience in the form of the arrival of the positive transference" (p. 93). In this same paper he also advises analysts not to be ashamed to "unreservedly confess" to their mistakes. This represents yet another break from standard technique, which considers such admissions a coloring of the blank screen.

By the time he published "The Principle of Relaxation and Neocatharsis," (1930) he no longer pretended to be staying within Freud's rules. "My own position in the psychoanalytical movement has made me a kind of cross between a pupil and a teacher," he says, "and perhaps this double role gives me the right and the ability to point out where we are tending to be one-sided, and, without foregoing what is good in the new teaching, to plead that justice shall be done to that what has proved its value in days past" (pp. 108–109). What he has in mind is the revival of catharsis in therapy. He refers to the early days, when Breuer and Freud perfected the cathartic method and then abandoned it in favor of free association. "The highly emotional relation between physician and patient, which resembled that in hypnotic suggestion, gradually cooled down to a kind of unending association-experiment," he laments. "The process became mainly intellectual" (p. 110). He notes that later Freud attempted to restore affectivity to the process by paying more attention to "transference of affect" and "affective resistance" in the analytic situation, but Ferenczi asserts that this restoration was not enough. So he developed the technique of relaxation and neocatharsis.

This new rendition of the cathartic technique differed from the Breuer/Freud version in that it was used only toward the end of an analysis, and its effects were permanent. "There is all the difference in the world between this cathartic termination to a long psychoanalysis and the fragmentary eruptions of emotion and recollection which the primitive catharsis could provoke and which had only a temporary effect" (p. 119). He contends, furthermore, that his new method has given him a deeper understanding of "traumatic primal repression." The first reaction to a traumatic shock, he believed, was a transitory psychosis—a turning away from reality:

> In every case of neurotic amnesia, and possibly also in the ordinary childhood-amnesia, it seems likely that a *psychotic splitting off* of a part of the personality occurs under the influence of shock. The dissociated part, however, lives on hidden, ceaselessly endeavoring to make itself felt, without finding any outlet except in neurotic symptoms. For this notion I am partly indebted to discoveries made by our colleague, Elisabeth Severn, which she personally communicated to me. [pp. 121–122]

This was the first of two references to Mrs. Severn, a beautiful dancer who, according to Masson (1984), had been in treatment with Ferenczi sometime between 1925 and 1926. She went on to become an analyst herself, and wrote a book in which she took credit for influencing Ferenczi's neocathartic method. Masson speculates that Ferenczi had begun to spend up to five hours with a single patient at a time, and that Mrs. Severn may have been one of the first with whom he did so. Like "Anna O." with Breuer, Mrs. Severn seemed to have had a strong emotional impact on Ferenczi. It may well be that she had herself been sexually abused as a child, and had developed a split personality, for it was subsequent to his work with her that Ferenczi began writing about the splitting that occurs after the early sexual abuse of a child.

In "Child Analysis in the Analysis of Adults" (1931) he further extends his use of neocatharsis. He writes of a young man "in the prime of his life" who today might have been diagnosed as a borderline personality. The young man had worked through much material and, at a certain point in the treatment, had begun to revive memories of his earliest childhood. He had apparently had a somewhat difficult relationship with his grandfather, and suffered from gender confusion. One day, having begun to transfer this grandfather onto Ferenczi, he suddenly turned to Ferenczi while discussing the old man, looked frightenedly into Ferenczi's eyes, threw his arms around his neck, and whispered into his ear, "I say, Grandpapa, I am afraid I am going to have a baby!"

Ferenczi's initial impulse was to interpret this behavior. However, upon further thought, he decided, in a moment of inspiration, to play the role of the grandfather. "Well, but what makes you think so," he replied (p. 129). This response helped the man get into his feelings.

He had by then begun to use trance states and regression as a matter of course, and he seems to have attracted patients with severe narcissistic and borderline features. In order to work with such patients, he contends, the analyst had to meet the patient as far as possible with "almost inexhaustible patience, understanding, good will, and kindness" (p. 132). Yet he also had to be real. If the patient was acting out hostile transference feelings, it would be wrong to always be kind. "It is better to admit honestly that we find the patient's behavior unpleasant, but we feel it our duty to control ourselves" (p. 133). He also recommended that analysts themselves regress to "this deep infantile stratum" in their training analyses.

His last and most controversial paper, "Confusion of Tongues Between Adults and the Child: The Language of Tenderness and Passion" (1933), goes a step further (some thought a step too far) in deviating from standard technique and reviving the seduction theory. In this work he proposes the idea of mutual analysis: while the analyst analyzes the patient, the patient analyzes the analyst. He also speaks, in rather plain language, of child sexual abuse in the family environment, citing molestations by fathers, mothers, brothers, sisters, governesses, and servants.

With respect to mutual analysis, he asserts that he came to see its value when he noticed that his patients were unable to trust him enough to reproduce their original traumas in his office so long as he remained hidden behind a blank screen. They sensed the hypocrisy of it, sensed a sometimes hidden dislike of themselves—a situation that replicated the environment that had led to their illness in the first place. In order to establish trust with the patient and provide a facilitating environment, one that contrasted to the toxic environments of their childhood, Ferenczi said he began to listen to patients, allowed them to analyze him, and admitted his mistakes. "The setting free of his [the patient's] critical feelings, the willingness on our part to admit our mistakes and the honest endeavor to avoid them in the future, all these go to create in the patient a confidence in the analyst. *It is this confidence that establishes the contrast between the present and the unbearable traumatogenic past*" (p. 160). This contrast is necessary, he believes, for the patient to be able to reexperience the past not as a "hallucinatory reproduction" but as an objective memory. (He does not actually use the term "mutual analysis" in this paper, although he does in his diaries [Masson 1984].)

Unfortunately, Ferenczi's life ended tragically, soon after this paper was presented at the 1932 Congress of the International Psychoanalytic Association. Freud and the psychoanalytic establishment had been critical of Ferenczi's experiments for several years. Then, some of Ferenczi's former patients reported to other analysts that he had held them in his lap as if they were children and had kissed them. These revelations seemed to be the final straw as far as Freud was concerned. He himself had turned away from hypnosis and catharsis when a patient had thrown her arms around him and a servant had walked in and caught them; the prospect of scandal was anathema to him. As a result, he and the establishment turned on Ferenczi. A year before the 1932 Congress, Ferenczi was considered the primary candidate to become president of the association he had founded, but as the date of the

Congress neared he was under pressure to remove his name from the candidacy and to withdraw his paper from its scheduled presentation. The paper was at that time entitled still, "The Passions of Adults and their Influence on the Sexual and Character Development of Children." Freud wrote to Max Eitingon on August 29, 1932:

He must not be allowed to give the paper. Either another one or none. He does not seem disinclined now to be chosen as president. Whether he can still be chosen by all of you after these revelations is another question. Our behavior will depend, in the first place, on whether he agrees to the postponement (of his paper) as well as on the impression that he makes on all of you in Wiesbaden. [Masson 1984, p. 170]

Ferenczi reluctantly withdrew his candidacy and was eventually allowed to read the paper to a silent, hostile audience. The paper was refused publication in the association's journal. The ideas in this paper seemed to have been tantamount to psychoanalytic heresy. Heartbroken by these events, feeling misunderstood and betrayed by all those closest to him, including his wife, he retreated to a sanatorium operated by Georg Groddeck. He died of pernicious anemia several months after the Wiesbaden Congress, at the age of 60.

Interpretation

For many years Ferenczi's work remained controversial within the psychoanalytic establishment, which held closely to the procedures Freud had suggested. However, more recently his papers on psychoanalytic technique have gained a certain acceptance and even grudging admiration. At the center of the debate about his work are the issues of regression and the use of active measures in order to facilitate therapy.

Freud, having abandoned the cathartic method soon after he and Breuer had gone their separate ways, attempted a compromise of sorts in his paper, "Remembering, Repeating and Working-Through" (1914), in which he suggested that abreaction was a byproduct of the analysis of transference and resistance. The primary aim "descriptively speaking . . . is to fill in gaps in memory; dynamically speaking, it is to overcome resistances due to repression" (p. 148). However, in overcoming these resistances, some abreaction occurs. "From a theoretical point of view one may correlate it with the 'abreacting' of the quotas of affect strangulated by repression," he notes, "an abreaction without which hypnotic treatment remained ineffective" (p. 156). With respect to analytic activity, Freud maintained it to be incorrect, yet he himself was frequently active in various ways: setting forced termination dates, giving commands, educating the patient, etc. However, for many years his followers did what he said, not what he did. It was believed that any activity on the part of the analyst represented a contamination of the procedure and merely lengthened and complicated the treatment.

Until the late 1960s, most psychoanalysts viewed regression as an aspect of the patient's psychopathology—a mechanism of defense, a factor in pathogenesis, or a potent form of resistance. Fenichel (1945) asserts that a "liberation of blocked emotions" takes place when any correct interpretation is given, but stresses that it is the building up of ego-strength that is most important in the curative process. "Abreaction is a source of material, sometimes significant, at other times only in the service of resistance; it is an occasion for demonstrating to the patient the existence and intensity of his emotions, and an introduction to the ensuing therapeutically effective working through of what has come to light in the patient's acting out" (p. 563).

Some analysts regard regression in therapy as a potential danger, a danger that might lead to a patient's decompensation or an analyst's overinvolvement. Fromm-Reichmann, while calling Ferenczi "one of the most impressive leaders in the early years of psychoanalysis" objects to his suggestion that analysts join patients in their reenactment of their childhood traumas. "My objection to this suggestion," she states, "stems predominantly from the danger implicit for many psychiatrists of losing track of their role as participant observer by becoming a gratified participant co-actor in relation to the patient's infantile needs" (1950, p. 123). She compares this with an erotic countertransference.

One of the few classical analysts during this period who speaks favorably about regression is Kris (1953), who sees it as essential to artistic creativity, for which regression is put to the service of the ego.

Balint (1968) brought the debate into sharp focus, and underscored the importance of regression as an aspect of therapy. He notes that the historic event of the disagreement between Freud and Ferenczi acted as a "trauma on the psychoanalytic world":

> Whether one assumed that a consummate master of psychoanalytic technique like Ferenczi, the author of a great number of classical papers in psychoanalysis, had been blinded to such an extent that even Freud's repeated warnings could not make him recognize his mistakes; or that Freud and Ferenczi . . . were not able to understand and properly evaluate each other's clinical findings, observations, and theoretical ideas, the shock was highly disturbing and painful. By tacit consent regression during analytic treatment was declared a dangerous symptom and its value as a therapeutic ally completely, or almost completely, repressed. [p. 153]

Balint confirms Ferenczi's discovery of the biphasic structure of infantile pathogenic traumas: the first phase consisting of over- or understimulation by caretakers, and the second phase consisting of attempts by the child to obtain reparation, comfort, or understanding from the caretakers and getting, instead, denials and rebukes. He calls this point at which the environment fails the infant the "basic fault" and contends that, in order for therapy to be effective, the analyst must facilitate regression back to this point. He also believes that Ferenczi was correct in assuming that classical analysts, who often deny or appear to deny their real thoughts and feelings about the patient, may replicate the hypocritical environment that produces childhood psychopathology.

Balint makes the point that Ferenczi was concerned with "two-person psychology" rather than one-person psychology. In contrast to classical analysts (ego psychologists), who discuss regression in terms of the patient only—i.e., how the ego is overwhelmed by regression, the conflicts between ego and id, the nature of the patient's ego when regression occurs during treatment—Ferenczi saw it as an event occurring between two people—the analyst and the patient, both contributing to the patient's regression. Hence, Balint asserts, Ferenczi was not only instrumental in reemphasizing the importance of regression in therapy, but also in exploring the newly emerging areas of countertransference analysis and object relations.

Kris, although known primarily as an ego psychologist, also commends Ferenczi for his work on countertransference analysis. He notes that "The interconnection between attention, intuition, and self-analysis in the process of interpretation has been masterfully described by Ferenczi" (1951 p. 251). He lauds Ferenczi's depiction of how the analyst must let the patient's free associations play upon him, while simultaneously allowing his own fantasies to bring forth associated material and still maintain a constant check on his subjective moods.

Kohut (1971) and Spotnitz (1985), who have both specialized in treating narcissistic patients, have acknowledged borrowing from and extending Ferenczi's work. Kohut's emphasis on creating an empathic therapeutic environment with positive mirroring by the analyst, mirroring that will compensate for the deficit that occurred during the patient's infancy, is an outgrowth of Ferenczi's relaxation technique. In addition, Kohut encourages analytic activity with narcissistic patients—parameters to be used only when necessary and to be explained as such to his patients. Like Ferenczi, he would advise a patient to stop some forms of acting out that impede the treatment, in order "to channel the unconscious, repressed incestuous drives, and the conflicts about them, toward a confrontation with the secondary processes of the ego, i.e., to encourage the formation of verbal fantasy derivatives in the form of free associations during the analytic sessions" (pp. 157–158).

Spotnitz observes that Ferenczi was the first to recognize the existence of a narcissistic countertransference, which provokes the patient into making flattering remarks about the analyst and suppressing negative thoughts and feelings. He has also incorporated other aspects of Ferenczi's theories into the modern psychoanalytic technique he uses in work with narcissistic patients: like Ferenczi, he actively encourages the development of the negative transference, believes in the importance of abreaction, understands the necessity for analysts to reveal their own thoughts and feelings and admit mistakes to patients, and in general feels analysts should do whatever necessary (including being active) to break an impasse and obtain therapeutic progress.

Citing Ferenczi's case history about the hysterical woman whom he forbade to masturbate, Spotnitz and Meadow (1976) write that Ferenczi was one of the first to discover "that there were periods of stagnation in analysis, during which new techniques were needed to hasten the exploration of unconscious material" (p. 147). Ferenczi, in working with this woman and others, had noticed how difficult it was for patients to follow the first rule of free association; they thought free association meant the complete thinking out of ideas rather than the complete utterance of what was in one's mind. "One of the points at which Ferenczi's active techniques coincides with modern psychoanalysis is in the use of the patient's contact function," they assert. "According to Ferenczi, active therapy is indicated when the patient asks questions or, in modern terminology, when the patient makes a contact with the analyst" (p. 148).

The debate about the use of active therapeutic interventions and abreaction continues to this day. Classical analysts still tend to view active techniques and abreaction as "wild analysis" and regard those who practice them as acting out unresolved narcissism or aggression. Active therapists argue that classical analysts are people who deny their own narcissism, aggression, and deeper infantile feelings, and therefore have a fear of dealing with those things in their patients. And, in fact, some active therapists may be acting out narcissistic or aggressive impulses, and some classical analysts may be limiting the range of their interventions due to the limits of their own self-awareness. However, things are changing, and many in both schools understand the need to modify their techniques according to the patient with whom they are dealing. Some patients need a blank screen; others cannot tolerate it. Some need to reexperience a deeply traumatic shock and release the feelings connected with it; others need to gain insight into an ongoing, destructive relationship. In working with an array of neurotic, narcissistic, borderline, and psychotic patients, one must be willing to use an array of interventions.

Ferenczi deserves credit as the first analyst to have the courage to ask these questions and to experiment with unorthodox techniques. He is not only the father of active therapy, but also, in another sense, of many other schools and techniques:

- His emphasis on mutual analysis was the predecessor of modern object relations theory.
- His active therapy experiments led to modern behavioral and gestalt therapy techniques.
- His acting-out of dramas with his patients was the precursor of psychodrama.
- His use of singing, dancing, and other arts foreshadowed the evolution of creative arts therapies.
- His work with regressive states preceded primal therapy.
- His attempts to create a nurturing environment laid the foundation for self psychology and is reminiscent of Winnicott's (1965) facilitating environment.
- His focus on the patient for the timing and nature of his interventions can be seen in aspects of humanistic and existential therapy.
- A great deal of his technique has reemerged in the techniques of the modern psychoanalytic school of Spotnitz (1976, 1984).

Though his death was tragic, his legacy lives on.

9

THE DEVELOPMENT OF CHILD ANALYSIS

Melanie Klein and Erna (1932)

It was at the First Conference of German Psychoanalysts at Würzburg in October, 1924 that Melanie Klein delivered one of the most gripping papers of her life. This was the story of Erna, upon which she based the third chapter in her first book, *The Psychoanalysis of Children* (Klein 1932). Before she presented this paper, which detailed her theories and analytic technique with a clarity and depth she had not previously attained, she had not been taken very seriously by most analysts. Indeed, at the Eighth International Congress at Salzburg that previous spring, another more theoretical and less graphic paper had aroused a great deal of controversy. In that paper she had begun to assert that the Oedipus complex started much earlier than Freud had put it—at the beginning of the second year. Members of the congress were stunned by what they saw as the impudence of a relative newcomer, a woman, who had no professional degrees and who based her findings on, of all things, the way children played with their toys.

Klein was born in Vienna in 1882, the youngest child of a physician named Moriz Reizes, who was from an Orthodox Jewish family. Her mother, Libusa, was his second wife. Melanie had a sister, Emily, six years older, a brother, Emmanuel, five years older, and another sister, Sidonie, about four years older. Sidonie suffered from scrofula and died when she was nine; before her death, she lovingly taught Klein everything she knew, and Klein never forgot her. Several years later, her brother died in his early 20s, of a rheumatic heart condition. These two deaths may have influenced Klein's tendency toward depression. She married Arthur Stevan Klein, a friend of her brother's, the day after she turned 21, and divorced him about twenty years later (at a time when divorce was still considered scandalous, particularly for a child analyst). She had three children, Melitta, Hans, and Erich.

Initially Klein had wanted to study medicine, and regretted for the rest of her life that she had not done so, believing that a medical degree would have won greater acceptance for her views. Instead while in her 20s she took humanities courses at the University of Vienna. When she read Freud's book *On Dreams* in 1914, she decided to become a psychoanalyst. She was analyzed by Ferenczi in Budapest and later by Karl Abraham in Berlin. She found Ferenczi supportive and engaging and was intellectually stimulated by Abraham; both encouraged her to become a child analyst.

Following the example set by Freud in his analysis of his daughter Anna, Klein's first patients included her own children. (Abraham is also said to have analyzed his own daughter and encouraged Klein to persevere with her children.) Erich seems to have required the most lengthy analysis. In early papers in which he was referred to as Fritz, Klein interpreted most of his problems as repressed incestuous desires toward his mother—herself (Grosskurth 1986). Unlike Freud and his daughter Anna (her chief rival, whom she would meet at the 1927 Conference on Child Analysis) Klein felt that children could develop a transference, and she analyzed their play the way therapists working with adults analyze free associations, dreams, or symptomatic acts.

Her book, *The Psychoanalysis of Children*, crystallized her basic theories about child development and analysis, and contained the paper, "An Obsessional Neurosis in a Six-Year-Old Girl," based on her treatment of Erna. This little girl, the only child of a wealthy Jewish family in Berlin, was brought to Klein because she had become extremely unruly at home and at school. Klein worked with Erna for about two-and-a-half years, which was then considered quite a long treatment for a child.

"There's something about life I don't like," Erna told Klein at the outset of the analysis (1932, p. 35). Depression was one of her main symptoms. The other was sleeplessness due partly to a fear of robbers and burglars and partly to obsessional activities. She would lie on her face and bang her head on the pillow; make a rocking movement, during which she sat, or lay on her back; and obsessively suck her thumb and masturbate. She masturbated even in the presence of strangers and almost continuously at her kindergarten.

Erna dominated her mother, left her no freedom of movement, and "plagued her continually with her love and hatred." As the mother put it, "She swallows me up" (p. 35). She was described as having a curiously unchildlike nature, of giving an impression of precocious sexuality, and of always having a suffering, brooding look on her face. In addition, she had a severe inhibition in learning. At the very beginning of the treatment, she turned to Klein and begged her in a sad voice, "Please help me." This showed Klein that the child herself was aware of her illness and this awareness "was of great assistance to me in analyzing her" (p. 36).

Most of this paper is a study of Erna's play. Generally Klein sat on the floor with Erna, participating in the play while interpreting its meaning to the child. Klein, a strikingly beautiful woman with brown, sensitive, penetrating eyes, a full, sensual, slightly pouting mouth, and a confident manner, was in her late 30s when she treated Erna. She believed in maintaining the blank screen and abstinence, even with children—differing with Anna Freud, who utilized a more sympathetic, educative attitude.

In the beginning Klein noticed that Erna's play often involved a triangular relationship. Once Erna ran a toy carriage toward Klein and said, "I've come to fetch you." She put a toy woman in the carriage, then a toy man, and had them "love and kiss one another." After a while she had another toy man in another carriage collide with the loving couple, run over them, kill them, and roast and eat them up. On another occasion she had the couple, now man and wife, defending their house against a burglar, represented by the second man. The house burned down and the husband and wife burst apart. The second man was the only survivor. On yet another occasion the second man paid a visit to the house and, while embracing the wife, bit off her nose. Klein interpreted that this second man represented Erna herself, symbolizing "her wish to oust her father from his position with her mother" or "to get rid of her mother and to win her father" (p. 36).

Often Erna had Klein play the child while she herself played the mother. On one of these occasions, Klein was told by her mother that one of her worst faults was thumb-sucking. In a stern, motherly tone, Erna told Klein to put a toy engine into her mouth. Klein writes:

She had already much admired its gilded lamps, saying, 'They're so lovely, all red and burning', and at once put them into her mouth and sucked them. They stood to her for her mother's breast and her father's penis. These games were invariably followed by outbreaks of rage, envy and aggression against her mother, to be succeeded by remorse and by attempts to placate her. [p. 37]

It was apparent from the beginning that Erna had a negative mother transference toward Klein, which got acted out in various ways. Once, when she was cutting patterns into paper, she told Klein that she was cutting "fringes" in Klein's nose. Klein interpreted that she wanted to bite her nose off, as the toy man had bitten the toy woman's nose off. Indeed, on a few occasions Erna actually attempted to bite Klein's nose. Klein interpreted this as a desire to bite off her father's penis, which she imagined her mother to have incorporated. Klein believed that cutting out paper and roasting and eating people also represented sadistic and cannibalistic impulses, derived, at its deepest level, from the child's innate aggression or death instinct; therefore, according to Klein, what was being transferred, in part, was the child's innate aggression toward her mother.

Other games led to the analysis of "oral-sadistic, urethral-sadistic, and anal-sadistic" fantasies. In one game Klein was told that she was a bad child who had dirtied her underclothes. Erna played a washerwoman (mother) who cruelly punished the child; but at times she would take the dirty linen (represented by cut up paper) and eat it. In another game she would pretend to sit on the toilet and eat her feces, or that she and Klein were giving feces to each other to eat; and in yet another game she would pretend that her mother had dirtied herself over and over and the whole room had been turned into feces, and the mother was thrown into prison and starved. When it was the child, played by Klein, who did the dirtying, Erna, as the mother, would sometimes have the father beat the naughty child. Once the father, as a magician, beat the child on the anus and head with a stick, and as he did so a "yellowish fluid poured out of the magic wand." On another occasion the child was given a powder to take, which cured her of her dirty habit of soiling and enabled her suddenly to talk and be as clever as her mother. "The magician stood for the penis, and knocking with the stick meant coitus," Klein interprets. "The fluid and the powder represented urine, feces, semen and blood, all of which, according to Erna's phantasies, her mother put inside herself in copulation through her mouth, anus and genitals" (p. 38).

Klein's use of the word "phantasies" here denotes that Erna was unconscious of such ideas. ("Fantasies," on the other hand, would denote consciousness or preconsciousness.) Often the phantasies revolved around a child being humiliated by her mother. Erna, as the queen, would taunt the child, played by Klein, through graphic displays of affection to her husband and would dress herself up in front of the child, always to stir the child's envy and wound her feelings. Then the child had to share her parents' bedroom and "be a spectator of sexual intercourse between them." If the child interrupted, she was beaten, and the mother would put the child to bed only to be with the father all the sooner, in order to copulate with him. The child was given a nasty pudding to eat that made her sick, while the mother and father were enjoying foods made of whipped cream or a special milk. "This special food, which was eaten by the father and mother alone, was used in endless variations to represent the exchange of substances during coition," Klein observes, adding that in her phantasies Erna believed that during coition "her mother incorporated her father's penis and semen and her father incorporated her mother's breasts and milk" (p. 40). These phantasies were the primary cause of her envy and hatred of her parents.

As an only child, Erna also had phantasies about siblings. Klein noted that for a long time Erna had attacks of rage at the beginning and end of her analytic sessions, which were "partly precipitated by her meeting the child who came to me for treatment immediately before or after her and who stood to her for the brother or sister whose arrival she was always awaiting" (p. 42). In her phantasies, brothers and sisters meant a child of her own, a reassurance that the attacks she had made on the children she supposed were inside her mother's body had not damaged them, a possible sexual outlet, and allies in her war against her parents. In one of her games, she and her siblings would unite and kill their mother and capture their father's penis.

Klein's method of working with Erna, as with all children, was to calmly interpret her phantasies in an attempt to bring her into complete touch with reality. She notes that, "With Erna, even after a good deal of analysis had been done, I had not succeeded in obtaining any detailed information about her real life. I got plenty of material regarding her extravagant sadistic impulses against her mother, but I never heard the least complaint or criticism from her about her *real* mother" (p. 43). Early in the analysis, Erna denied that her phantasied attacks were against her real mother. Then she admitted that they were directed against her real mother, but did not acknowledge being angry at her. Again and again Klein tried to get Erna to talk about her real life, but to no avail. Finally she succeeded in analyzing her deepest reasons for wanting to cut herself off from reality—that is, her resistance.

For the most part Erna avoided reality and lived in a dream world; whenever real thoughts entered her head, she would be seized by rage and depression. For instance, she might be playing with toy carriages and coachmen, pretending that she was a queen, with toy women as her servants, when suddenly her expression would grow dark and sullen. She would run to the bathroom and phantasize aloud while she defecated, then come out and fling herself onto the couch, passionately sucking her thumb, picking her nose, and masturbating. "By means of these pleasurable satisfactions and the phantasies bound up with them she was trying forcibly to continue the same dream-state which she had been keeping up while playing. The depression, anger and anxiety which seized her during her play were due to a disturbance of her phantasies by . . . reality" (p. 44).

Erna's sadistic impulses against her parents, particularly her mother, led to megolomanical phantasies and an excessive fear of both parents. She developed a paranoid character—which Klein would later in her career designate as the paranoid-schizoid position—along with the depressive position, one of two phases of normal development in children. (In the first position, the child reacts to sadistic impulses; in the second, the child, fearing persecution and overcome by the reality principle, becomes masochistic and sinks into a depression.) Klein writes of Erna's paranoia:

> The severe, punishing mother and the hating child, between whom she perpetually alternated in her play and phantasies, showed the action of an over-harsh superego in many details. It needed a very deep-going analysis to elucidate these phantasies, which corresponded to what, in adult paranoiacs, are known as delusions. [pp. 44–45]

The deepest layer of her paranoia was linked to a homosexual attachment to her mother. The most difficult work of the analysis involved the uncovering of these homosexual phantasies. "Beneath Erna's homosexual attachment . . . lay an extraordinarily intense feeling of hatred against her mother, derived from her earliest oedipal situation and her oral sadism" (p. 45). This hatred brought about a deep anxiety that in turn became the determining factor of her phantasies of persecution. The "deepest foundation" of her hatred was her "oral envy" of the genital and oral gratifications she imagined her parents were enjoying with each other in bed. She had phantasies of attacking them, especially her mother, with poisoned feces, sometimes delivered by a flea, who flew up her mother's anus.

After these phantasies had been analyzed, Erna's homosexual fixation began to diminish and she began to turn to her father more and more in a genuine way. Until then, he had been merely an object with which her mother made her jealous or she made her mother jealous. In this period of the analysis, as Klein analyzed her phantasies, Erna would often say in astonishment, "But Mother can't really have meant to do that? She's very fond of me *really*" (p. 47). When her unconscious hatred of her mother became more conscious, she began to criticize her openly, and her relationship with her began to improve. Alongside this improvement, she also became genuinely motherly and tender with her own play children. "Should I *really* have treated my child like that?" she asked Klein one day (p. 47).

Analyzing the etiology of Erna's illness, Klein notes that she had been toilet-trained at an unusually early age—the training was completed by the time she was 1 year old. She had eagerly complied with this training, and it had been outwardly successful. "But this outward success went along with a complete internal failure. Erna's tremendous anal-sadistic phantasies showed to what degree she remained fixated at that stage and how much hatred and ambivalence flowed from it" (p. 48). In addition, Erna had never gotten over her weaning. Finally, there was a third factor that led to her obsessional neurosis. When she was between 6 and 9 months old her mother noticed that the child responded with sexual pleasure when she took particular care in cleaning her genitals. As Erna grew older, her mother began to deliberately avoid washing her vulva as thoroughly as she had before. The child looked upon this development as a kind of seduction and abandonment. Then, when she was 2 years 6 months, and again at 3 years 6 months, she shared her parents' bedroom during a summer holiday, and witnessed their lovemaking. It was this witnessing of the primal scene during those holidays that first brought on the obsessional symptoms.

Klein interprets Erna's symptoms as follows: the thumb-sucking was related to phantasies of sucking, biting, and devouring her father's penis and her mother's breasts; her fear of robbers and burglars was a fear of her parents' retaliation against her sadistic impulses; her banging her head against her pillow at night represented an identification with her father's movements during coitus (identification with the aggressor); rocking back and forth harkened to a longing to be masturbated by her mother; and the various ways in which she masturbated represented her playing at times her father's active and at times her mother's passive role in coitus.

Klein asserts that the handling of the child's fits of anger and sadistic impulses constituted the most difficult part of child analytic technique. During the early stage of analysis, Erna would have outbreaks of rage each time Klein told her the session had ended. She would break her toys, cut them up, knock down chairs, fling cushions about, stamp her feet, spill water, smudge paper, dirty her toys or the sink, or hurl abusive language at Klein. Klein allowed all forms of expression, except for physical attacks on her. However, eventually she would open the double doors, knowing that the child would not want her mother to see her having such outbursts, and the child would quiet down. Later in the analysis, Erna would hurriedly throw down cushions at the end of the sessions; and still later, toward the end, she would calmly leave the room without any display. Klein divides her technique for handling a child's outbursts into three phases: (1) the child was required to keep his emotions under control only if there were a necessity for it in reality; (2) he could otherwise give vent to affects in abuse and in the other ways; (3) affects were lessened or cleared up by continuous interpretation and by tracing them back to the original source.

The analysis with Erna was terminated successfully after 575 hours of treatment. By then her obsessional symptoms had diminished, her anxiety was reduced, and her sleeplessness cured. Her attacks of depression also ceased. Klein kept in touch with Erna throughout her childhood, and in 1939 Erna, like Klein, was one of the many Jews to flee Germany. While in London she visited Klein at a party, and was described as "a tall young woman" who was warmly embraced by the analyst. She was about to emigrate to Australia and seemed to have turned out fine (Grosskurth 1986).

In 1941 Klein analyzed a 10-year-old boy named Richard, who became the subject of a book-length case history upon which she worked until her death. *Narrative of a Child Analysis* (1961), at nearly 500 pages, is the longest case history in psychoanalytic literature. It provides a session-by-session account of her work with a depressed boy—93 sessions in all, over a period of four months. Klein states in her preface, "this book is intended to illustrate the psycho-analytic procedure, which consists in selecting the most urgent aspects of the material and interpreting them with precision" (p. 12). Her technique was to show the patient, through direct interpretations, how his relationship with her and with his parents aroused anxiety or guilt, and how he altered relationships in phantasy to avoid pain. For example, during the third session Richard told Klein that he had heard on the radio that the British battleships were being blockaded by the Germans, and he was afraid they'd be trapped. Klein interpreted that Richard was also unconsciously worried that Daddy's genital might get trapped inside Mommy, like the British ships in the Strait of Gibraltar. Although she succeeds in demonstrating her technique, her paper about Erna represents more of a turning point in psychoanalytic thinking. There was really nothing new in Richard's case, only a recapitulation of all Klein's ideas. Session-by-session accounts become repetitious and monotonous to read, even for analysts. *Narrative* suffers from an overabundance of material.

Klein's career was beset with power struggles from the time she moved to England. First there was a struggle with Anna Freud over whose theories and methods of child therapy were more correct. Then one of her chief supporters, Edward Glover, began to attack her as a "heretic," and he was joined by her own daughter, Melitta Schmidelberg, who had herself become an analyst. The British Psychoanalytic Association was split into factions by these conflicts, and there were attempts made to oust Klein from the association, not only because of her work but because she herself had developed a reputation as an arrogant and difficult person (Roazen 1984). She also became a crusader for child analysis, proposing that analysis should be a normal part of every child's education. By the time of her death, due to anemia and complications from a broken hip, she had become alienated from her two surviving children, Erich and Melitta. Neither came to her funeral.

Interpretation

At the time she treated Erna, Klein regarded herself as a staunch follower of psychoanalytic principles. However, her footnotes to the case show she recognized that she had departed radically from Freud's ideas in some ways. For example, she observes that Freud stated that "it is the quantity of anxiety present which determines the outbreak of a neurosis," but she adds that "anxiety is liberated by the destructive tendencies, so that the outbreak of a neurosis would, in fact, be a consequence of an excessive increase of those destructive tendencies" (p. 50). In Erna's case, Klein continues, it was the envy and hatred engendered by her seeing the primal scene that led to her neurosis, not anxiety. Anxiety was a by-product. Klein had begun to disagree with Freud in this paper and in others she wrote around this time. Thus, it marks her divergence from mainstream psychoanalysis, and the beginning of a journey that would end in her establishment of an entirely new school of thought.

Grosskurth (1986), in her biography of Klein, contends that Klein's paper about Erna demonstrated that she had "reached a new level of understanding not touched in her previous papers. If Freud was led to an understanding of the development of libido through the behavior of a hysteric, so Melanie Klein was led to an understanding of early psychic conflict through the observation of a cruelly disturbed child" (p. 116). Grosskurth's analogy makes sense: what Dora was to Freud, Erna was to Klein. Her study of Erna provided her with the basic material from which to fashion her ideas about child psychoanalysis, children's phantasies, obsessional neuroses, paranoia, and an array of other phenomena.

"Freud discovered the repressed child in the adult," Segal (1979) notes. "Investigating children, Melanie Klein discovered what was already repressed in the child—namely the infant" (p. 44). Referring to the Erna case, Segal, who was analyzed by Klein, retells how Erna had phantasies of being cruelly persecuted by her mother, and considered every step in her education, every frustration, and even every pleasure her mother enjoyed with her father as a persecution and punishment. Segal notes that Klein demonstrated how the child protected herself against the anxiety produced by threatening internalized figures by splitting them off, projecting them outside, and trying to introject idealized parental figures in their stead. "In discovering the child's primitive Oedipus complex she uncovered a whole new world of the child's complex and rich phantasies and anxieties relating to its mother's body" (p. 47).

Although she acknowledges that Klein's theories have not yet been proven—depending on how one evaluates the psychoanalytic evidence—she argues that Klein's work should be considered as "still in progress" and therefore judgment should be suspended. Klein, Segal thinks, opened up areas of investigation in what Freud called "the dim and shadowy era" of early childhood—that is, the more primitive layers of the unconscious. "She has provided both a conceptual framework for understanding them and a technical tool for their investigation" (p. 177).

Jacobson (1971) also lauds Klein's understanding of the internalizations of children. In studying depressed individuals, Jacobson found that the normal boundaries between self and object representations either had dissolved or were in the process of dissolving. This phenomenon, she asserts, was accompanied by symptoms and fantasies related to "introjected objects" and "body objects" as described by Klein, that is, "bad" introjects that were experienced as the bad, worthless part of the self, or used to characterize the dangerous objects which threaten the self. "It is M. Klein's great merit to have observed and described fantasy material in small children and in psychotic adults" (p. 251).

Klein's detractors usually maintain that her interpretations of children's play is far-fetched. Anna Freud writes that in Klein's cases, such as the Erna case, "If a child upsets a lamp-post or one of the figures in the game, she interprets the action probably as due to aggressive tendencies toward the father, while if the child makes two cars collide, it is construed as implying observation of parental coitus" (1927, p. 240). Freud wonders if there could not be a simple explanation for such play; if, perhaps, it represents something that the child had witnessed during the day.

Kernberg (1975) credits Klein with being one of the first to understand the dynamics of borderline personality organization, particularly the importance of pregenital aggression. However, he strongly disagrees with her on certain points: he thinks that the Oedipus complex begins from the second to third year, rather than from the first year; he does not feel, as Klein does, that children have an innate, unconscious knowledge of the genital organs of both sexes; and he believes that she disregards structural concepts in her conceptualization of internalized objects and the superego. He also chastises her for her "rather peculiar language," a strange criticism coming from a writer who himself is noted for his rather peculiar and pedantic style.

Blum (1953) argues that while the clinical evidence for unconscious fantasies in children is generally accepted by the psychoanalytic community, Klein's contention that these fantasies (or phantasies, as she called them) are in extensive operation even in the first few months of life "taxes one's gullibility." He concedes that some may be willing to characterize the 6-month-old as "an ungrateful wretch who wishes to 'dismember mama,'" but most of us will probably prefer to delay this appellation for a year or two, at which time we can watch him carefully aim a rock at her head" (p. 54).

Geleered (1963), reviewing "Narrative of a Child Analysis" and noting Klein's conviction that anxiety must be activated during therapy, asks, "But how, when anxiety reappears, does Mrs. Klein know whether it is due to the progress of the analysis, or to the anxiety which the direct symbolic interpretation had aroused in the child?" (p. 495). Nelly Wollfheim, who ran the kindergarten which Erna attended, claimed that before beginning the analysis with Klein, Erna was quiet and well behaved in the kindergarten—her only problem being excessive masturbation. According to Wollfheim, she suddenly became aggressive, hitting other children and getting irritated over trivial matters, about two weeks after the analysis began. An analyst herself, Wollfheim felt that Klein was more interested in making discoveries than she was in the real, everyday life of Erna (Grosskurth 1986).

Balint (1968) criticizes Klein's therapeutic technique, finding it oppressive and biased. He contends that she and her followers created their own language and special way of interpreting, using words like "good breast" and "bad breast" and "good introjects" and "bad introjects," and the like. Their interpretations create an impression of overwhelming authority, which, Balint asserts, might be one of the reasons why so much aggressiveness, envy, and hatred emerges in their patients' associations. In addition, they are always looking for introjection and idealization, and so are bound to find them. "These are the two most frequently used defense mechanisms in any partnership in which an oppressed, weak partner has to cope with an overwhelmingly powerful one" (p. 107).

Greenberg and Mitchell (1983) are critical of the "fuzziness" of Klein's conception of internalizations as phantasies. On the one hand, Klein depicts all internalizations as phantasies, while on the other hand she suggests that the child internalizes all significant others and all experiences. "In this formulation . . . the distinctions between phantasied objects, perception, and memory become blurred" (p. 149). They wonder if internal objects are kept separate from the day-to-day perceptions of others, or if all phantasied internal objects continually intermingle with current perceptions. They contend that she does not adequately distinguish between current perceptions of real others, durable representations of others, phantasies of internal objects, and identifications with internal objects. They also see fuzziness in Klein's work concerning the relationship between phantasy and the establishment of character structure. Noting the "enormous fluidity" of phantasies, they wonder, "How does a patterned existence emerge from this rich, kaleidoscopic fluidity? How does the personality become organized into patterns or structures which have durability and constancy? . . . Klein leaves an unfilled gap between her vivid and fluid account of the phenomenology of experience and the organization of personality and behavior" (p. 148).

Perhaps the most universal criticism of Klein is that she placed too much emphasis on the death instinct and neglected environmental factors. As Roazen (1984) puts it, "Her postulation of inborn emotions in a child, such as envy, seemed to some a modernized version of original sin" (p. 481). Grosskurth (1986) speculates that Klein had never really separated from her own mother, and always had a protective attitude toward her. Perhaps, through identification, she also wished to protect herself. By viewing aggression as innate, parents were spared from responsibility for their children's emotional problems. As in Erna's case, Klein did not really feel parents were persecuting their children; these were merely phantasies, brought about by the children's projected sadism. In this sense Klein was following Freud, who had decided that most of his adult patients' memories of childhood seductions were fantasies; however, she was going against the theories of her former analyst, Ferenczi.

While there is a great deal of evidence to suggest the presence of an innate aggressive instinct, there is also a great deal of evidence to suggest that environmental factors have an impact on aggression, particularly on the degree of aggression and how it is expressed. All animals are aggressive by nature, but normally this aggression is utilized to sustain life or to vie for territory. M. F. Ashley Montagu (1968), an ethologist, asserts that a certain degree of aggression may be phylogenetically programmed, but that excessive aggression and destructive behavior is usually the result of environmental frustration. He is critical of anthropologists, ethologists, and psychoanalysts who wish to attribute all aggression to the genes. "What we are unwilling to acknowledge as essentially of our own making, the consequence of our own disordering in the man-made environment, we saddle upon 'Nature,' upon 'phylogenetically programmed' or 'innate' factors," he states. This blaming of Nature, he believes, serves to "divert attention from the real sources of man's aggression and destructiveness, namely, the many false and contradictory values by which, in an overcrowded, highly competitive, threatening world, he (man) so disoperatively attempts to live. It is not man's nature, but his nurture, in such a world, that requires our attention" (p. 16).

Although the mother figures more prominantly in Klein's theories than in Freud's or Ferenczi's, her actual role in the child's developmental process was to a great extent neglected by Klein. In her writings, the mother was more an object upon which the child projected phantasies. Nor does Klein allow for the impact of the mother's and the father's special defects or particular strengths. She does not consider the character of the mother, father, and other siblings and their impact on the child—the impact, for example, of a depressed mother on a newborn infant. This would be left for later analysts to delineate.

There is no doubt, however, that Klein made original and lasting contributions to psychoanalysis. In many ways she was more rigorous than Freud, and in some she extended his theories. She was one of the few major psychoanalysts to adopt fully Freud's death instinct, and work out its clinical implications. She also added to the structural theory, throwing new light on the origin, composition, and functioning of the superego, and agreeing with and extending Freud's later formulations on guilt and envy. Her emphasis on the relationships between children and objects, external and internal, was such that she became known as the founder of "object relations theory." (Later that term was more often used to categorize those who had completely departed from Freud's instinct theory.) Indeed, in 1962, when she was invited by Jones to come to England, she began what was to be known as the "British School of Object Relations Theory." Finally, by focusing on the child's oral and anal stages of development, rather than on the phallic/oedipal stage, she demonstrated the importance of pregenital fixations, and underscored for the first time the importance of the mother's, rather than the father's, relationship to the child, even though that relationship was seen more in symbolic than in real terms.

10

THE MASOCHISTIC CHARACTER

Wilhelm Reich and the Masochist (1933)

It was sometime during the late 1920s that a young man came to Wilhelm Reich's office in Vienna, complaining of being in a "masochistic bog." Reich worked with him for almost four years. Afterward, he produced a paper that shocked the psychoanalytic establishment, led to his break with Freud and, a few years later, with the International Psychoanalytic Association.

"The Masochistic Character" was first submitted for publication in the *International Journal of Psychoanalysis* in 1932, when Freud was the editor. The paper, which was eventually incorporated into Reich's most famous book, *Character Analysis* (1933), dismissed Freud's theory of the death instinct and its relationship to masochism, held mental health to be synonymous with orgasmic potency, and demonstrated a radical confrontational form of therapy. Disturbed by its contents, Freud at first decided to publish the paper only on the condition that it be accompanied by an editorial disclaimer saying that Reich did not speak for psychoanalysis, since psychoanalysis was nonpolitical. Freud contended that the paper "culminated in the nonsensical statement that what we have called the death instinct is a product of the capitalistic system" (Jones 1957, p. 477). However, after consulting with colleagues, Freud was persuaded to publish the paper without a disclaimer (so as not to offend the Soviet Union), but to follow it with a critical review by Siegfried Bernfeld. Reich, who had previously written about a kind of psychoanalytic Marxism, did not feel "The Masochistic Character" was political; he claimed Freud wanted to believe the paper had been written "in the service of" the Communist Party because he was angry that Reich had disproved the death instinct theory. At the time, Freud was 76 and Reich was 35.

The sons of a prosperous farmer, Reich and his younger brother were educated by a series of tutors and lived isolated lives. At 14 Reich found out that his mother was having an affair; he told his father about it, and his mother committed suicide. This event was to fill him with guilt for the rest of his life. In medical school he began to read psychoanalytic books: Stekel, Adler, Freud, and several others. Eventually he paid each a visit, in order to choose a mentor. Stekel, he said, sought to be impressive. Adler railed against Freud. Freud was natural, personable, impressive without trying to be. "Freud did not put on any airs. He spoke with me like a completely ordinary person. He had bright, intelligent eyes, which did not seek to penetrate another person's eyes in some sort of mantic pose, but simply looked at the world in an honest and truthful way" (Reich 1942, p. 31). Freud was impressed with Reich as well, welcoming him into the Vienna Psychoanalytic Society that same year (as the youngest member at that time). However, Freud refused to become Reich's training analyst; instead he was analyzed by Paul Federn, Isidor Sadger, and later Sandor Rado. His first wife, a former patient of his, reported that "it was the refusal of Freud to take Reich for personal analysis that led to the serious break. . . . Reich reacted to this rejection with deep depression" (Roazen 1984, p. 504).

Nevertheless, Reich quickly established himself as the wunderkind of the society, founding—with Freud's encouragement—the Vienna Seminar on Psychoanalytic Technique, and becoming its chairman in 1924, at the age of 27. Many thought him arrogant. At one of the private meetings at Freud's home, Freud seemed to want to put him in his place, saying to him, "You are the youngest here; would you close the door" (Roazen 1984, p. 504). The Vienna Seminar was supposedly founded in order to keep Reich within bounds. He was asked to study current technique to see where it had become misguided; instead, he came up with a new technique.

Reich began to notice that psychoanalysts were hesitant about encouraging patients to express their aggression. (Ferenczi had also noticed this.) He asserted that unconsciously analysts trained their patients to be polite; when patients were positive and cooperative, analysts responded positively, but when they were critical, analysts were silent. Reich explained, "It may be more agreeable to treat a polite patient than it is to treat an impolite, highly outspoken patient who might, for example, tell the analyst straight off that he is too young or too old, hasn't a beautifully furnished apartment or has an ugly wife, is not very bright or looks too Jewish, acts like a neurotic, should be undergoing analysis himself" (Reich 1933, p. 32). In response to this problem, Reich developed a method he called "character analysis," which suggested that an analyst draw out a patient's negative transference by confronting, through interpretation or other means, his characterological resistance. Characterological resistances, he felt, could be detected through body language.

His case history, "The Masochistic Character," provides an excellent example of this technique. Reich begins by describing the patient's initial complaints:

> He had been wholly incapable of work and socially apathetic since he was sixteen. In the sexual sphere, there was a severe masochistic perversion. He had never cared for intercourse with girls but had masturbated nightly for hours in the way characteristic of the pregenital libido structure. He would roll around on his stomach, squeeze his penis while fantasizing that a man or a woman was beating him with a whip. [Reich 1933, p. 238]

Whenever the patient was about to ejaculate, he would hold back and begin anew. He would go on all night in this way, and sometimes all day as well, until he would exhaustedly yield to an ejaculation in which "the semen did not spurt out rhythmically but merely flowed out" (p. 238). This had been going on for many years—how many Reich does not indicate. From this description, and others throughout the case history, the patient would appear to have been in his late 20s or early 30s.

"It's hard to drag myself out of bed in the morning," the patient told Reich. "But in spite of an overwhelming sense of guilt, I can't put a stop to this loafing in bed. Most of the time I feel like I'm in some kind of masochistic bog. The more I rebel against it, the more deeply I seem to become engulfed in it" (p. 239).

Reich's first impression of his patient was that he scarcely had the energy to keep himself going. He made an effort to appear composed and well bred, however, and often spoke of becoming a mathematician. When Reich asked him to elaborate on this ambition, it turned out to be a narcissistic fantasy of wandering through the woods of Germany for years, devising a mathematical system that would change the whole world. Reich lost no time in interpreting this façade. "That's the outer shell of your personality," he told him. "It serves as a compensation for your feeling of complete worthlessness, a feeling intimately related to and continually reproduced by your experience of masturbation as something dirty and squalid. From childhood on, the 'mathematician' has served to cover up the 'man of squalor'" (p. 239).

Once this façade had been relinquished, the patient's masochistic attitude appeared "in its full magnitude." Each session began with a complaint, followed by openly childish provocations. The patient would complain about not being able to control his "loafing in bed."

"Could you supplement that?" Reich would ask.

"No, I won't," the patient would reply in a spiteful, childish voice.

The patient would talk vaguely about some chronic, subjective feeling of being worthless.

"Could you give me a more precise formulation?" Reich would ask.

"No, I won't! No, I won't!"

The patient would mumble about life's unfairness.

"Could you say more about that?" Reich would ask.

"No, I won't! No, I won't! No, I won't!" (p. 239).

In this way, Reich notes, the patient attempted to reduce the therapist's efforts to absurdity. However, despite the patient's character resistances during the first few months, Reich began to learn some basic facts of his childhood. He discovered that a traumatic scene had occurred when the patient was 3 years old. He had been playing in the garden when he soiled his pants. Since guests were present, his "psychopathic, sadistic father" got upset, carried the boy into the house, threw him onto the bed, and whipped him. On the bed, the patient immediately turned over on his stomach to protect his genitals "and waited for the blows with great curiosity, which was mixed with anxiety" (p. 240).

Between the ages of 4 and 5 the patient went through a phase of violent stubbornness (similar to that experienced by the Wolf Man), during which he would have screaming and kicking fits. The most trivial incident could bring on the fits, which reduced the patient's parents to despair and rage. These fits would last until he was exhausted. (Later on in the analysis the patient was able to identify this period as the precursor of his masochism.) His first fantasies of being beaten appeared when he was 7; sometimes he would imagine he was being put across someone's knees and beaten, while at other times he would go into the bathroom, lock the door, and actually beat himself. Describing the way he masturbated from the age of 16 on, the patient said, "It was as if I were turned from my back to my stomach with screws" (p. 241). This posture, Reich theorized, represented an unconscious fixation back to the moment of the first beating, at the age of 3, when the child had first protected his genitals from his father; he had a compulsion to repeat this traumatic scene again and again, protecting his penis, assuaging his castration fear.

Reich further theorized that the apparent desire of the masochistic patient (and of all masochists) for punishment was actually a desire to relieve the dread of an even more severe punishment. "Masochistic self-punishment is *not* the execution of the feared punishment but rather the execution of a milder, substitute punishment. Thus, it represents a special kind of defense against punishment and anxiety" (p. 241). On another level this desire to be beaten is a homosexual desire to give himself in a passive-feminine way.

The first six months of the analysis was a struggle of wills. Reich would open the door of his office each day to find the patient standing there "with a sullen, pain-distorted, spongy face, the epitome of a bundle of misery" (p. 244). Reich himself would put on the same face, mocking the patient. Whenever the patient said, "No, I won't! No, I won't! No, I won't!" Reich would respond in a like manner. The struggle of wills heated up. One day the patient began kicking the couch as he shouted the usual "No, I won't!"

"Do that again," Reich said. "Let yourself go completely."

"I don't understand how anybody could ask me to do such a thing," the patient replied (p. 242).

Finally he plucked up his courage and began thrashing around on the couch, crying in defiance and bellowing "inarticulate animal-like sounds." While he screamed, Reich interpreted his behavior. When he told him that he defended his father merely to mask the hatred he felt for him, the patient became particularly violent. When he suggested that there was a rational justification for his hatred, he bellowed so horribly that neighbors became frightened. "We could not allow ourselves to be deterred by this, for we knew that this . . . was the only way he could reexperience his childhood neurosis completely and affectively—and not merely as a recollection" (p. 242).

The patient was stuck in the kicking and screaming stage that represented a reactivation of the stage he had gone through between the ages of 4 and 5. He had wanted to provoke his parents; now he wanted to provoke Reich. But why? Reich's initial interpretation was that the patient's provocation was a desire to make the analyst/parent respond cruelly, in order to justify his uncon-scious hatred of him. It was as though the patient were saying, "You are a bad person; you don't like me; on the contrary, you treat me horribly; I am right in hating you" (p. 243).

As time went on it dawned on the patient that he could not reduce Reich to a frenzy as he had his parents. His behavior took on a different meaning: he began to enjoy letting himself go in the analysis. He consumed the entire hour with childish screaming and kicking. Reich interpreted to him that originally his provoca-tion had a secondary goal of testing how far he could go before his parents would withdraw their love and attention and switch to punishment. Moreover, "by continually conducting himself in a disagreeable fashion, he neutralized the steadily flowing fear of punishment; therefore, being bad was a source of pleasure" (p. 244). To break through this new resistance, Reich himself joined the action. One day he lay on the floor and began kicking and screaming along with the patient. The patient gawked at Reich, stopped his kicking and screaming, and began to laugh. "The breakthrough had been effected, but only temporarily," Reich explains. "I continued these procedures until he himself began to analyze. Now we were able to continue" (p. 244).

Having confronted the patient's character resistances and forced him out of his defensive posture, Reich was able to get him to cooperate with him in the work of analyzing. Reich went back to the standard analytic technique of interpreting whatever mate-rial came up. The patient lay on the couch and free-associated; Reich sat behind him. (Later he would change his format and begin to sit face-to-face with patients.) This phase of the treatment took about three years more.

First they analyzed the patient's pattern of provoking the people closest to him. Reich speculates that a "deep disappoint-ment in love" lay beneath the provocations. "The masochist is especially fond of provoking those objects through whom he suffered a disappointment" (p. 243). In addition, the provocation was his way of asking for love. He needed proofs of love to reduce his inner tension. "This demand for love was directly dependent upon the degree of tension produced by his unsatisfactory form of masturbation" (p. 244). His complaints were an attempt to gain sympathy. If he did not get sympathy, he would become spiteful. Reich further speculates that masochistic characters have a predisposition to anxiety. This anxiety represents a fear of losing love. Because they fear losing love, they take desperate measures to prevent this from happening; but instead of preventing the loss of love, these measures end up bringing about such a loss. "The masochistic character seeks to bind the inner tension and threat of anxiety by an *inadequate* method, namely by *courting love through provocation and defiance*" (p. 246). In this way, masochists torture the people they love, and eventually lose them, which in turn keeps them in a state of anxiety, sapping them of their energy.

Masochists also have a desire for contact with others, Reich asserts, especially for "warmth of the skin." This is why they have fantasies of being pinched, rubbed, whipped, tied up, roughed up, and of anything else which causes their skin to bleed and makes them burn inside. Their desire is not for pain, but for contact, and for the burning sensation. Masochists constantly feel cold because of the chronic contracting of their muscles and veins; rough bodily contact is the antidote to this. The coldness they feel is a replication of an infantile memory of being abandoned, left alone in the cold, unprotected. And the ultimate antidote is the physical contact with another person in sexual intercourse, culminating in orgasm, which serves to change blood circulation and bring about "peripheral vessel dilation and discharge of tension in the center (splanchnic vessels)" (p. 248).

Further analysis revealed that the patient had been on the one hand overindulged and seduced by his mother, and on the other sexually rejected by her. He was allowed to lie in bed with her, embrace her, and press his body against hers, until he was 16. But if he expressed interest in exploring further possibilities, he was met by the "full severity of parental authority" (p. 249). Her behavior, combined with the punitive behavior of his father, served to keep him fixated at the anal stage.

From the ages of 3 to 6 the patient developed a fear of the bathroom; he was afraid that an animal would crawl up his anus. He began to hold on to his bowel movements, which in turn aroused a fear that he would soil his pants. This then led to a fear of being beaten by his father, and of castration. It also got him special attention from his mother, who took a special interest in his bowel movements and accompanied him to the bathroom until the age of 10. "His mother was pleased with and took care of his bowel functions, whereas the father beat him for it. In this way, his Oedipus complex became predominantly anchored in the anal zone" (p. 258).

The patient also had a conflict about exhibiting himself and about releasing his semen. One day he showed Reich his penis and asked, "Is this erosion on my skin a sign of an infection?" It was clear to Reich that the intent behind this was exhibitionism. It turned out that when he reached the phallic stage, his mother had strictly forbidden him to exhibit his genitals. (As an adult, during his rare encounters with women he did not want them to see him naked.) This fear of exhibiting himself had several consequences. It caused him to depreciate himself, in part to gain sympathy and in part so that he would not stand out; to stand out aroused the fear of being castrated. The conflict about exhibitionism also led to problems with getting and maintaining an erection. When they had analyzed this, the patient began to develop a new career: he became a photographer. Eventually, as the analysis came nearer to its termination, he became successful. Photography became a sublimation of his wish to peep at his mother and a displacement of his wish to exhibit himself.

His tendency to hold back his semen was traced to the times when he had slept with his mother. On occasion he would quietly masturbate as he lay beside her, but he was afraid of ejaculating. He became convinced that if he did so, his mother would become pregnant. On other occasions he could ejaculate only if he had a fantasy that his mother was beating him; Reich interpreted this to mean that he could only ejaculate if his mother took responsibility for it, and at the same time exonerated him. The function of the beating fantasy was, "Beat me so that, without making myself guilty, I can release myself" (p. 265).

He had a fear of vaginas. They digusted him; he viewed them as a mire of swarming snakes and vermin, which would nip off the tip of his penis. When, as the result of the analysis, he got over that fear, he developed a fear of rivals, and the feeling that his penis was smaller than theirs; whenever a rival appeared he would retreat from his relationship with a woman. All of this was connected with his unresolved castration fear and oedipal guilt. As this was analyzed, his relationships with women began to improve.

However, his attempts at establishing intimate relations with women were, in the beginning, fraught with difficulties. At the core of his difficulties was a "disturbance of the pleasure mechanism. He *avoided every increase of the sensation of pleasure*" (p. 263). Reich interpreted this as a fear of disintegrating or melting. "It is impossible to allow these sensations to pour into one—it is wholly unbearable," the patient told him (p. 263). Orgasm itself was seen as a disintegration and as a punishment, or as an act that might bring about the feared punishment of the oedipal father. As the patient understood this, he was able to tolerate more pleasure, and to maintain his erections with women. By the end of the treatment, after many relapses, he had achieved a measure of orgasmic potency.

Reich concludes that Freud's assumption that masochism stems from a primary biological tendency toward self-destruction (a death instinct) is unsubstantiated. Originally, Freud had maintained that masochism was the result of environmental frustration. Masochistic suffering derived from the outer world, from the family, and from society. In the light of the new "death instinct" theory, masochistic suffering was said to derive "from the biological will to suffer." Reich points out that in Freud's new theory human suffering is said to be ineradicable because destructive impulses and impulses striving toward self-annihilation cannot be mastered, whereas his earlier formulation of the psychic conflict, "on the other hand, leads to a critique of the social system" (pp. 232–233).

Freud's original formulation was that sadism (aggression) was originally directed to the outer world—to the primary object that frustrated the infant's oral, anal, or genital drives; this sadism was then turned against the self when it too was frustrated by the primary objects. It then became masochism. The frustrating object was introjected by the superego, and the superego became a representative both of the person responsible for the original frustration and of society. "The neurosis is brought on by the conflict between an ego which strives for pleasure and an outer world which frustrates these ego strivings," Reich paraphrases Freud. "The superego retains its power on the basis of the repeated experience that sexual pleasure is something punishable" (p. 259). Reich asserts that his work with masochistic patients, such as the one described in this case, essentially validates Freud's original thesis.

Reich saw the treatment of masochism as divided into three tasks. The first task was to reduce masochism back to its original condition of sadism, by attacking the masochistic character resistance. The second task was to help the patient work through his pregenital blocks, so that he could advance to genitality. The third was the analytic dissolution of the anal and phallic "spastic attitude," which experiences pleasure as unpleasure. Reich concludes that curing a masochistic patient is one of the analyst's most difficult tasks, but "reincorporating the problem of masochism into the framework of the pleasure–unpleasure principle" will facilitate its solution, "which was delayed by the hypothesis of the death instinct" (p. 269).

After publishing *Character Analysis* and breaking from the International Psychoanalytic Association in 1934 (Jones had asked him to choose between psychoanalysis and politics), Reich moved further and further away from the psychoanalytic establishment. He left Vienna to live in Scandinavia, where his abrasive manner soon stirred up another controversy. He then moved to the United States and set up a laboratory in Rangley, Maine. There he became the leader of a cult, creating a new science he called "orgonomy." It had its own terminology, at the core of which was his discovery of "physical orgone energy" and "orgone energy accumulators." The latter were upright boxes in which he placed patients, attempting to heal them of physical ailments such as cancer as well as mental illness. Since he required patients to be naked when they sat in these boxes, his experiments aroused still more controversy and set the U.S. Food and Drug Administration against him.

Angered at what he saw as a breach of his scientific freedom, he refused to appear at an FDA hearing. He was then charged with contempt. At his trial he appeared to be mentally disturbed (Roazen 1984). He refused to have a lawyer speak for him and delivered a diatribe against the U.S. government. He was sentenced to a short term in federal prison, where he died in 1957. His writings were confiscated by the U.S. government and were unofficially censored for several years after his death.

Interpretation

Although he has come to be regarded as the "madman" of psychoanalysis, Reich's work on psychoanalytic technique, particularly with respect to the handling of character resistances or, as he sometimes put it, "defensive armoring," is still considered an important addition to psychoanalysis by most psychoanalysts and psychotherapists. He was one of the first psychoanalysts to criticize Freud's death instinct theory, which is unacceptable to most analysts today. His paper about the masochistic character is still regarded as a classic. In addition, several of his analytic trainees were influenced by his ideas: Erich Fromm wrote widely about the effects of the social system on the individual psyche; Clara Thompson broadened the meaning of penis envy to incorporate envy of the male role in society; A. S. O'Neill founded the famous Summerhill School in England, incorporating Reich's notions about sexual freedom; and Alexander Lowen and Elsworth F. Baker founded schools of therapy grounded in Reichian principles.

Some psychoanalysts applaud Reich's emphasis on character analysis but not his method. Fenichel (1935) agrees with Reich that the main focus in analysis should go to transference interpretation, but objects to Reich's aggressive way of "shattering the armor plating." He asserts that Reich is in error when he says that the only correct method is the consistent working through of character resistances. It overlooks the fact that if a patient experiences this kind of analysis, which invariably arouses anxiety, he or she may develop a transference resistance, which would be even more superficial than the character resistance. Sterba (1953) agrees with Fenichel on this point; furthermore, he believes that not every transference is a resistance. He questions Reich's suspicion that every positive transference at the beginning of treatment is a façade, asserting that there are times when a patient really does feel positive toward the therapist, and such positive feelings are useful in establishing an alliance.

Thompson asserted in 1950 that *Character Analysis* was "still among the best practical guides on the subject [of resistance analysis] for the student" (p. 189). Indeed, she claims that Reich "out-Freuds Freud" as far as stressing the libido is concerned, praising his advocacy of a "frontal attack" on the character resistance and noting that it provides analysts with the first effective approach to the analysis of character structure. She adds, however, that most analysts are not as active as Reich, preferring to treat character trends "like other neurotic symptoms. Insight into them is to be presented to the patient only when he is ready for it and can therefore utilize the knowledge constructively" (p. 190).

Kohut (1971) notes that Reich was one of the first to call attention to narcissistic resistances. Spotnitz and Meadow (1976) praise Reich's attention to the resolution of resistance and the analysis of transference, particularly his suggestion that analysts not try to nip transference resistances in the bud (especially negative transferences), but to allow them to develop fully so that the full affects which are transferred can be used for the treatment. They also note that one of Reich's dicta was that if the patient was left to determine for himself the number and timing of interventions, the transference would unfold; this is the approach of the modern psychoanalytic school. (When Reich's work with the masochistic patient is viewed in this light, one must question whether he allowed the patient in this instance to determine the number and timing of the interventions, particularly during the first six months. Reich seemed overly aggressive and quick to attack the patient's character resistances. However, it might be argued that in this instance the patient's provocations called for such interventions, and an analyst who ignores such provocations might be silently forestalling the negative transference.)

Jacobson (1971) also appreciates Reich's improvements in technique, particularly in allowing the transference to develop to the extent that "intensive emotional responses" are invoked in the patient. "Even though we now know that the production of affective storms is often a therapeutically undesirable side effect," she observes, "the handling of the emotional attitudes and reactions of our patients is still one of the central problems in our clinical work" (p. 3).

Gill (1982) asserts that Reich "inaugurated a major chapter in psychoanalytic technique by arguing that resistance is primarily lodged in the character and that the therapist's interpretations should be first directed to that resistance" (p. 34). However, he makes a distinction between character as a defense in *intrapsychic* terms and character resistance expressed interpersonally in the transference. "Character defense has concomitant expressions in the transference; these are the *resistances*, which, in my opinion, should receive priority in interpretation" (p. 35).

Reik (1941) generally agreed with Reich about the psychology of masochism. "On some points no abyss separates my opinion from W. Reich's, but what is more, a nuance" (p. 164). He cites Reich's observations of the defiance element in masochism, the use of provocation in grasping for love, the relationship between masochism and exhibitionism, and the tendency toward self-depreciation. However, he differs with Reich about the death instinct theory. He feels that the death instinct theory does not rule out psychological factors. "My explanation of the phenomena of masochism is restricted to their psychological aspects. It considers them as results of psychic processes, which does not mean it denies the existence of biological factors" (p. 199). My own view (Schoenewolf 1989) of the death instinct—I prefer to call it the aggressive instinct—also accommodates both the biological and psychological; I see the biological as primary, and the psychological as secondary aggression.

Reik also disagrees about the cause of masochism. Reich felt that the father's punishment when the boy was 3 was the originating trauma. Reik cites similar cases and alludes to Freud's "A Child is Being Beaten" (1919), in which a child remembers not himself or herself being beaten but a brother or sister's beating. Reik speculates that even in cases where there is such a traumatic punishment, the child usually provokes it because of precipitating factors earlier in development.

Although Ferenczi (1933) did not write about masochism, his two-phase theory about the etiology of severe narcissism probably comes closer to explaining the cause of masochism than did Reich. If, during the earliest infancy, parents behave in such a way as to over- or undergratify an infant's needs, the child becomes hurt and angry. If the child cries out for a hug, a smile, or a reassurance, and instead is ignored, rebuked, or deceived, the child's anger is turned back on the self. It is the cumulative effect of these moments over time that causes the child to become masochistic. And these moments can begin right after birth.

Thompson (1950) takes issue with "much of Reich's thinking" in his paper on "The Masochistic Character," but basically supports his dismissal of the death instinct theory and his view of the relationship between character structure and social order. "His seeing the character structure as created by the social order is one of the early indications of the developing interest in cultural factors in neurotic difficulty" (p. 191).

The debate about Reich and his work continues. There are many psychoanalysts who will not quote Reich in their papers, though privately they might acknowledge his contributions to technique and to the understanding of character. He succumbed to madness—a form of paranoid schizophrenia—at the end of his life, and his work is still stigmatized. Like the masochistic character, he too could be quite provocative, and his work is permeated with a crusading quality, an "us" against "them" tenor, that is bound to offend. He was a fighter for genitality—the full, healthy expression of one's sexuality—and against *homo normalis*, whom he accused of bringing about an "emotional plague" through blocked sexuality and envy of those whose sexuality was healthy; he was a friend to schizophrenics, who, he felt, saw through the hypocrisy of *homo normalis* and were then driven crazy by him—a sentiment later expressed by Laing (1969); and he opposed orthodox psychiatrists and psychoanalysts, who he perceived as being representatives of *homo normalis*, and therefore unconsciously committed to maintaining the established order of things.

Stolorow and Atwood (1979) advance the theory that Reich's obsession with sexual freedom and crusade against *homo normalis* was an acting out of unresolved feelings about his mother's suicide. They assume that in betraying his mother's unfaithfulness, Reich was enacting an identification with his father's authoritarian and puritanical values. "Since in acting on the basis of a narrow code of sexual morality he was responsible for the death of the one person he loved above all others, an immense burden of pain and guilt must have been generated. What could be a better way to atone for his fateful act of betrayal than devoting himself to the eradication of all those values and ways of thinking which had motivated him?" (p. 121). They point out that Reich idealized his mother after her death, while derogating his father, implying on occasion that he was not really his father's son. The anti-sexual death forces (*homo normalis*) envisioned by Reich were, according to them, Reich's guilty self (the one identified with his father) projected onto the external world, while the life-affirming, sexually free forces (orgone energy) corresponded to his idealized image of his mother and himself.

Leaving his madness aside, Reich's message was not too different from that of several other psychoanalysts. Laing (1969), Ferenczi (1933), Balint (1968), Sechehaye (1956), Rosen (1962), Little (1981), Guntrip (1969), Winnicott (1947), Fromm-Reichmann (1950), Jacobson (1971), and Spotnitz (1985)—to name a few—all believed, as Reich did, that narcissistic patients could only be cured if the therapist was willing to deviate from standard procedure, gratify some of their narcissistic needs, encourage the verbalization of their aggression, and allow them to work through their deepest infantile feelings of rage, hurt, and longing. Classical psychoanalysts, according to Reich, are themselves blocked and spend their sessions trying to understand the minute workings of the ego, id, and super-ego rather than seeing the patient's deeper and more obvious character symptoms. Such therapists, Reich asserts, tend to work only with patients of the *homo normalis* variety, and they look in askance at anybody who is not doing classical analysis.

Theories about masochism and its treatment continue to evolve. Most analysts today recognize that one seldom meets a purely masochistic character type such as that described by Reich. Indeed, masochism is a feature of all character types, from neurotic to borderline to psychotic, since all forms of mental illness bring about additional suffering and are to an extent self-destructive. And even today, there is no one universally accepted definition of the masochistic process, and masochistic patients are still recognized among the more difficult to cure.

One has to admire Reich's willingness to try "heroic" measures, such as lying down on the floor to kick and scream with his patient. Not everybody can do such things, and when such an intervention is attempted there is a higher risk that it will fail. One also has to admire his clear, direct writing, and his originality. While Freud's method began at the surface and worked its way inward, Reich went directly to the deepest layers of character, trying to get energy moving, muscles relaxed, libido flowing. Freud was a city boy, an intellectual, a sophisticate; Reich was a country boy, a sensualist, and an *enfant terrible*. Freud's method was intellectual and urbane. Reich's was sensual, daring, physical. It was this accent on the physical that may have been his most important contribution, along with his capacity to relate on an emotional level to his patients.

"The schizoid person sees through hypocrisy and does not hide the fact," Reich once wrote. "He has an excellent grasp of emotional realities, in sharp contradistinction to *homo normalis*" (1933, p. 401). Was Reich the schizoid person? Was Freud *homo normalis*? Was Reich's lifelong battle against this somewhat abstract foe an enactment of his bitterness toward Freud? Or was his battle with Freud a reenactment of a similar battle with his father and with his own disowned "bad" self? If so, in this as in so many cases, revenge, not accident, is the real mother of invention.

11

EXISTENTIAL ANALYSIS

Ludwig Binswanger and Ellen West
(1944-1945)

When *"Der Fall Ellen West"* (The Fall of Ellen West) was first published in three consecutive volumes of *Schweizer Archiv für Neurologie and Psychiatrie* (1944-1945), it stunned the European psychoanalytic community with its radical existential perspective and its haunting beauty. The first part of this 130-page case history reads as if it were a novel rather than a scientific paper, while the main part is a fairly dense elucidation of the principles of *Daseinsanalyze*, or existential analysis. This case was later published in 1958 in English, sending off shock waves in America and England as well.

Ludwig Binswanger was born in Kreuzlingen, Switzerland, in 1881, into a family of distinguished physicians. After completing his medical studies in Zurich (under Jung), he succeeded his father (and grandfather) as director of Sanatorium Bellevue in Kreuzlingen. On March 6, 1907, he attended his first meeting of Freud's Vienna Psycho-Analytical Society, and then went into analysis with Freud. He later reminisced that during this analysis, "Freud's interpretation of . . . [a] dream, which I found rather unconvincing . . . was that it indicated a wish to marry his eldest daughter, but, at the same time, contained a repudiation of this wish . . ." (Binswanger 1957, p. 2). Roazen (1984) observes that Freud frequently claimed to discern, both in his students and in regular patients such as the Rat Man, a desire to marry one of his daughters. In his book, Binswanger recalls his many visits to Freud's home, and the three-day visit Freud made to his sanatorium on Lake Constance, Switzerland, noting that his friendship with Freud was the only instance of Freud's continuing a relationship with a colleague who had deviated radically from his views. "You, quite different from so many others," Freud once wrote Binswanger, "have not let it happen that your intellectual development—which has taken you further and further away from my influence—should destroy our personal relations, and you do not know how much good such fineness does to one" (Binswanger 1957, p. 10). Whether this friendship survived because, as May (1983) observed, the conflict between the two men was like the "proverbial battle between the elephant and the walrus," or because of Binswanger's diplomatic attitude (for which Freud mildly chided him), is a matter of debate. At any rate, survive it did. Unfortunately, Freud died five years before Binswanger published the Ellen West case, thereby missing Binswanger's most famous and controversial work.

After completing his major book on existential analysis, *Basic Forms and Cognition of Human Existence* (1943), Binswanger wanted to demonstrate his views through a case history. He went back to the archives of the sanatorium of which he was director to select the case of "Ellen West," a talented young writer and poet who reminds one of Sylvia Plath. She had come to the sanatorium in 1918, when psychoanalysis was still being formulated. Binswanger uses the case to contrast the crude methods of that day with the way Ellen West would have been understood by existential psychoanalysis. At the time, her long illness was variously diagnosed as obsessional neurosis, manic-depression, and schizophrenia, while today her condition would be diagnosed as severe anorexia nervosa. Binswanger stays clear of psychiatric labels, however, wanting to relate to her as a human being on her own terms.

He begins by providing background information about the "human individuality" to whom he gave the name Ellen West. She was the only daughter of a father "for whom her love and veneration know no bounds" (Binswanger 1944, p. 237), a stiffly formal, reserved, and willful man, who suffered from nocturnal depressions and states of fear. Her mother was a kindly, suggestible, nervous woman, who underwent a three-year depression when she became engaged to be married. Ellen had an older and a younger brother. The younger brother was admitted to a psychiatric clinic because of suicidal ideas. Her father's sister became mentally ill on her wedding day, and of his five brothers, one shot himself, a second committed suicide in some other manner (details are lacking), a third was "eccentric," and the other two fell ill of dementia arteriosclerosis and died of strokes. The mother's mother was said to be manic-depressive and to come from a family "which produced many outstandingly capable men but also many psychotics, one of whom I have treated (an eminent scholar)" (p. 238).

When she was 9 months old, Ellen reportedly refused milk, and was then fed "meat-broth." In later years she could never tolerate milk at all. As she grew up she continued to like meat, but there were certain vegetables and desserts that she did not like. If they were forced on her, she resisted them mightily. Binswanger sees this as an early act of renunciation. Little else was known about her early childhood; during her two periods of psychoanalytic treatment in later life she reported few memories about her first ten years. Defiance seems to have been a strong character trait:

> According to her own statements and those of her parents, Ellen was a very lively but headstrong and violent child. It is said that she often defied an order of her parents for hours and did not carry it out even then. Once she was shown a bird's nest, but she insisted that it was not a bird's nest and nothing would make her change her

opinion. Even as a child, she said, she had had days when every-thing seemed empty to her and she suffered under a pressure which she herself did not understand. [p. 238]

At the age of 10 she moved with her family from her home-land, which Binswanger does not identify, to Europe, where she went to a school for girls. She could "weep for hours" if she did not rank first in her favorite subjects—German and history. She never wanted to miss school, even when her doctor ordered it, fearing she might fall behind. She was said to be a tomboy and to have sucked her thumb until her 16th year. She preferred to wear trousers at a time when it was considered highly inappropriate to do so, and her motto was: *aut Caesar aut nihil* (Either Caesar or nothing)! In a poem written when she was 17, she expresses the ardent desire to be a boy, to be a soldier, to fear no foe, and "die joyously, sword in hand." At around that time she suddenly gave up her thumb-sucking and trousers to devote herself to her first infatuation, which lasted two years. Binswanger does not say who the object of her infatuation was.

Other poems from her 17th year already showed a marked variability of mood. "Now my heart beats with exultant joy," goes one poem, "now the sky is darkened, the winds blow weirdly, and the ship of life sails on unguided, not knowing whither to direct its keel" (p. 239). In another poem "the wind rushes about her ears," and she wants it to cool her feverish brow; when she runs blindly against this wind, unconcerned with pro-priety, she feels as if she's stepping out of a confining tomb or flying through the air in an "uncontrollable urge to freedom"; she believes that she must achieve something great and mighty, but as she flies her gaze falls back onto the world, and a saying comes to her: "Man, in small things make your world." Horrified, her soul cries out, "Fight on" (p. 239). In still another poem from her late adolescence, entitled "Kiss Me Dead," she writes of the sun sink-ing into the ocean like a ball of fire, a mist over the sea and beach, and a pain coming over her. She asks, "Is there no rescue any-more?" and calls upon the cold, grim Sea-King to come to her, "take her into his arms in ardent love-lust, and kiss her to death" (p. 239).

During this period of her life she considered herself to be "called to achieve something special." She read voraciously and occupied herself with social problems, feeling deeply her own social privilege in contrast to the plight of the masses, drawing up plans for improving the lot of poor people everywhere. Upon reading a novel about a disillusioned idealist called *Niels Lyhne*, popular with young people at that time, her attitude changed from deep religiosity to atheism.

Her eighteenth year was full of praise for the blessings of work. In her diary she calls work "the opiate for suffering and grief" and says that if there were no work they would have to enlarge the cemeteries for those who went to death of their own accord. "When all the joints of the world threaten to fall apart, when the light of our happiness is extinguished and our pleasure in life lies wilting, only one thing saves us from madness: work. Then we throw ourselves into a sea of duties as into Lethe, and the roar of its waves is to drown out the death-knell pealing in our heart" (p. 240). She also writes of "great, undying fame"—and of her name still ringing out on the lips of mankind after hundreds of years, so she will "not have lived in vain" (p. 240).

Her mood was lifted by a journey across the ocean with her parents when she was 19. Calling this period "the happiest and most harmless time of my life," she writes in her diary of "floods of light" and "golden hands" resting on grainfields, villages, and valleys, and only the mountains standing "in darkness." When she returned to Europe later that year, her spirits were still high as she developed an interest in riding horses. Soon she was vying with experienced riders in jumping competitions; as with everything else, she cultivated horseback riding with great intensity, as if her very life depended on it. Her mood remained upbeat as she turned 20, her diary replete with poems of "the wild ecstasy of life," of the sun standing high, spring gales blowing, her blood "racing and roaring," youthful zest bursting her breast asunder, stretching "her young, strong body," as she wondered how one could lag behind and lock oneself "into the tomb of a house" (p. 241). She yearns for the man of her dreams:

> Oh, if "He" would come now. . . . He must be tall, and strong, and have a soul as pure and unblemished as the morning light! He must not play life nor dream it, but live it, in all its seriousness and all its pleasure. He must be able to be happy, to enjoy me and my children, and to take joy in sunshine and work. Then I would give him all my love and all my strength. [p. 241]

Toward the end of her twentieth year, she took another trip abroad. She became engaged to a "romantic foreigner," but at her father's wish she broke the engagement. On the return trip she wrote an essay called "On the Woman's Calling." In her diaries she writes that her god is "the god of life and of joy, of strength and hope" and that she is filled with a consuming thirst to learn. She has already, she says, had a glimpse of the "secret of the universe" (p. 242). She did not seem to mind her father's breaking her engagement, but soon afterward she began to feel a new dread for the first time, a dread of getting fat.

At 21 her mood became depressive. She was constantly tormented about getting fat, constantly on a diet, so that her friends began to tease her about it. She was highly nervous and took long hikes into the woods, never stopping to rest. Once, on a hike with her friends, when they stopped to view a beautiful scene, she continued to circle around them. In her poems she writes of feeling absolutely worthless and useless and being in dread of everything, "of the dark and of the sun, of stillness and of noise" (p. 242). She reports that "grim distress sits at her grave, ashly pale—sits and stares, does not flinch nor budge; the birds grow mute and flee, the flowers wilt before its ice-cold breath." Death no longer appears to her as terrible, not a man with a scythe but "a glorious woman, white asters in her dark hair, large eyes, dream-deep and gray." She welcomes death. "Such a delicious stretching out and dozing off. Then it's over. . . . Back of every word I really hide a yawn" (p. 242).

She began to write about a revolution. "I will make no concessions," she says, asserting that the existing social order is "rotten, rotten down to the root, dirty and mean." She is a "human being with red blood and a woman with a quivering heart" who cannot breathe in this atmosphere of hypocrisy and cowardice. "No, no, I am not talking claptrap. I am not thinking about the liberation of the soul; I mean the real, tangible liberation of the people from the chains of their oppressors. Shall I express it still more clearly? I want a revolution, a great uprising to spread over the entire world and overthrow the whole social order" (p. 243). She began to work on a pet project—the establishment of children's reading-rooms, which she saw during her trip to America. Before long, though, this project no longer satisfied her.

In the fall of her twenty-third year, after an unpleasant love affair with a riding teacher, she broke down for the first time. Now her dread of getting fat was accompanied by a great longing for sweets that became most intense when she was with people. She began to study for an examination to enter a university, gave that up after a while, instead took an examination to become a teacher, and started auditing courses. She fell in love with a student, and became engaged, but her parents demanded a temporary separation, so she retreated to a seaside resort and sank into a severe depression. The next year she remained depressed, took long hikes, and swallowed thirty-six to forty-eight thyroid tablets a day. In her diary she writes:

> I'd like to die just as the birdling does
> That splits his throat in highest jubilation;
> And not to live as the worm on earth lives on,
> Becoming old and ugly, dull and dumb!
> No, feel for once how forces in me kindle,
> And wildly be consumed in my own fire. [p. 246]

The following year she made another trip overseas, where a physician diagnosed her as having Graves' disease, a condition of exophthalmic hyperthyroid goiter. She stayed in bed for six weeks, rapidly gained weight, and wept about her fate. By the time she returned home, her weight had jumped to 165 pounds, and shortly afterward she broke her engagement to the student. She entered a public sanatorium during the spring, studied gardening in the summer, and enrolled at the university again in the fall. Then a cousin took an interest in her, and she fell in love with him. At 26 she made plans to marry her cousin, but for two more years she vacillated between her cousin and the student, with whom she had resumed her relationship. At 28 she married her cousin.

From the day of her marriage to the day of her arrival at Binswanger's Kreuzlingen Sanatorium on January 14, 1918, at the age of 33, her condition steadily deteriorated. At 29 her menstruation ceased, and she was torn between a desire to have a child and the dread of getting fat. At 30 and 31 she became intensely interested in social work, slept twelve hours a day, took laxatives to keep her weight down, and often went out on the street in a feverish state in hopes of catching pneumonia. At 32 she increased her dosage of laxatives, using sixty to seventy tablets a night, causing tortured vomiting at night and violent diarrhea by day. Later that year she underwent her first analysis with "a young and sensitive analyst." The analyst told her that her main goal was "the subjugation of all other people" (p. 250), an interpretation she felt was "marvelously correct." Nevertheless, she soon tired of analysis. When she was 33 the analysis was terminated "for external reasons." Later that year she attempted suicide twice, once by taking fifty-six tablets of Somnacetin, and once by taking twenty tablets of a barbiturate compound. She began treatment with a second analyst, who told her she had a father-complex and described her eating problem as "anal-erotic," equating eating with getting pregnant: "Eating = being fertilized = pregnant = getting fat" (p. 260). Before entering the sanatorium, she was diagnosed by Kraeplin as having melancholia, and her body weight had fallen to 102 pounds. In her diary she writes, "I am surrounded by enemies. Wherever I turn, a man stands there with drawn sword. As on the stage: The unhappy one rushes toward the exit; stop! an armed man confronts him. He rushes to a second, to a third exit.

All in vain. He is surrounded, he can no longer get out. He collapses in despair" (p. 258).

She remained at the Kreuzlingen Sanatorium with her husband from January 14 to March 30, 1918. She saw Binswanger daily. While at the sanatorium, her dreams were always about food and death. In one dream, war breaks out and she goes into a field joyful that she will soon die, glad that she can now eat anything she wants. In another she dreams she orders goulash but only wants a small portion; she complains to her old nursemaid that people are torturing her and says she wants to "set herself on fire in the forest" (p. 263).

On one occasion she offered a farmer 50,000 francs if he would shoot her quickly. She continued to take laxatives but lied to her doctors about it. She complained that all she wanted was to be left alone to die. Binswanger, impressed with her will to die, had her husband gather material on this theme, which had permeated her existence. Even as a child, the husband reported, Ellen had been fascinated by suicide. While ice skating, she had thought it would be interesting if the ice broke and she fell through. During her riding period she performed foolhardy tricks, once falling and breaking her clavicle, and fantasized about having a fatal accident. Later she stood naked on her balcony after taking a hot bath, hoping to catch pneumonia, and still later she stood in front of a streetcar.

Again and again she demanded that she be discharged from the sanatorium, so that she could kill herself. She accused the doctors of being sadists who took pleasure in tormenting her. She expressed the feeling that a ghost was stalking her in order to kill her. In her diary she writes that she is only waiting until "insanity comes and, shaking its black locks, seizes me and hurls me into the yawning abyss" (p. 264). Binswanger gave her two options: she could either be put into the locked ward, or be released in her husband's custody. Her husband asked if there were any chance of cure. Binswanger shook his head, but suggested that they call in two other experts for second and third opinions on the matter. He also advised the husband that if she were released, there was a very good chance that she would commit suicide.

A consultation was scheduled on March 24 with Bleuler and another, unnamed psychiatrist. Bleuler diagnosed her as a schizophrenic, and the other man labeled her as having a "psychopathic constitution progressively unfolding." All three definitely agreed that there was no reliable therapy available for her. Binswanger notes, "If shock therapy had existed then, it would have offered a temporary way out of the dilemma and a certain postponement, but it would certainly have changed nothing in the final result" (p. 266). Finally, the three psychiatrists resolved to give in to Ellen's request for a discharge.

On returning home, she found that life with her relatives made her feel worse. For two days she fasted, hiked, and took laxatives. On the third day she woke up "transformed." She ate butter and sugar for breakfast, gulped down a lunch that completely sated her, and had a dessert of chocolate creams and Easter eggs. In the afternoon she went for a walk with her husband and read poems by Rilke, Goethe, and Tennyson, saying she was in a "positively festive mood." That evening she took a lethal dose of poison. By morning she was dead. It was reported she looked "as she had never looked in life—calm and happy and peaceful" (p. 267).

In the existential analysis of this case, Binswanger begins by rejecting the use of labels, including the label "Ellen West." "On the basis of the life-history, her specific name loses its function of a mere verbal label for a human individuality" (p. 267). He adds that the conception of a human individuality depends on the "varying standpoint and viewpoint of the person or group making it. Love alone and the imagination originating from it, can rise above this single point of regard" (p. 268).

He interprets Ellen's "peculiarity and stubbornness in regard to taking food"—which began at 9 months when she first refused milk and continued until her death—as a peculiarity of "sensory communication" and "behavior toward the world." In refusing milk, Ellen separated from, rather than united with, the *Umwelt* (around-world, or environment), setting it in opposition to herself. "Concurrently with this opposition to the *Umwelt*, there may already have existed a resistance to the *Mitwelt* (with-world, or fellow humans), a resistance to those persons who tried to oppose Ellen's idiosyncrasy" (p. 270). When Ellen refused to acknowledge that a bird's nest was a bird's nest, repudiating something recognized as obvious by the *Mitwelt*, this demonstrated that she also failed to unite successfully with the *Mitwelt*, and that the "upbuilding of the *Eigenwelt* (own-world, self) here proceeds in sharp opposition to the *Mitwelt*" (p. 270). As a result, the *Mitwelt* makes judgments about her: she is defiant, stubborn, overly ambitious, violent. Binswanger concludes that Ellen's experiencing of the *Umwelt* and *Mitwelt* as oppositional forces, and her "rigid assertion" of the *Eigenwelt* in contrast to these forces, "constricts the span of the existential possibilities and reduces this span to limited sectors of possible behavior" (p. 271).

But it is not only her opposition to the *Mitwelt* and *Umwelt* that constricted, oppressed, and emptied out Ellen's life, but also her opposition to her "world-of-fate," her role as a woman. She played only boys' games, wore trousers, and wanted to be a soldier until she was 16, and she also sucked her thumb until that age. Binswanger sees a connection between these two factors. "With her self-willed 'separation' between the *Eigenwelt*, on the one hand, and the *Um*-, *Mit*-, and fate-world, on the other, goes a certain own-worldly self-sufficiency, expansiveness, and aggressiveness. There is evidence for the former in her thumbsucking, strikingly protracted until her 16th year, for the latter too, in her 'ambitious' all-or-nothing principle: *aut Caesar aut nihil*" (pp. 271–272).

It is only love, Binswanger asserts, "the dual mode of existence," the "I–Thou" relationship, which can transform defiance, stubbornness, and the ambition and "infinite unrest of existence" born of defiance and stubbornness. It is only authenticity that could save her, but such authenticity evaded her. Instead, her defiance and stubbornness led her further and further toward isolation, dread, and death, and were in turn directly related to her ideals, social betterment and revolution, and to her fear of getting fat.

Her oppositional situation in turn affected her mode of *Dasein* (being there, being-in-the-world). Her existence did not stand "with both feet firmly on the ground"—that is, "neither its independence nor its possibilities of orientation can take root in practical action" (p. 275). Her existence moved only with an effort, convulsively, and "its standing-on-earth is constantly opposed by a swaying and flying in the air and a being-confined in and under the earth" (p. 275). Binswanger explains that existential autonomy means that an individual is comfortable with the world on the earth (of practical action), the world of the air (of "winged" wishes or highest ideals), and the world in or under the earth (the "down-to-earth" demands, desires, burdens of the world). Ellen's poems and other diary entries reveal not only her inability to move comfortably on the earth—to take practical actions such as passing exams or making decisions about marriage—but also a conflict between her desires to fly (her high ideals) and her down-to-earth burdens (death wishes). Her life became a struggle to fuse these two worlds and achieve peace and contentment.

When Ellen, at her father's request, broke her engagement with the "romantic foreigner," she experienced this as the failure of her last chance to bring her ethereal world into harmony with the earthly world. It was soon after this that she was, even at her most exuberant moments, beset by "pains and spasms." Nowhere, Binswanger observes, did her existence find a "loving shelter," nor a firm footing. "This means that her existence is threatened by its own nothingness. This being-threatened we call, with Heidegger, *Angst* (dread) or, as the life-history has it, fear and trembling" (p. 280). In Ellen's case, the dread was a particular one—the dread of getting fat:

> With the dread of becoming fat and the wish to be thin, the cosmological contrast undergoes a further, in fact a final, alteration. From the macrocosm it spreads over to the microcosm, into psychophysical structure. The contrast between light and dark, between rising and descending life, is now enacted in the *Eigenwelt*, without in the least losing thereby its macrocosmological features. [p. 280]

The external conflict between the ethereal and earthly worlds became an internal, psychological struggle between an "ethereally spiritualized young soul and ethereal young body" and a "spiritless and clumsy soul and a deteriorating, aging body" (p. 280). The dread of becoming fat, which began in her 20th year, was in an anthropological sense, the end of the "encirclement process"; Ellen was no longer open to existential possibilities. She was now definitively stuck in the contrast between light and dark, flowering and withering, thin and fat. Trapped in this circle, the only authentic act left to her was the act of suicide. She did not want to live as the worm lived, dumb and dull and fat. She wanted to die as the bird died who burst his throat with supreme jubilation; she wanted to be consumed in her own fire. "The existential exultation itself, the festive existential joy, the 'existential fire' are placed in the service of death" (p. 285).

Binswanger asserts that, in view of her existential dilemma, suicide represented a viable solution. In her death, he perceives "with especial impressiveness" the existential meaning—or contrameaning—of her life. "This meaning was not that of being herself, but rather that of being not herself" (p. 297). Because of her willful relatedness to herself, her mode of existence was not authentic. "If we want to designate such a mode of existence with one word, none is more fitting than despair" (p. 310). Existential analysis must suspend any judgment derived from any viewpoints, he asserts, be they ethical, religious, psychiatric, or psychoanalytic. One must neither tolerate or disapprove of the suicide of Ellen West, nor "trivialize it with medical or psychoanalytic explanations, nor dramatize it with ethical or religious judgments" (p. 292).

Binswanger compares the existential analytic view with that of psychoanalysis. Psychoanalysis places its chief emphasis, he contends, on the ethereal world—the world of phantasies and dreams—whereas existential analysis "undertakes to work out all possible world-designs of human existence, faithful to the fact established by Hegel that the individuality is what its world is, in the sense of its own world" (p. 314). He agrees with Ellen's psychoanalysts that there were definite signs of anal-eroticism in her character structure. Her defiance and self-willedness, and the meticulous manner in which she filled up her time, all point to such traits. However, here the agreement stops, for the existential analyst now asks first of all what world-design is basic to anality. For Ellen West, anality represents the world-design of an emptiness, a tomb, a grave:

> The entire life-history of Ellen West is nothing but the history of a metamorphosis of life into mold and death. It is, in the words of Paul Claudel, a most impressive example of the '*dismal alchemy of the tomb.*' What psychoanalysis calls anality is only a special segment of the history of this alchemy. Expressed in another way, anality belongs in the realm of the dull, moldering, rotting swampworld and its 'end-product,' the cold grave. [p. 318]

Existential analysis, Binswanger concludes, cannot revert to an anal-erotic drive-component as the cause of the rotting swampworld or the cold grave. Anality in the psychoanalytic sense is only a segment of the total *Gestalt*, a segment which is restricted "to the bodily share in the *Eigenwelt*." Likewise, Ellen's dreams can be interpreted in terms of their anal-eroticism or their orality, but such interpretations again lose sight of the total Gestalt, the total existential individuality that was Ellen West.

Regarding diagnosis, Binswanger believes she suffered from a form of polymorphous schizophrenia. He notes Ellen's stiff and empty facial expression, a gaze at times empty and at times abnormally "drenched with feeling," and a rather stiff posture. "All these are expression-forms of existential emptiness in the sense of the schizophrenic process" (p. 359). Added to this was her feeling that all inner life had stopped, that everything was unreal and senseless. She was no longer able to be absorbed in the "being-with-each-other" of love or friendship, or to open herself up to "existential care." Her turning to herself, her preoccupation with her weight, and her suspicion that people did not want to help her and were in fact tormenting her, all prevented her from forming a relationship of mutual understanding; attempts to transfer her to the present and to open her to the future were bound to fail.

Binswanger was 37 when he treated Ellen West and 63 when he published her case. He died in 1966 at the age of 85.

Interpretation

Binswanger contends that existential analysis does not aim to displace psychoanalysis, but rather to broaden it to include the phenomenological realm of existence. However, in making this "disclaimer" he may be guilty of the diplomacy of which Freud often accused him. Existential analysis is not just another deviation from classical analysis; it is a radical departure from the medical–scientific model to which psychoanalysis subscribes. In addition, as May (1983) points out, it would be a mistake to identify existential psychoanalysis as another of the schools of therapy that have broken off from mainstream psychoanalysis. In one way, he says, it is like other deviations, such as those by Jung, Adler, Ferenczi, Rank, and Reich. Otto Rank's emphasis on the present emerged when classical analysis was bogged down in arid intellectualized discussion of the patient's past; Wilhelm Reich's character analysis arose as an answer to the need to break through the "ego defenses" of the character armor; the cultural approach of Horney, Fromm, and Sullivan was brought forth by the narrow focus of analysis on the individual and his drives. Existential analysis also covered a psychoanalytic blind spot—it was an attempt to be less judgmental, or, as May puts it, "The existential analysis movement is a protest against the tendency to see the patient in forms tailored to our own preconceptions or to make him over into the image of our own predilections" (p. 45). It is very different than the other schools, though, in two important respects: It is not the creation of any one leader, but grew up spontaneously in diverse parts of Europe; and it does not purport to be a new school opposed to other schools or a new technique opposed to other

techniques, but rather seeks to broaden existing schools through
an analysis of the structure of human existence.

With regard to therapeutic technique, May asserts that existential analysts do not differ from other therapists in the way in
which they would interpret a dream or respond to a patient's
outburst. But the context would differ, always focusing on the
question of how a dream throws light on a patient's existence in his
world. "The context is the patient not as a set of psychic dyna-
misms or mechanisms but as a human being who is choosing,
committing, and pointing himself toward something right now"
(p. 152).

Reviewing Binswanger's case history of Ellen West, May sees
Binswanger's aim as using existential analysis to throw light on a
given case, and then comparing it with other methods of understanding. He contends that Binswanger was not interested in the
technique of treatment, but with understanding the individual
called Ellen West. Her apparent love of death fascinated him; she
seems to him to be a vivid example of Kierkegaard's description of
despair as a "sickness unto death." "Whether or not Binswanger is
successful in explicating existential principles in this case is for the
reader to judge," May concludes. "But anyone who reads this
long case will feel the amazing depth of Binswanger's earnestness
in his search together with his rich cultural background and schol-
arliness" (p. 42).

Ellenberger (1958) characterizes Binswanger's *Daseinanalyze*
as a synthesis of psychoanalysis, phenomenology, and existential-
ist concepts, modified by original insights. "It is a reconstruction
of the inner world of experience of psychiatric patients with the
help of a conceptual framework inspired by Heidegger's studies
on the structure of human existence" (p. 120). When he started his
case histories, Binswanger organized his descriptions around how
his subjects related to the *Umwelt*, *Mitwelt*, and *Eigenwelt*. By the
time he wrote about Ellen West, he had begun to add the concept
of the "existential mode," an additional system of looking at the
self in the context of the "dual," "plural," "singular," or "anon-
ymous" modes of existence. In Ellen West's case, she was unable

to achieve the dual mode—that is, achieve a loving, intimate relationship with one other person—nor could she achieve authenticity in any other existential mode, including the singular (relating to herself). Binswanger's concept of the singular mode, Ellenberger notes, extends the psychoanalytic concept of narcissism to include a wide range of other intrapsychic relationships.

Fromm-Reichmann (1959) calls Binswanger "an outstanding psychiatrist" who understood the constructive aspect of anxiety as the tension aroused in a person who is able to face the universe and "the task which is set to men, to conquer the emanations of the universe by action" (p. 316). She also cites Binswanger's descriptions of the anxiety that is beyond anxiety—"the naked horror"— a severe loneliness with a specific character of paralyzing hopelessness and unutterable futility. She agrees with him that psychoanalytic concepts only go so far in understanding human conditions such as loneliness. "In the last analysis, anxiety and fear of real loneliness merge where they are an anticipation of the fear of the ultimate isolation and separation, of the inconceivable absolute loneliness of death" (p. 330). At this point of merger, defense and remedy, she concludes, seem out of reach; for when people experience this naked horror they are devoid of any interest or any goal. Such was the case with Ellen West.

Critics of Binswanger's way of analyzing things usually accuse him of fuzzy or romantic thinking. Hanly (1979), for instance, claims that Binswanger makes a fundamental mistake when he speaks of subjective temporality as an a priori form of consciousness that exists independently of the life processes of the body and psyche. "To say, as Binswanger does, that Ellen West had already lived her adult psychical existence in her childhood and that her adult physical existence had no subjectivity with which to live, is a confused way of saying that her instinctual life remained fixated in a precocious infantile form, which, as an adult, she could no longer either abandon or enjoy" (p. 206). Hanly also believes that Binswanger rationalizes and idealizes the suicide of his patient by substituting a problem of temporal structure for the problems of regressed instinctual life, viewing her suicide as a

courageous act of unification, rather than the outcome of a mel-
ancholic psychopathic process over which she had no control.
"Phenomenological concepts of subjective temporality cannot
satisfactorily substitute for an adequate concept of the psychic
unconscious," he states, because they "lose their specificity and
thus their phenomenological accuracy" (p. 206).

Nor, Hanly adds, is existential dream analysis a tenable substitute for psychoanalytic dream analysis. While existentialists
accept the fact that dreams have a manifest and a latent content,
they cannot accept the causal explanation for this fact. They suffer
from a "categorical rigidity in the use of basic concepts," which
results in a failure on their part to realize that self-comprehension
"is not preserved in an authentic form by denying that intrapsychic processes are causal. On the contrary, it is precisely their
causal nature that provides for the possibility of self-comprehension" (p. 95).

Fromm (1973) also takes Binswanger to task for attempting
to substitute imprecise descriptions of the interpersonal process
(incorporating somewhat vague philosophical notions) for precise
clinical data. He notes that a number of psychoanalysts—most of
whom have been influenced by Adolf Meyer—have been developing an ever-deepening understanding of the unconscious processes that go on during interpersonal relationships, and many of
them speak of authentic and inauthentic relationships. However,
those who have successfully done so have achieved this success
because of the precision of their formulations, the very thing
lacking in Binswanger's work.

Chessick (1989) contends that Binswanger's argument that
Ellen West's suicide was the solution to her existential dilemma
is "patent nonsense." "I believe that the entire history of Ellen
West is a tragic demonstration of what can go wrong in the
treatment of a psychotic patient when psychoanalytic listening is
improperly carried out . . ." (p. 67). He explains that in his clinical experience, people with eating disorders possess a deep characterological depression, often with core paranoid features, a fixed
derogatory self-image, cynicism, hopelessness, and a profound

narcissistic rage. "Thus a long and difficult intensive psychotherapy is to be expected with such patients, because we are dealing
with a profound preoedipal disorder characterized by severe, early
structural defects. The case of Ellen West is an extreme example of
such a disorder" (p. 69).

I believe that Binswanger and other existentialists are guilty
of the hypocrisy of which they accuse psychoanalysis. Binswanger criticizes psychoanalysts for judging and labeling individuals, thereby robbing them of their essential humanity, and he
asserts that such judgments have negative connotations. However,
the same could be said about existential judgments. When Binswanger speaks about Ellen West's problems in establishing effective relationships with the *Umwelt*, *Mitwelt*, and *Eigenwelt*, and
when he describes her as "self-willed," "defiant," and "stubborn,"
is he not making judgments that also rob her of her humanity and
have negative connotations? At the same time, he is also judging
psychoanalysts, saying that they are bad because they use labels,
and assuming that he and other existentialists know better than
Freud and are morally superior since they do not make judgments.
Indeed, all those who start new schools of psychology, philosophy, politics, science, and the like, with claims that their psychology, philosophy, science, or politics is morally superior to their
predecessors, are guilty of such hypocrisy. To study something,
whether it is man or mineral, requires one to make judgments. To
say, "I am against labeling or judging people," is to make the most
pious judgment of all, a self-righteous condemnation of those who
presumably do. Unfortunately, there is a streak of this kind of
moral hypocrisy not only in existential psychoanalysis, but also in
other schools of therapy.

Finally, Binswanger's diagnosis of Ellen West was wrong;
she was not a schizophrenic, but rather, as previously noted,
suffered from a severe form of anorexia nervosa. Neither his
existential view of her, which placed an emphasis on existential
dread, nor the psychoanalytic emphasis on anal-erotic factors
which prevailed in those days, came to grips with the basic cause
of her condition. Today, bolstered by many years of research with

anorexics, our knowledge of this condition is much greater. Harrison (1979) states that anorexia nervosa occurs predominantly in adolescent girls and that "the mother (or occasionally the father) has usually been strongly overcontrolling toward the patient, with an ambivalent and hostile–dependent relationship existing between mother and daughter" (p. 590). (In Ellen West's case, both parents seem to have been strongly overcontrolling. It was their overcontrolling attitude that probably caused her to refuse milk at 9 months of age, and to insist a few years later that a bird's nest was not a bird's nest.) Harrison goes on to say that the relationship of the girl with her father may have an overtly seductive quality. We are not given detailed information about Ellen's relationship with her father, but certainly his interference with her engagements suggests an unhealthy attachment to her. Finally, Harrison states that "Food intake then becomes the area in which patients can assert their control" (p. 591). Ellen's parents were internalized, introjected into her superego, and then converted into an overcontrolling attitude toward herself. She was paralyzed by a conflict between ideal self-image and negative self-image.

I agree with Hanly and Chessick that Binswanger rationalized and idealized the suicide of his patient. One reason for this was that he was unable or unwilling to understand how angry Ellen was at her parents and how that pent-up anger was being taken out on herself and had given her (to use Reich's term) a suicidal "character armor." Indeed, had she gone to Reich or Ferenczi instead of Binswanger, they would probably have attacked her suicidal armor, gotten her to scream at them or at the world, had her give vent to her rage by play-acting with her the traumatic relationship with her father and mother, and might then have rescued her from her dilemma.

However, on the plus side, Binswanger and other existentialists made an important contribution to psychoanalysis by calling our attention to the fact that the psychoanalytic view of the human condition is often rather narrow in focus. Since existential analysis also incorporates phenomenology, it recognizes that human development can be viewed from a multitude of perspectives, and that humans are not just motivated by their drives, phantasies, or interactions with their family environment. They are also influenced by their own innate sensibilities, which help them give meaning to their lives, and face the inevitability of death; by the cultural climate in which they live; by their genetic endowment; by the relative state of peace or war in the world during their lifetimes; and by a host of other, perhaps more subtle, factors. In terms of therapy, the existential outlook provides clinicians with a wider framework; by seeing a patient's dilemma in a broader context, one can relate to the patient more effectively.

Binswanger's existential analysis was a forerunner of many later schools of therapy, such as Gestalt therapy, humanistic therapy, and psychosynthesis. His concepts have also been influential in other fields.

AFTERWORD

Breuer, Freud, Jung, Adler, Ferenczi, Klein, Reich, Binswanger: they were there during the golden age of analytic therapy. They formulated the first theories, set up guidelines for therapy, and laid the framework around which later analysts would build an enduring edifice. (Another of my books, *Turning Points in Analytic Therapy: From Winnicott to Kernberg* [Northvale, NJ: Jason Aronson, 1990] considers the work of these later analysts, reviewing the most famous cases of the second half of the twentieth century.)

Looking back at the classic cases in this book, one can follow the development of analytic therapy from case to case and from analyst to analyst. There was Breuer, a kindhearted, insightful, but rather timid man, who ran both from Anna O. and from the truth he had uncovered about the etiology of hysteria. He passed the torch to Freud, whose burning ambition provided him with the boldness to follow that truth, and who had the profound intellect to elaborate on it. And so it was Freud who tried dream interpretation with Dora, validated the Oedipus complex through Little Hans, intellectually indoctrinated the Rat Man, and tried to mold the Wolf Man. He was nervous, obsessive, and defensive, but he knew himself about as well as anyone ever has, and he stood firm against the enormous, often vicious attacks on psychoanalysis and on his own character.

There were the mystical Jung and the practical Adler, two characterological opposites who took the torch from Freud and went their separate ways. Jung was not only a mystic, but also a scholar who extended the range of applied psychoanalysis, and Adler shed light on the inferiority complexes that form the core of narcissism, a topic that has since taken on major importance. There was Ferenczi, dauntlessly reconsidering the rules about neutrality, the blank screen, and abstinence, and, like Breuer, getting in over his head—yet, also like Breuer, leaving behind a trail for others to follow. There was Melanie Klein, taking Freud's death instinct and running with it, driven Freudlike by her own burning ambition and profound intellect, unable to withstand the rigors of leadership. Her research on children's phantasies is still a useful tool. There was the feisty Reich, brilliant and mad, cracking the armor of patients and colleagues, making enemies, yet delineating character structure as few have before or since. And there was the gentle Binswanger, who denied his own aggression and misunderstood the inward aggression of Ellen West. He took the mantle of mysticism from Jung, added a little of Heidegger, and came up with existential psychoanalysis, setting the stage for future humanistic and existential therapists to dance around on.

If it does nothing else, this volume dispels the popular notion that all analysts are alike: passive, emotionless individuals who sit in their chairs and never say a word. Each of these explorers had different personalities, and they went at analytic therapy in their own particular ways. Each specialized in one kind of patient—that is, Freud stuck mainly with neurotics, Jung attracted those of a mystical bent, Ferenczi appealed to narcissistic and borderline types, and Reich worked well with neurotic characters other than the usual hysterics and obsessives who inhabited the offices of most early analysts. Each had theories peculiar to his own upbringing and personality.

All analysts are not alike, and almost every kind of experimental therapy that exists today grew out of experiments by the earlier analysts. Similarly, the theories that are accepted today had their developmental roots in these and other classic cases. My only regret, having completed this first volume, is that I could not have known each of these people myself. Having immersed myself in their cases, I feel as though I have had a training analysis with each analyst, and have personally treated each patient and supervised each case. I hope readers of this volume will share that feeling. If so, I will have achieved an important aim.

REFERENCES

Adler, A. (1908). The aggressive drive in life and neurosis. *Fortschrift Medicine* 26:577–584.

—— (1929). *Problems of Neurosis: A Book of Case Histories*. New York: Harper, 1964.

—— (1931). The differences between individual psychology and psychoanalysis. In *Superiority and Social Interest*, ed. H. L. Ansbacher and R. R. Ansbacher. New York: Norton, 1964.

Balint, M. (1968). *The Basic Fault*. London: Tavistock.

Binswanger, L. (1943). *Basic Forms and Cognition of Human Existence*. Zurich: Max Neihaus.

—— (1944). The case of Ellen West. In *Existence, a New Dimension in Psychiatry and Psychology*, ed. R. May, E. Angel, and H. F. Ellenberger, pp. 237–364. New York: Basic Books.

—— (1957). *Sigmund Freud: Reminiscences of a Friendship*. Trans. Norbert Guterman. New York: Grune and Stratton.

Blanck, G., and Blanck, R. (1974). *Ego Psychology: Theory and Practice*. New York: Columbia University Press.

Blum, G. (1953). *Psychoanalytic Theories of Personality*. New York: McGraw-Hill.

Blum, H. (1980a). The borderline childhood of the Wolf Man. In *Freud and His Patients*, ed. M. Kanzer and J. Glenn, pp. 341–358. North-vale, NJ: Jason Aronson.

——— (1980b). The pathogenic influence of the primal scene: a reevaluation. In *Freud and His Patients*, ed. M. Kanzer and J. Glenn, pp. 367–371. Northvale, NJ: Jason Aronson.

Bowlby, J. (1979). *The Making and Breaking of Affectional Bonds*. London: Tavistock.

Breuer, J., and Freud, S. (1895). Studies in hysteria. *Standard Edition 2*. New York: Norton.

Brunswick, R. M. (1928). A supplement to Freud's "history of an infantile neurosis." In *The Wolf Man by the Wolf Man*, ed. M. Gardiner, pp. 153–171. New York: Basic Books.

Chessick, R. D. (1989). *The Technique and Practice of Listening in Intensive Psychotherapy*. Northvale, NJ: Jason Aronson.

Donn, L. (1988). *Freud and Jung: Years of Friendship, Years of Loss*. New York: Charles Scribner's Sons.

Ellenberger, H. F. (1958). A clinical introduction to psychiatric phenomenology and existential analysis. In *Existence*, ed. R. May, E. Angel, and H. F. Ellenberger, pp. 92–126. New York: Basic Books.

Erickson, E. H. (1962). Reality and actuality. *Journal of the American Psychoanalytic Association* 10:451–474.

Esman, A. (1973). The primal scene: a review and a reconsideration. *Psychoanalytic Study of the Child* 28:49–81. New Haven, CT: Yale University Press.

Eysenck, H. J. (1952). The effects of psychotherapy: an evaluation. *Journal of Consulting Psychology* 16:319–325.

Fairbairn, W. R. D. (1954). *An Object-Relations Theory of the Personality*. New York: Basic Books.

Fenichel, O. (1945). *The Psychoanalytic Theory of Neurosis*. New York: Norton.

——— (1953). Concerning the theory of psychoanalytic technique. In *The Collected Papers of Otto Fenichel*, first series, pp. 332–348. New York: Norton.

Ferenczi, S. (1919). Technical difficulties in the analysis of a case of hysteria. In *Further Contributions to the Theory and Technique of Psycho-Analysis*, pp. 189–197. New York: Brunner/Mazel, 1980.

—— (1921). Further development of an active therapy in psychoanalysis. In *Further Contributions to the Theory and Technique of Psycho-Analysis*, pp. 198–217. New York: Brunner/Mazel, 1980.

—— (1924). On forced fantasies: activity in the association technique. In *Further Contributions to the Theory and Technique of Psycho-Analysis*, pp. 68–77. New York: Brunner/Mazel, 1980.

—— (1928). The elasticity of psycho-analytic technique. In *Further Contributions to the Theory and Technique of Psycho-Analysis*, pp. 87–101. New York: Brunner/Mazel, 1980.

—— (1930). The principles of relaxation and neocatharsis. In *Further Contributions to the Theory and Technique of Psycho-Analysis*, pp. 108–125. New York: Brunner/Mazel, 1980.

—— (1931). Child-analysis in the analysis of adults. In *Further Contributions to the Theory and Technique of Psycho-Analysis*, pp. 126–147. New York: Brunner/Mazel, 1980.

—— (1933). Confusion of tongues between adults and the child. In *Further Contributions to the Theory and Technique of Psycho-Analysis*, pp. 156–167. New York: Brunner/Mazel, 1980.

Freeman, L., and Strean, H. (1981). *Freud and Women*. New York: Frederick Ungar.

Freud, A. (1927). Symposium of child analysis. *International Journal of Psycho-Analysis* 8.

—— (1951). Observations on child development. *Psychoanalytic Study of the Child* 6:18–30. New York: International Universities Press.

Freud, E. I. (1960). *The Letters of Sigmund Freud*. New York: Basic Books.

Freud, S. (1895). On the grounds for detaching a particular syndrome from neurasthenia under the description "anxiety neurosis." *Standard Edition* 3:112–120.

—— (1905a). Three essays on the theory of sexuality. *Standard Edition* 7:125–248.

—— (1905b). Fragment of an analysis of a case of hysteria. In *Collected Papers of Sigmund Freud* 3:13–148. New York: Basic Books.

—— (1909a). Analysis of a phobia in a five-year-old boy. In *Collected Papers of Sigmund Freud* 3:149–295. New York: Basic Books.

—— (1909b). Notes upon a case of obsessional neurosis. *Standard Edition* 10:155–237.

—— (1910). Five lectures on psycho-analysis. *Standard Edition* 11: 1–58.

—— (1914a). Remembering, repeating and working through. *Standard Edition* 12:147–156.

—— (1914b). On the history of the psychoanalytic movement. *Standard Edition* 14:3–66.

—— (1916–1917). Introductory lectures on psycho-analysis. *Standard Edition* 15/16:313–340.

—— (1918). From the history of an infantile neurosis. In *Collected Papers of Sigmund Freud* 3:473–605. New York: Basic Books.

—— (1919). A child is being beaten. *Standard Edition* 17:175–204.

—— (1925). An autobiographical study. *Standard Edition* 20:3–76.

—— (1926). Inhibitions, symptoms and anxiety. *Standard Edition* 20:75–175.

—— (1933). New introductory lectures on psycho-analysis. *Standard Edition* 22:3–184.

—— (1937). Analysis terminable and interminable. *Standard Edition* 23:216–253.

Fromm, E. (1973). *The Anatomy of Human Destructiveness*. New York: Fawcett Crest Books.

Fromm-Reichmann, F. (1950). *The Principle of Intensive Psychotherapy*. Chicago: Phoenix Books.

Gardiner, M., ed. (1971). *The Wolf Man by the Wolf Man*. New York: Basic Books.

Geleerd, E. R. (1963). Evaluation of Melanie Klein's narrative of a child analysis. *International Journal of Psycho-Analysis* 44:393–506.

Gill, M. M. (1982). *Analysis of the Transference*. Vol. 1. New York: International Universities Press.

Glenn, J. (1980a). Freud's adolescent patients: Katerina, Dora and the "homosexual woman." In *Freud and His Patients*, ed. M. Kanzer and J. Glenn, pp. 23–47. Northvale, NJ: Jason Aronson.

—— (1980b). Freud's advice to Hans' father: the first supervisory sessions. In *Freud and His Patients*, ed. M. Kanzer and J. Glenn, pp. 122–127. Northvale, NJ: Jason Aronson.

Glover, E. (1927). Review of Ferenczi's collected papers. *International Journal of Psycho-Analysis* 8:417–421.

Graf, M. (1942). Reminiscence of Professor Sigmund Freud. *Psychoanalytic Quarterly* 11:465–476.

Greenberg, J. R., and Mitchell, S. A. (1983). *Object Relations in Psychoanalytic Theory*. Cambridge, MA: Harvard University Press.

Grinstein, A. (1980). *Sigmund Freud's Dreams*. New York: International Universities Press.

Grosskurth, P. (1986). *Melanie Klein: Her World and Her Work*. Harmondsworth, England: Penguin Books.

Guntrip, H. (1969). *Schizoid Phenomena, Object Relations and the Self*. New York: International Universities Press.

Haley, J. (1973). *Uncommon Therapy*. New York: Norton.

Halpert, E. (1980). Lermontov and the Wolf Man. In *Freud and His Patients*, pp. 386–397. Northvale, NJ: Jason Aronson.

Hanly, C. (1979). *Existentialism and Psychoanalysis*. New York: International Universities Press.

Harrison, S. I. (1979). *Basic Handbook of Child Psychiatry*. Vol. 3. New York: Basic Books.

Hartman, H. (1958). *Ego Psychology and the Problem of Adaptation*. New York: International Universities Press.

Jacobson, E. (1946). The effect of disappointment on ego and superego formation in normal and depressive development. *Psychoanalytic Review* 33:129–147.

—— (1964). *The Self and the Object World*. New York: International Universities Press.

—— (1971). *Depression*. New York: International Universities Press.

Jones, E. (1957). *The Life and Work of Sigmund Freud*. Ed. and abridged by L. Trilling and S. Marcus. New York: Anchor Books, 1963.

Jung, C. G. (1927). The structure of the psyche. In *The Portable Jung*, ed. J. Campbell, pp. 23–46. Harmondsworth, England: Penguin Books, 1971.

—— (1928). The relations between the ego and the unconscious. In *The Portable Jung*, ed. J. Campbell, pp. 70–138. Harmondsworth, England: Penguin Books, 1971.

———— (1951). Avion: phenomenology of the self. In *The Portable Jung*, ed. J. Campbell, pp. 139–162. Harmondsworth, England: Penguin Books, 1971.

Kanzer, M. (1980a). The transference neurosis of the Rat Man. In *Freud and His Patients*, ed. M. Kanzer and J. Glenn, pp. 137–144. Northvale, NJ: Jason Aronson.

———— (1980b). Freud's human influence on the Rat Man. In *Freud and His Patients*, ed. M. Kanzer and J. Glenn, pp. 232–240. Northvale, NJ: Jason Aronson.

———— (1980c). Further comments on the Wolf Man: the search for the primal scene. In *Freud and His Patients*, ed. M. Kanzer and J. Glenn, pp. 359–366. Northvale, NJ: Jason Aronson.

Kernberg, O. (1975). *Borderline Conditions and Pathological Narcissism*. Northvale, NJ: Jason Aronson.

Kernberg, O., Selzer, M. A., Koenigsberg, H. W., Carr, A. C., and Appelbaum, A. H. (1989). *Psychodynamic Psychotherapy of Borderline Patients*. New York: Basic Books.

Kestenberg, J. S. (1980). Ego-organization in obsessive-compulsive development: a study of the Rat Man, based on interpretation of movement patterns. In *Freud and His Patients*, ed. M. Kanzer and J. Glenn, pp. 144–179. Northvale, NJ: Jason Aronson.

Klein, M. (1932). *The Psychoanalysis of Children*. Trans. Alix Strachey. New York: Delacorte Press, 1975.

———— (1961). *Narrative of a Child Analysis*. New York: Delta, 1975.

Kohut, H. (1971). *The Analysis of the Self*. New York: International Universities Press.

———— (1984). *How Does Analysis Cure*. Chicago: University of Chicago Press.

Kris, E. (1951). Ego psychology and interpretation in psychoanalytic therapy. *Psychoanalytic Quarterly* 20:15–30.

———— (1953). Psychoanalysis and the study of creative imagination. In *Selected Papers of Ernst Kris*, pp. 473–493. New Haven: Yale University Press.

Laing, R. D. (1969). *The Politics of Family*. Harmondsworth, England: Penguin Books.

Langs, R. (1980a). The misalliance dimension in the Dora case. In *Freud and His Patients*, ed. M. Kanzer and J. Glenn, pp. 58–71. North-vale, NJ: Jason Aronson.

—— (1980b). The misalliance dimension in the case of the Rat Man. In *Freud and His Patients*, ed. M. Kanzer and J. Glenn, pp. 215–231. Northvale, NJ: Jason Aronson.

—— (1980c). The misalliance dimension in the case of the Wolf Man. In *Freud and His Patients*, ed. M. Kanzer and J. Glenn, pp. 372–385. Northvale, NJ: Jason Aronson.

Little, M. (1981). *Transference Neurosis and Transference Psychosis*. North-vale, NJ: Jason Aronson.

Mahler, M. S., Pine, F., and Bergman, A. (1975). *The Psychological Birth of the Infant*. London: Maresfield Library.

Malcolm, J. (1981). *Psychoanalysis: The Impossible Profession*. New York: Vintage Books.

Masson, J. M. (1984). *The Assault on the Truth: Freud's Suppression of the Seduction Theory*. New York: Farrar, Straus and Giroux.

May, R. (1983). *The Discovery of Being*. New York: Norton.

Montagu, M. F. A. (1968). *Man and Aggression*. London: Oxford University Press.

Nunberg, H., and Federn, E., eds. (1962). *Minutes of the Vienna Psycho-Analytic Society*. Vol. 1. New York: International Universities Press.

Obholzer, K. (1982). *The Wolfman Sixty Years Later*. New York: Continuum.

Olsen, D. A., and Koppe, S. (1988). *Freud's Theory of Psychoanalysis*. New York: New York University Press.

O'Regan, B., ed. (1985). Multiple personality—mirrors of a new model of the mind. In *Investigations*, vol. 1, Institute of Noetic Sciences, Chicago.

Orgler, H. (1963). *Alfred Adler: The Man and His Work*. New York: New American Library.

Reich, W. (1933). *Character Analysis*. 3rd ed. Trans. V. R. Carfagno. New York: Touchstone Books, 1972.

—— (1942). *The Function of the Orgasm*. Trans. V. R. Carfagno. New York: Pocket Books, 1973.

Reiff, P. (1959). *Freud: The Mind of the Moralist*. Chicago: University of Chicago Press.

Reik, T. (1941). *Masochism in Sex and Society.* Trans. M. H. Beizel and G. Kurth. New York: Pyramid Books, 1976.

Roazen, P. (1984). *Freud and His Followers.* New York: New York University Press.

Roiphe, H., and Galenson, E. (1981). *Infantile Origins of Sexual Identity.* New York: International Universities Press.

Rosen, J. (1962). *Direct Psychoanalytic Psychiatry.* New York: Grune and Stratton.

Rosenbaum, M., and Muroff, M., eds. (1984). *Anna O.: Fourteen Contemporary Reinterpretations.* New York: Free Press.

Rosenfeld, E. (1956). Dream and vision. *International Journal of Psycho-Analysis* 37:97–105.

Schlesinger, H. (1969). Family: a study of family member interactions. In *The Psychoanalytic Forum*, vol. 3, ed. J. A. Lindon, pp. 13–65. New York: Science House.

Schoenewolf, G. (1989). *Sexual Animosity between Men and Women.* Northvale, NJ: Jason Aronson.

—— (1990). *Turning Points in Analytic Therapy: From Winnicott to Kernberg.* Northvale, NJ: Jason Aronson.

Schur, M. (1972). *Freud: Living and Dying.* New York: International Universities Press.

Sechehaye, M. (1963). Transference psychosis in the psychotherapy of chronic schizophrenia. *International Journal of Psycho-Analysis* 44:249–281.

Segal, H. (1979). *Melanie Klein.* Harmondsworth, England: Penguin Books.

Shengold, L. (1980). More on rats and rat people. In *Freud and His Patients*, ed. M. Kanzer and J. Glenn, pp. 180–202. Northvale, NJ: Jason Aronson.

Silverman, M. A. (1980). A fresh look at the case of Little Hans. In *Freud and His Patients*, ed. M. Kanzer and J. Glenn, pp. 95–120. Northvale, NJ: Jason Aronson.

Slap, J. (1961). Little Hans' tonsillectomy. *Psychoanalytic Quarterly* 30:259–261.

Spotnitz, H. (1961). *The Couch and the Circle: A Story of Group Therapy.* New York: Alfred A. Knopf.

———— (1976). *Psychotherapy of PreOedipal Conditions*. Northvale, NJ: Jason Aronson.

———— (1985). *Modern Psychoanalysis of the Schizophrenic Patient*. 2d ed. New York: Human Sciences Press.

Spotnitz, H., and Meadow, P. (1976). *Treatment of the Narcissistic Neurosis*. New York: Manhattan Center for Advanced Psychoanalytic Studies.

Sterba, R. F. (1953). Clinical aspects of character resistance. *Psychoanalytic Quarterly* 22:1–20.

Stern, P. J. (1976). *The Haunted Prophet*. New York: Braziller.

Stolorow, R. D., and Atwood, G. E. (1979). *Faces in a Cloud: Subjectivity in Personality Theory*. Northvale, NJ: Jason Aronson.

Thompson, C. (1950). *Psychoanalysis: Evolution and Development*. New York: Grove Press.

Weiss, S. S. (1980). Reflections and speculations on the psychoanalysis of the Rat Man. In *Freud and His Patients*, ed. M. Kanzer and J. Glenn, pp. 203–214. Northvale, NJ: Jason Aronson.

White, R. W. (1957). Adler and the future of ego psychology. *Journal of Individual Psychology* 13:112–124.

Winnicott, D. W. (1953). Symptom tolerance in paediatrics. In *Through Paediatrics to Psycho-Analysis*, pp. 101–117. New York: Basic Books, 1975.

———— (1965). *The Maturational Process and the Facilitating Environment*. New York: International Universities Press.

———— (1986). *Holding and Interpretation: Fragment of an Analysis*. New York: Grove Press.

Wolman, B. B. (1960). *Contemporary Theories and Systems in Psychology*. New York: Harper and Row.

INDEX

Abandonment, 186
Abraham, Karl, 64, 162
Abreaction, 16, 155, 158
Absence, 5, 8
Active therapy, 141–159
Adler, Alfred, 64, 65, 123–139, 142, 180
  biography of, 124, 134
  Freud and, 83, 84, 96, 124–125, 134–136
Aggression
  active therapy and, 158–159
  Adler and, 123
  child analysis, 169–170, 175–176
  Ferenczi and, 149, 150
  Little Hans case and, 59
  masochism and, 189
  Reich and, 181
  repression and, 16–17
  Wolf Man case and, 91
Anality
  existential analysis and, 209–210
  Ferenczi and, 148
  masochism and, 186–187
  Rat Man case and, 76–77
  Wolf Man case and, 86, 90, 92

Anal-rapprochement phase, 60
Analysis of a Phobia in a Five-Year-Old Boy (Freud), 44
"Analysis Terminable and Interminable" (Freud), 96
Anna O. case, vii, 1–19, 21, 35
Anorexia nervosa, 199, 215–216
Anxiety
  Binswanger and, 213
  child analysis and, 171–172, 174
  ego and, 59–60, 62
  masochism and, 183, 184, 186
  masturbation and, 48
  phobias and, 51
  Wolf Man case and, 91
Anxiety hysteria, 44. *See also* Hysteria
Apathy, 86, 87
Archetype, 115
Artistic creativity. *See* Creativity
Atwood, G. E., 194

Baker, Elsworth F., 190
Balint, M., 15, 16, 156, 157, 174, 194
Basic Forms and Cognition of Human Existence (Binswanger), 198

Bauer, Philip, 21–22. *See also* Dora case
Bed-wetting, 32–33. *See also* Urination
Bernfeld, Siegfried, 180
Billinsky, John M., 107
Binswanger, Ludwig, vii, 197–217
  biography of, 197–198, 211
Birth order, 131, 133
Bisexuality, 46, 61
Bleuler, Eugen, 106, 206
Blum, G., 118–119, 173
Blum, H., 83, 86, 97, 98, 100
Body language, 181
Borderline personality
  Ferenczi and, 152
  Klein and, 173
  Wolf Man case and, 86, 98–99
Bowlby, J., 82
Breuer, Joseph, vii, 1–19, 21, 35, 146, 150
  biography of, 1–3
  Freud and, 23, 43
Brunswick, Ruth Mack, 94, 97, 100, 139

Campbell, J., 106, 116, 122
Castration complex, 26–27
  Jung and, 121
  Little Hans case and, 45, 49–50
  masochism and, 187, 188
  Wolf Man case and, 89–91
  womb envy and, 60–61
Cathartic method, vii, 1–19, 146, 150–151
Catholic church, 5, 15
Character Analysis (Reich), 179, 189, 191
Chessick, R. D., 136, 214
Child analysis, vii, 161–177
"Child Analysis in the Analysis of Adults" (Ferenczi), 152

Child-rearing
  Adler and, 133
  culture and, 102
  masochism and, 183, 186–187, 193
  trauma and, 156–157
Children, 47
Child sexual abuse, 152–153
Claudel, Paul, 210
Cognitive therapy, 139
Collective unconscious
  dream analysis and, 113–117
  Jung and, 108, 118–119
Compulsion neuroses, 57
Concentration method, 23
Confession, 15
Confrontation
  Adler and, 129–130
  Ferenczi and, 146
"Confusion of Tongues Between Adults and the Child: The Language of Tenderness and Passion" (Ferenczi), 152
Consciousness, 44, 59
Conversion hysteria. *See also* Hysteria
  Anna O. case and, 3
  society and, 18, 102
Corporal punishment, 102
Countertransference. *See also* Transference
  Anna O. case and, 2, 13
  Breuer and, 14–15, 19
  Ferenczi and, 157
  Freud and, 35, 38–39
  Jung and, 119–120
  narcissistic countertransference, 158
  Rat Man case and, 76, 81
  Wolf Man case and, 97–98
Creativity, 156
Culture
  Adler and, 135
  character and, 102
  conversion hysteria and, 18, 102

Darwinism, 102
Daseinsanalyze (Binswanger), 197, 212
Death
    Adler and, 124
    Klein and, 162
    Rat Man case and, 66–67, 70, 71,
        81, 82
    repression and, 16
    unconscious and, 10
Death instinct
    Klein and, 175
    Little Hans case and, 59
    masochism and, 188
    Reich and, 179–180, 190, 192–193
Defecation. *See* Excrement
Depression
    Adler and, 125–129
    child analysis and, 170
    Klein and, 162, 163
    Wolf Man case and, 87, 94, 101
Deutsch, Felix, 36, 41
Developmental child analysis, 161–
    177
"Differences Between Individual
    Psychology and Psychoanalysis,
    The" (Adler), 125
Displacement
    Breuer and, 19
    Dora case and, 27
Donn, L., 108
Dora case, 21–42
Dream interpretation
    Adler and, 133, 135, 136
    Freud and, 117–118
    hysteria and, 21–42
    Jung and, 105–122
    Little Hans case and, 50, 54, 55–
        56
    Wolf Man case and, 87–89, 100–
        101
Drive theory, 59
Drugs, 5, 8, 19

Ego
    abreaction and, 155
    Adler and, 123, 136
    anxiety and, 59–60, 62
    Ferenczi and, 158
    Jung and, 117
Ego psychology
    Adler and, 136–137
    regression and, 157
Eigenwelt, 207
Eissler, Kurt, 94, 95, 97
Eitingon, Max, 154
"Elasticity of Psycho-Analytic
    Technique, The" (Ferenczi), 150
Electricity, 24
Electric shock treatment, 5
Elimination. *See* Excrement;
        Urination
Enuresis. *See* Bed-wetting
Epstein, Raissa, 133
Erikson, E. H., 37, 38
Erna case, vii, 161–177
Esman, A., 98
Excrement
    child analysis and, 165
    disgust and, 26
    Little Hans case and, 50, 55, 60
    masochism and, 187
    money and, 75
Exhibitionism, 187
Existential analysis, vii, 139, 197–
    217
Existential philosophy, 122
Exorcism, 5
Eysenck, H. J., 139

Fairbairn, W. R. D., 121
False self, 121
Family, 102. *See also* Child-rearing
Fantasy
    child analysis, 165–167, 168, 169,
        172–174

Fantasy (*continued*)
  Ferenczi and, 149–150
  free association and, 158
  Freud and, 118–119
  internalization and, 174–175
  Jung and, 116
  masochism and, 182, 188
  primal scene and, 96
  Rat Man case and, 73–74
  Wolf Man case and, 94
Federn, E. 64
Federn, Paul, 180
Feminism, 13, 17, 18, 36, 121
Fenichel, O., 155, 191
Ferenczi, Sandor, 64, 141–159, 193,
    194
  aggression and, 181
  biography of, 141–142, 153–154
  contributions of, 159
  Freud and, 142–143, 150,
    153–154
  Klein and, 162
Fliess, Wilhelm, 40
Forel, August, 14
Free association
  development of concept, 23, 24
  fantasy and, 158
  Ferenczi and, 146, 157
  Little Hans case and, 50
  Rat Man case and, 64, 65
  Reich and, 185
Freeman, L., 2, 13, 14
Freud, Anna, 98, 162, 171
Freud, E. I., 40, 102
Freud, Sigmund, vii, 2, 3, 5, 139,
    150
  abreaction and, 155
  Adler and, 124, 134–136
  Binswanger and, 198
  Breuer and, 12, 13, 14, 23, 43
  description of, 64–65
  Dora case and, 21–42
  Ferenczi and, 142–143, 146, 150,
    153–154, 156
  hostility toward, 43, 83
  hysteria and, 9, 19
  infantile sexuality and, 17–18
  Jung and, 105, 106–108, 117–118,
    121
  Klein and, 162, 171, 176, 177
  Little Hans case and, 43–62
  masochism and, 188–189
  narcissistic countertransference and,
    158
  punishment and, 193
  Rat Man case and, 63–82
  Reich and, 179–181, 195–196
  repression and, 16
  Wolf Man case and, 83–103
Fromm, E., 137, 190, 211, 214
Fromm-Reichmann, F., 155–156,
    195, 213
"From the History of an Infantile
    Neurosis" (Freud), 84
"Further Development of an Active
    Therapy in Psycho-Analysis,
    The" (Ferenczi), 146

Galenson, E., 60
Gardiner, Muriel, 94, 95, 97, 101
Geleered, E. R., 174
Gestalt therapy, 217
Gill, M. M., 192
Glenn, J., 37–38, 57–58
Glover, E., 150, 171
God, 113, 114–115
Graf, Max, 43, 44, 47, 48, 56–57.
    See also Little Hans case
Graves' disease, 203
Greenberg, J. R., 174
Grinstein, A., 39
Groddeck, Georg, 154
Grosskurth, P., 162, 170, 172,
    174

Guilt
  Adler and, 127
  Anna O. case and, 11, 16–17
  Breuer and, 13, 19
  Jung and, 117
  Rat Man case and, 70–71
  Reich and, 180, 194
Guntrip, H., 194

Hallucination, 8, 10, 17
Halpert, E., 98, 99
Hanly, C., 213–214
Harrison, S. I., 216
Hartmann, H., 123
Heidegger, M., 208
History of the Psychoanalytic
    Movement, A (Freud), 117,
    134–135
Homosexuality
  child analysis and, 167–168
  culture and, 102
  Dora case and, 39–40
  lesbianism, 18
  masochism and, 184
  Rat Man case and, 66
  Wolf Man case and, 91, 92, 93
Horney, K., 137, 211
Humanistic therapy, 217
Human potential movement, 122
Hydrotherapy, 24, 63
Hypnosis
  Anna O. case and, 2, 4–5, 10,
    15–16
  Freud and, 23, 153
Hysteria
  Anna O. case and, 1–19
  culture and, 102
  Dora case and, 21–42
  Ferenczi and, 143–146
  sexuality and, 30
Hysterical childbirth, 13
Hysterical neurosis, 109

Id, 117
Incest, 90, 91
Individuation, 116. See also
    Separation-individuation
Infantile neurosis, 101
Infantile sexuality
  challenges to, 84
  Rat Man case and, 67
  Wolf Man case and, 90
Inferiority complex, 123–139
Inhibitions, Symptoms, and Anxiety
    (Freud), 59
Instinct theory, 59
Internalization, 174–175
Interpretation of Dreams, The (Freud),
    22, 43, 106, 124, 142

Jacobson, E., 121, 173, 192, 195
Jones, E., 12–13, 43, 64, 77, 83, 103,
    107, 124, 142, 143, 177, 180,
    189
Jung, C. G., 64
  biography of, 105–106, 116, 136,
    142
  dream analysis and, 105–122
  Freud and, 83, 84, 96, 106–108,
    134

Kanzer, M., 78–79, 100–101
Kaplan, Marion A., 18
Kernberg, O., 138, 173
Kestenberg, J. S., 79–80
Kierkegaard, Søren, 212
Klein, Melanie, vii, 161–177
  biography of, 161–162, 171
Kohut, H., 119, 121, 157, 191
Koppe, S., 15, 35, 57, 80
Kraepelin, E., 85, 204
Kris, E., 78, 156, 157

Laing, R. D., 194
Langs, R., 38, 81, 99

Language, 6–7, 10
Lesbianism, 18. *See also*
    Homosexuality
Libido theory
    Adler and, 125, 136
    Jung and, 117, 121
    Reich and, 191
Little, M., 194
Little Hans case, 43–62
Lowen, Alexander, 190

Mahler, M. S., 60, 121
Malcolm, Janet, 36–37
Manic-depressive disorder, 85
Marxism, 180
Masculinity, 135
Masochism
    child analysis and, 167
    Reich and, 179–196
    sources of, 186, 188–189, 193
    Wolf Man case and, 91, 92
Masson, J. M., 142, 151, 154
Masturbation
    anxiety and, 48
    child analysis and, 163, 167, 169,
        174
    Dora case and, 33, 37
    Ferenczi and, 144, 145, 146, 158
    Little Hans case and, 45, 47, 49
    masochism and, 183, 186, 187–188
    obsessional neurosis and, 64
    Rat Man case and, 74
May, R., 198, 211–212
Meadow, P., 158, 191
Meyer, Adolf, 214
Mirroring, 157
Mitchell, S. A., 174
Mitwelt, 207
Montagu, M. F. A., 176
Mourning, 72
Multiple personality, 18
Muroff, M., 18

Mutual analysis, 153
Mysticism, 118, 119

Narcissism
    Adler and, 123
    culture and, 102
    Ferenczi and, 152, 157
    masochism and, 193
    Reich and, 191, 195
    Wolf Man case and, 96, 101
Narcissistic countertransference, 158
Narrative of a Child Analysis (Klein),
    170
Neocatharsis. *See* Active therapy
Nietzsche, F., 136
Nunberg, H., 64

Obholzer, Karin, 85, 87, 94, 95,
    96–97
Object relations
    Adler and, 123
    child analysis and, 173
    Klein and, 177
Obsessional neurosis, vii, 63–82
    Ferenczi and, 145, 147–149
    homosexuality and, 102
    Wolf Man case and, 84, 95
Obsessive-compulsive disorder,
    91–92
Oedipus complex
    child analysis and, 168, 172
    countertransference and, 39
    Dora case and, 29, 30
    Ferenczi and, 149
    Jung and, 117, 118
    Klein and, 161
    Little Hans case and, 43–62
    masochism and, 187, 188
    Rat Man case and, 66
Olsen, D. A., 15, 35, 57, 80
On Dreams (Freud), 162
O'Neill, A. S., 190

"On Forced Fantasies: Activity in the
    Association-Technique"
    (Ferenczi), 149
"On the History of the
    Psychoanalytic Movement"
    (Freud), 96
Oral sadism
    child analysis and, 168
    Rat Man case and, 80
O'Regan, B., 18
Orgler, H., 124, 125, 134
Orgonomy, 190
Outcomes, 139

Pankejeff, Sergesius, 83–103
Pappenheim, Bertha. See Anna O.
    case
Paralysis. See Hysteria
Paranoia
    resistance and, 41
    Wolf Man case and, 94
Paranoid-schizophrenia
    child analysis and, 167
    Reich and, 193–194
"Passions of Adults and their
    Influence on the Sexual and
    Character Development of
    Children, The" (Ferenczi), 154
Passive-feminine identification,
    60–61
Penis
    Dora case and, 26
    Little Hans case and, 44–45, 49–
        50, 58
    Rat Man case and, 77
Penis envy, 27, 190
Person-centered approach, 139
Phantasy. See Fantasy
Phenomenology, 216–217
Phobia
    compulsion neuroses and, 57
    Ferenczi and, 147–149

Little Hans case and, 44, 46–47,
    51–52
repression and, 53
Wolf Man case and, 84
Plath, Sylvia, 198
Play, 163–164, 173
Preoedipal factors
    emphasis on, 60
    Wolf Man case and, 99
Primal scene, 83–103, 166, 169
"Principle of Relaxation and
    Neocatharsis, The" (Ferenczi),
    150
Problems of Neurosis (Adler), 125
Pseudocyesis, 13
Psychoanalysis
    Adler and, 134–135
    Breuer and, 14
    children and, 47
    critique of, 96–97
    dream analysis and, 23
    existential analysis and, 209–210,
        211
    outcomes and, 139
    overzealous use of, 55
    preoedipal factors and, 60
    Rat Man case and, 64, 77–78
    transference and, 117
    trauma and, 101–102
    Wolf Man case and, 84,
        95–96
Psychoanalysis of Children, The
    (Klein), 161, 162–163
Psychosynthesis, 122, 217
Punishment
    masochism and, 183–184
    orgasm and, 188

Rado, Sandor, 180
Rank, Otto, 211
Rat Man case, vii, 63–82
Rauschenback, Emma, 107

Reaction formation
    Anna O. case and, 17
    Rat Man case and, 80
Reality therapy, 139
Real self, 121
Regression
    Anna O. case and, 15
    Ferenczi and, 154, 155–157
Reich, Wilhelm, 179–196
    biography of, 180–181, 189–190
    Freud and, 195–196
Reik, Theodore, 192–193
Reizes, Moriz, 161
"Remembering, Repeating and
    Working-Through" (Freud),
    155
Repression
    aggression and, 16–17
    Anna O. case and, 3–4, 9
    anxiety and, 60
    child analysis and, 172
    dream analysis and, 23
    Ferenczi and, 148
    Freud and, 16
    Jung and, 117
    Little Hans case and, 46
    Oedipus complex and, 47, 54
    phallic stage of development and,
        61
    phobia and, 53
    Rat Man case and, 71
    unconscious and, 30
Resistance
    abreaction and, 155
    Adler and, 125, 137, 138
    Anna O. case and, 7
    Dora case and, 28, 41
    masochism and, 184–185
    Rat Man case and, 68
    Reich and, 190, 192
    Wolf Man case and, 86
Rieff, P., 37, 59, 78

Rilkin, Franz, 64
Roazen, P., 136–137, 171, 175, 180,
    181, 190, 198
Roiphe, Herman, 60
Rosen, J., 194
Rosenbaum, M., 18
Rosenfeld, E., 97, 98

Sadger, Isidor, 64, 180
Sadism. See also Masochism
    child analysis and, 165, 167,
        169–170
    Wolf Man case and, 91
Schizophrenia
    Anna O. case and, 4, 18
    child analysis and, 167
    Reich and, 194
    Wolf Man case and, 99
Schlesinger, H., 38
Schmidelberg, Melitta, 171
Schoenewolf, Gerald, 60, 193
Schur, M., 59, 98, 103
Sechehaye, M., 194
Seduction theory, 152–153
Segal, H., 172
Self-realization, 121
Separation-individuation. See also
    Individuation
    Little Hans case and, 58
    Wolf Man case and, 99
Severn, Elizabeth, 151
Sexual abuse, 152–153
Sexuality
    Anna O. case and, 2, 3–4, 16
    Breuer and, 14
    child analysis and, 163, 173
    childhood development of, 44
    Dora case and, 25–26, 27, 32
    education about, 48, 60
    Ferenczi and, 143, 145, 146
    hysteria and, 30
    Jung and, 106, 117, 118

masochism and, 181–182, 186
patient–therapist relationship,
     107–108
Reich and, 194
Shengold, L., 80
Siblings, 166
Silverman, M. A., 58, 59, 60
Slap, J., 58
Social factors
  Adler and, 137
  Anna O. and, 18
  existential analysis and, 203
Speech. *See* Language
Speilrein, Sabrina, 107–108
Split personality, 18
Splitting
  Ferenczi and, 151
  Rat Man case and, 77, 80
Spotnitz, H., 15, 16, 157, 158, 191,
     195
Stekel, Wilhelm, 43, 64, 83, 142,
     180
Sterba, R. F., 191
Stern, P. J., 106, 118
Stolorow, R. D., 194
Strachey, L., 96
Strean, H., 2, 13, 14
Sublimation, 19
Suicide
  Adler and, 129–131
  Dora case and, 26
  existential analysis and, 199, 206,
     209, 214
  obsessional neurosis and, 63, 72
  Reich and, 180, 194
  Wolf Man case and, 84, 93, 94, 99
Sullivan, Harry Stack, 136, 137, 211
Superego
  Klein and, 177
  masochism and, 189
Symbolism
  Anna O. case and, 16–17

child analysis and, 164–165
  dream analysis and, 31–32, 40, 118
Symptoms, 28
Syphilis, 21

Talking cure, 11–12, 19
"Technical Difficulties in the
     Analysis of a Case of Hysteria"
     (Ferenczi), 143
Termination of treatment
  child analysis and, 170
  Ferenczi and, 143
  Jung and, 111, 114–115, 119–120
  Wolf Man case and, 92–93, 96, 97,
     101
Thompson, C., 119, 136, 190, 193
Three Essays on the Theory of Sexuality
     (Freud), 43–44, 45, 62
Toilet training
  child analysis and, 168–169
  Little Hans case and, 53
  preoedipal factors and, 60
Tonsillectomy, 48, 58–59
Transactional analysis, 139
Transference. *See also*
     Countertransference
  abreaction and, 155
  Adler and, 125, 137, 138
  Anna O. case and, 9
  Breuer and, 13–15, 19
  child analysis and, 162, 164
  Dora case and, 32
  Ferenczi and, 143–144, 150, 152
  Freud and, 39
  hypnosis and, 23
  Jung and, 111–112, 113, 117, 119
  Little Hans case and, 59
  Rat Man case and, 66, 76, 78–79
  Reich and, 181, 191, 192
  Wolf Man case and, 87, 99–100,
     101
Transference neurosis, 75, 82

Trauma
  borderline personality and, 99
  Ferenczi and, 151
  masochism and, 183
  psychoanalysis and, 101–102
  Rat Man case and, 81–82
  regression and, 156
  Wolf Man case and, 90
Two Essays on Analytical Psychology
  (Jung), 119

Umwelt, 206–207
Unconscious
  Adler and, 136, 138
  Anna O. case and, 5
  child analysis and, 172–174
  death and, 10
  Dora case and, 29–30
  Freud and, 28, 117
  Jung and, 108, 113, 115
  Little Hans case and, 59
  masochism and, 183
  Rat Man case and, 71

Unterweger, Albin, 95
Urination. *See also* Bed-wetting
  Ferenczi and, 145–146
  Little Hans case and, 46, 53
  Rat Man case and, 79
  Wolf Man case and, 90, 93

Voigtländer, Else, 102

Weiss, S. S., 81
West, Ellen, vii, 197–217
Weygandt, Wilhelm, 83
White, R. W., 137
Winnicott, D. W., 121, 194
Wolf Man case, 83–103, 139
Wollfheim, Nelly, 174
Wolman, B. B., 137
Womb envy, 60–61
Women, 18, 36. *See also* Feminism
Wundt, Wilhelm Max, 44

Zola, Emile, 75
Zweig, Stefan, 12